Managing Fashion and Luxury Companies

ERICA CORBELLINI
STEFANIA SAVIOLO

ETAS

Traduzione dall'italiano di Jill Marie Connelly
Redazione di Fabio Ceresoli

Fotocomposizione: Nuova MCS - Firenze

ISBN 978-88-453-1520-6

Copyright © 2009 RCS Libri S.p.A.
Prima edizione Etas: febbraio 2009

I libri Etas sono disponibili con particolari sconti quantità per l'utilizzo
promozionale o nell'ambito di programmi di formazione aziendale.
Per ulteriori informazioni scrivere a etaslab@rcs.it.

www.etaslab.it

MANAGEMENT

From Erica to Tancredi and Zoe

From Stefania to Isa and Giorgio

CONTENTS

Foreword

Renzo Rosso [*]

Fashion is inspiration, creativity and intuition. But it is also organization, strategy and management. These two apparently contrasting sets of elements have to come together to ensure the success of a business idea.

The current scene presents new challenges, such as the increasing sophistication of consumers, the constant need to innovate, the importance of attaining specific critical masses in order to meet growing investment requirements in retailing and communication, the micro-segmentation of the market, hyper-competition, and brand management, just to mention a few.

It is increasingly difficult to find professionals in the fashion industry that are capable of "managing creativity", that means leading creativity without impeding or deforming it. Firms and managers have to know how to innovate, breaking free from competitive rules while still remaining loyal to the core values of their brand. The fashion market is in a constant state of excitement, the consumer constantly wants new stimuli, and it is up to the actors in the industry to create and maintain a relationship with their own target.

---

[*]   President and Founder of Diesel.

A fashion firm always works in a circle. Any decision, any action undertaken, has decisive consequences on brand and corporate image. Let us take the example of retail directly managed by the firm. This affects only one functional department of the firm, retailing, but how can one forget the overall effects in terms of brand image, let alone business organization? Production, logistics, information-gathering, reporting, and communication at the retail level all have to operate effectively and efficiently in order to maintain overall consistency.

There is another key point that should not be forgotten, the enlarged concept of communication. In the past one hardly talked about advertising, and the product was the focus of all the company's efforts. In the 1980s, and above all in the 1990s, communication became a key success factor in the fashion world. Today, communication does not just mean advertising or public relations. An advertisement (whether on press or on television) no longer has a rational motivation ("to inform and persuade") as much as an emotional content ("to seduce"). Communication means working with the new technologies (from the Internet to videogames), and above all expressing the corporate philosophy in every way, not only through business communication but also through shop windows, direct marketing, and customer service.

The brand has to be created, managed, sustained and protected. A brand is much more than a simple logo for a fashion firm. It evokes values, atmospheres, benefits that can never be ignored. This list of tangible and intangible factors attracts the consumer and ensures his loyalty. It ensures an economic advantage and represents a genuine weapon in the fight against competitors. It is also vital for the firm's growth (if not for its survival as well).

The clients of fashion products often do not have national limits or national taste. Thinking internationally, but at the same time respecting diversity among markets is another key success factor within an industry that is becoming global. A book like this helps to analyze and understand the complexity and potential of the fashion system. But it is only a start. I strongly believe in learning by doing. Making mistakes does not matter to me; it is reaction time that makes the difference. This is why I let my managers make mistakes. This way they will develop the necessary antibodies for what is increasingly a daily fight.

Foreword

*Federico Marchetti**

When I was invited to write this foreword, the first thing I asked myself was – What's an Internet entrepreneur like me doing in a book about fashion and luxury? When I thought a bit more about the question's context, I discovered some answers that centre on three key points: 1) my own experiences; 2) the centrality of "the store" for brands; 3) the brand as a digital form.

I founded YOOX in 2000, and since then have been something of a liaison, a sort of simultaneous translator, between the world of Internet and Fashion. I honestly feel closer to Fashion than the Internet in many ways through my interests, background, passions, culture, and language and although I shouldn't admit it, my relationship with technology is not a particularly close one. I find it fascinating of course, but there are times when I can't stand it, and I dive back into the past with all things vintage.

Above all however, I'm an entrepreneur who has managed to explain the opportunities and the beauty of Internet in simple terms to fashion, luxury and design brands. The Internet is what's driving brands towards New Luxury: accessible from everywhere yet always

* Founder and CEO of YOOX Group.

exclusive. YOOX has done the same thing for end consumers, who are often experimenting with purchasing online for the first time - we created a site that isn't just a site; first and foremost it's an online store.

This brings me to my second point. When all is said and done, my job is the oldest in the world - I'm a shopkeeper. Yes, it may be true that YOOX is an Internet store, but as far as customers are concerned, it's no different, whether they're buying from their home in Sicily in front of a computer or in a boutique in Via Montenapoleone in Milan.

The store is the most important space for a brand. It's where the final customer sees every facet of the product, the communication style, the location, the atmosphere, and so on. The bottom line is that the store is the final outcome of all the upstream work. So an online store is not so very different from a real one. In fact, with a virtual store the brand can create a virtuous circle linking multimedia/editorial content and the product, coupling the power of communication and distribution capacity to perfection. For example, just think of having the chance to buy products directly from the video of the fashion show, putting a product on virtual display into an exceptional container. What's more, the fact that Internet customers can't touch the product is actually a false problem. Actually, you can do so at home, in front of your wardrobe, in the privacy of your bedroom. And you only have to wait a few days for "your gift to yourself", knowing that you have some time to change your mind for any reason and send it back.

Finally, I want to go out on a limb and give some advice to those of you who are taking the trouble to read my foreword. I start from the assumption that for anyone who works in a fashion house, interpreting a brand in the digital arena is your daily bread. 1) Prepare yourself to be able/obliged to interact a great deal with customers in the digital world; most importantly, treat them well: people on the Internet are real, not avatars! 2) Technology, special effects, in short, innovation: these are not the only ways to create a brand on the Internet. Creativity, entertainment, and the element of surprise are always imperatives. 3) Don't listen to Internet gurus; follow your instinct. Every brand has a different story, and gurus tend to apply the same success story to all of them. 4) Concentrate solely on creating something incredible, something never seen before. This is what I always say to the brands YOOX has developed online stores for: you have to think of your online store as your most beautiful (and biggest) in the world!

Coming to the end of this piece, I understand more as to why I was asked to write this foreword: in the end, the Internet isn't so distant, different or difficult to understand. The rules of the game online and offline are the same.

Introduction

Since ancient times, fashion and luxury have been a part of the human experience as much as these two phenomena relate to our culture, to our need for identification and differentiation and hence to our social identity. But just as human societies have evolved dramatically over time, what fashion and luxury represent has also continued to change, once over a period of centuries, now in the span of decades.

The system of fashion and luxury goods found fertile ground in the Italian and international sphere in the late 1970s to the 1980s. Today, however, these favorable conditions no longer exist. In fact, there is no longer a single concept of fashion or luxury; instead, we have a variety of fashions and luxuries, given the ever-expanding yet simultaneously ever-more segmented market in terms of customers, competitors, channels, and media. Once willing to pay ample price premiums for given brands, today customers are bored with the proliferation of brands and products with little or nothing that distinguishes one offering from another. In fact, consumers are now more selective and more oriented toward value, yet always and forever searching for the "dream factor". Growth comes primarily from new markets such as India and China, which have different characteristics and needs than Western customers.

Competitors have become bigger and more international, especially since 2001. Often listed on the Stock Exchange, these players need to balance operational management and (often short-term) economic results with creativity and innovation.

The independent multibrand stores which once dominated apparel and accessories distribution in Europe have given way to large international vertically integrated chains with own brands in fashion, and networks of monobrand boutiques in luxury. New channels appear to point toward a revolutionary way of doing business: Internet, travel retail, and outlets. Social networks, celebrity marketing, and Customer Relationship Management are innovative communication tools for a progressively sophisticated and critical customer/user.

On the global scene, serious doubts regarding the international economic situation do not encourage luxury consumption. On the contrary, present circumstances favor ethical consumption, and demand greater corporate social responsibility of all companies. At the same time, the benefits and experiences sought after through luxury and fashion are redefined by a maturing population.

A new world requires a fresh, more sophisticated way of approaching markets, products, brands, and communication. Strategies once based on a single product and a single brand for a single consumer today must be able to segment the offering through a different value proposition for different segments on different markets in terms of product, store, communication, and service.

From this perspective, our text is intended, on one hand, as a management handbook for fashion and luxury companies. On the other, our aim is to slot management tools into a context undergoing a radical evolution; providing substantiation through real-life examples makes the book topical. The purpose of part one, defining fashion and luxury, is to offer an analysis of what the fashion and luxury system represents today from an etymological standpoint and in terms of the structure of business pipelines. In the second part, the focus of our analysis lies on the major competitor nations and different country models. The third part explores the competitive system, i.e. industry segments, business models, and consumption drivers. Finally, in the last part we discuss the following levers available to management: brand storytelling, and stylistic, retail, and communication identity. Fashion and luxury are treated like two business logics which are separate yet convergent when they serve the same customer in the same channel with the same "reason why".

Throughout this book, we argue that traditional managerial science developed and established for fast-moving consumer goods industries must be enriched with different perspectives in order to be truly helpful for fashion and luxury companies. These perspectives deal with the relation between managers and creative people; the role of tradition versus innovation; the relation between core and extended product categories. Managers, the "rational spirit" of fashion firms, are more and more important to drive these companies into new markets, new channels and new product categories; but still managers need to respect and interact with the creative people who represent the "reason why" of these firms. At the same time creative people need to understand the market and the consumer and see the commercial results of their efforts. Brand heritage and iconic products should be leveraged and presented as sources of legitimacy, but at the same time these companies need to be innovative and ground-breaking in terms of their products. Extending the brand into different segments and products is needed in order to preserve growth, but at the same time the core business and client should be maintained and respected in order to avoid losing relevance and confusing the market. The book also argues that from fast consumer goods industries, fashion and luxury companies should learn a more quantitative, precise and scientific approach to the business in the areas of consumer insight, retail and operations. Now this is a necessity, no longer an option.

This book is intended to be among the first European and Italian contributions to international students, researchers and managers in the field of both fashion and luxury management. The objective is to deal with all management issues and business processes that are most significant for these companies. We provide the support of many real examples coming from almost 15 years of experience of the two authors in the field of teaching, researching and consulting these companies. We also adopt a European perspective, considering the reality of small and medium sized firms, generally managed by an entrepreneur or a family, willing to improve their managerial skills.

This work is the fruit of research by the authors, enriched by continually exchanging and sharing ideas.

Erica Corbellini wrote *Chapters 3, 4* (with Leandré D'Souza), *6, 8, 13*, and *Sections 1.4, 2.4, 11.4, 12.1, 12.4* (on the Internet), *12.6*, and *14.4*.

Stefania Saviolo wrote *Chapters 1, 2, 5, 7, 9, 10, 11, 12, 14*, and *Sections 3.5, 6.1, 6.2*.

Introduction and *Conclusions* were written by both authors, likewise Sections *2.3, 3.4, 7.4, 8.1, 8.2, 8.3*, and *14.3*.

Many thanks go to our students, who never for a moment let us grow old.

Special thanks also to the companies who have generously and passionately shared their experiences in our classrooms or through direct interviews. In particular: Altagamma, Bain & Co (Italy), Bottega Veneta, Cotonificio Albini, Diesel, Ermenegildo Zegna, Giorgio Armani, Gucci, L'Oréal – Luxury Division, Louis Vuitton, Luxottica, Prada, Salvatore Ferragamo, Swarovski, Tod's, Valentino, and Versace.

Defining fashion and luxury

1   Defining fashion

1.1 What is fashion?

Much has been said and written about fashion. Great historians
have described the customs and manners of dress in their societies in detail. Men of letters, poets, sociologists, psychologists
and economists have all discussed fashion. Consumers, journalists, retailers, creative people, managers and entrepreneurs
are involved in it on a daily basis. And yet, like every issue that
is hard to define but that affects the life and taste of us all, it
seems that everything is the opposite of what could still be said.
It is claimed that fashion is a pointless subject, but also a very
serious one, that it is about shows and glossy magazines, but
also about jobs and creating wealth. It is said that fashion only
exists in the minds of those who create it, but that everyone can
create his own fashion. Fashion has been celebrated but also considered as something useless and even "atrocious". In his essay
on fashion, Georg Simmel[1] writes:

---

1. G. Simmel, "Fashion", *The American Journal of Sociology*, 1957, p. 544.

"... fashion is merely a product of social demands. ... This is clearly proved by the fact that very frequently not the slightest reason can be found for the creation of fashion from the standpoint of an objective, aesthetic or other expediency. ... Judging from the ugly and repugnant things that are sometimes in vogue, it would seem as though fashion were desirous of exhibiting its power by getting us to adopt the most atrocious things for its sake alone".

It is hard to provide an unambiguous definition of the word fashion, as there is no objective and unanimous interpretation of it, above all at an international level. The Italian dictionary *Garzanti* defines fashion as "the more or less changeable usage that, deriving from the prevailing taste, is imposed on habits, ways of living, and forms of dress"[2]. Another Italian source asserts that clothes represent only one aspect of fashion. This author argues that "fashion is a universal principle, one of the elements of civilisation and social custom. It involves not only the body but all the means of expression available to people"[3]. According to Wikipedia, the free online encyclopaedia, fashion "refers to styles of dress (but can also include cuisine, literature, art, architecture, and general comportment) that are popular in a culture at any given time. Such styles may change quickly, and 'fashion' in the more colloquial sense refers to the latest version of these styles".

Going back to the etymological roots of the word, the Italian word for fashion, *moda*, introduced into the language around 1650, derives from the Latin word *mos*, and has the different but related meanings of: a) usage, custom, habit, tradition, b) law, rule, c) regulation, good manners, morality. However the fashion phenomenon existed long before the introduction of the word *moda* into the Italian language. Right from the start it was considered a strange and absurd phenomenon. In fact, even Leonardo da Vinci, in his *Codex Urbinate*, gives a humorous description of the changes in the manner of dress of Florentines.

This list of meanings makes it clear that although taste is the expression of an individual orientation, it has to contend with a system of social rules that defines what can be considered "fashionable" at any time or place. A presumed etymological overlap

2. AA. VV., *Grande dizionario della lingua italiana*, Garzanti, 1993.
3. G. Devoto, *Il dizionario della lingua italiana*, Le Monnier, 1995.

between fashion (*moda*) and "modern" is not thus the result of pure chance. It emphasises the developing and institutional aspect of taste. The French, English and German words *mode* confirms this matrix. This word derives from the Celtic words *mod* and *modd*, which have the same meaning as the Latin word *mos*: usage, custom or manner.

The commonest word in the international setting, fashion, seems less interesting and explanatory. It derives from the French word *façon*, through the Latin *facere*: do, build, make.

Modern sociologists define fashion as a system of meanings where the notions of style and aesthetics predominate over functional benefits. The way we dress talks about us, shapes our social identities. For centuries, individuals or societies have used clothes and other body adornment as a form of nonverbal communication to indicate occupation, rank, gender, sexual availability, locality, class, and wealth and group affiliation. According to Breward, fashion possesses many facets simultaneously, as indicated in *Figure 1.1*.

According to the vision, fashion is the direct result of both a creative and an industrial process. It is a system of innovation engineered to meet and encourage seasonal consumer demand, fulfilling a cultural requirement to define ever-shifting social identities and relationships. The phenomenology of fashion is therefore made up not only of design but also production, distribution and consumption processes, within an ever-evolving

FIGURE 1.1   **FASHION AS A SYSTEM OF MEANINGS**

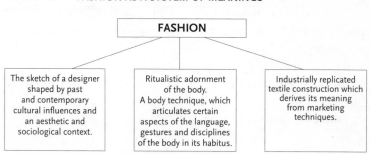

Source: adapted from C. Breward, *Fashion*, Oxford University Press, 2003.

context. Fashion cannot be understood out of context. What you wear, how you wear it and why you wear it depends on time and place. A product, a service, or even a social behaviour, is considered "fashionable" if it is widely approved by a specific public in a specific time and social context. If the consumption of a fashionable item is removed from its specific social context then it loses any meaning, and changes in fashion do not entail any improvement in product quality. The specific public may be intended according to a geographical perspective, New York rather than the Italian city of Parma, or it may be socio-demographic: the provincial middle-class, urban women working in the service industry, shop-assistants, or teenage snowboarders.

Modern fashion, as we know it today, is a recent phenomenon. After the Second World War and up to the 1970s the concept of seasonal fashion was only associated with clothing, in particular with some specific womenswear segments: *haute couture* and *ready-to-wear*. Since the 1980s, however, fashion has increasingly spread to additional segments – fur and hosiery, perfumes and cosmetics, eyewear, accessories (watches, jewels, pens, mobile telephones), furniture and household goods, and even travel destinations and domestic pets. We can talk about fashion in some contexts, such as computers and academic theories, that are a long way from the dimension of aesthetics and style.

Up to now there has been no other field of human activity where the systematic change of the product has been institutionalised as it has in clothing and the consumer goods closely related to apparel (accessories, perfumes, eyewear). Here, in fact, seasonal change has truly become quite an obsession.

This is due to the fact that clothing is, or ought to be, the expression of a development in customs, social context, culture and lifestyle, in a phenomenological context that is much wider and more complex than clothing itself.

Knowledge of the meaning of fashion, of the whys and hows of its creation, spread and consumption, is central to understanding the fashion business and its management.

1.2 The fashion cycle

The product life cycle concept suggests that goods go through four stages of evolution: introduction, growth, maturity and decline. As a product evolves and passes through each stage, profit is affected, and different strategies have to be employed to ensure that the item is a success within its market. The length of the product lifecycle in fashion-related industries is short compared to other industries; it can range from a few weeks to a few seasons. We define the fashion cycle as the period of time between the introduction of a certain fashion (a new product, a new look) and its replacement by a new one.

The degree of innovation of the replacement may involve basic features (product concept, style, basic materials, accessories), or variants (colors). The process of change is partly driven by the cycle of the seasons (Spring/Summer and Autumn/Winter), and partly by the fashion cycle itself (introduction, peak, and decline of a certain fashion). Why such an obsessive rate of change? The fashion cycle can be explained from two perspectives:

- Seasonal change is brought about by the industrial, retail and communication system of fashion. This is tied to the need to encourage and control a certain level of product turnover. "Planned obsolescence" encourages new demand season after season for products that could last much longer considering their functional and technical features alone. The fashion cycle plays out within the structure of seasonal collections that are connected to seasonal trade fairs and fashion shows. These events were once the exclusive domain of women's *haute couture* and ready-to-wear clothing, but have now been penetrated by the whole clothing system and pipeline, including fibres, textiles, leather goods and hosiery (menswear, children's wear, sportswear, leather goods and hosiery, fabrics, yarns and finishing, and so on).
- Change, intended as great product variety and variability over time, is designed to guarantee the consumer a wide range of choice and the greatest satisfaction in terms of how the product fits personal needs. The existence of trends

and new products coming out in the market follows the increasing individualisation of the consumer. This is particularly true in the case of so-called "fast fashion".

It is important to remember that a certain trend in terms of colors or shapes or materials must gain wide consumer acceptance to become a fashion. In other words, consumers must buy and wear a style to make it a fashion. Of course, it isn't fashion if nobody buys it. Not all fashion products go through a short, seasonal lifecycle. Companies also customarily sell basic products, such as polo-shirts and blue jeans, for years with few style changes. Such items never become completely obsolete, but remain accepted for an extended period of time. Companies selling basic products can count on a long product life cycle with the same customers buying multiple units of the same product at the same time or over time. For these products, decline is often related to structural changes in people's habits and lifestyles (for instance, the use of a hat or suspenders or overcoats in menswear, the use of large shoulders or pointed shoes in womenswear). In addition to the seasonal fashion cycle and the longer cycle of basics, there is a third cycle in fashion, the so-called "fad". A fad is usually a short lived fashion, one that comes and goes, and that lacks the character to hold consumer attention for very long. *Figure 1.2* shows the three cycles. We will come back to this in *Chapter 11* on product development.

FIGURE 1.2 **LIFE CYCLE FOR FAD, FASHION AND BASIC PRODUCTS**

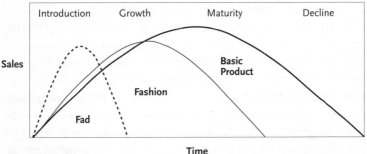

FIGURE 1.3   **FASHION ADOPTION CONSUMER TYPES**

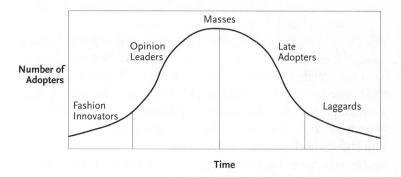

As we said, each fashion has its own life cycle made up of three stages: introduction, peak, and decline. Various actors participate in the adoption and diffusion of fashion trends in the different stages. Fashion innovators create the trend and opinion leaders are the first to adopt the new fashion during the initial stage, when it is emerging. Opinion leaders are the so-called VIPs or small groups of consumers and distributors who want to look different from the mainstream for several reasons (class differentiation, identification with a particular system of values and so on). There is a process of diffusion and adoption by much wider segments of the market during the second stage through the masses first (when volume sales peak) and then late adopters. There is often an aspirational element supporting the diffusion of fashions to mainstream consumers, the desire to be trendy among those who follow an imitative model of behaviour. The final stage (*Figure 1.3*) is decline and adoption by laggards who are the last to co-opt a particular fashion.

When did the cycle of fashion start historically? Despite disagreements about the beginnings of fashion in history, scholars agree that, despite a certain variability in the duration of cycles, the flow of change underwent an initial acceleration in the 13th and 14th centuries. The institutional origin of the concept of fashion, in the sense of a systematic process of socially accepted variations in a particular custom and clothing style, took place early in the Renaissance in the Italian cities. It later spread to the whole of Europe, in particular to the Boulogne courts, an early sign of the crucial role of Paris as the place where new fashions were created in later centuries. A second acceleration of the phenomenon seems to relate to the emergence of the merchant social class, alongside the established social groups such as the nobility, the army, the clergy and farmers. The diffusion of rich merchants throughout Europe encouraged the creation of a new dress code, one no longer conditioned by ostentation (the nobility and clergy), poverty (farmers), or usefulness (the army), but by the search for social legitimacy. Thus the association between clothing and cyclical change was strengthened.

The rhythm of the fashion cycle underwent a considerable intensification in the 19th century. At first the role of designers was fundamental; later industry and distribution played a part in supporting or anticipating the development of the end consumer. A further acceleration in the fashion cycle took place in the late 1970s with the relative democratization of fashion. This was the result of the emergence of ready-to-wear collections that bore the name of the designer on the label of the industrial product, and the move from Paris to Milan for the exhibition of seasonal collections. Ready-to-wear designers (Giorgio Armani, Valentino Garavani, and Gianni Versace) also helped to create a much more complex relationship between the designer and an increasingly demanding market, less willing to accept a standardized industrial product but at the same time unable to buy *couture* dresses.

1.3 The rise of fast fashion

If, as we have already stressed, the dominance of the institutional fashion system has prevailed over the last thirty years, today it has to come to terms with greater consumer awareness and independence. Consumers are increasingly mobile, wired, connected and they are creating their own fashion, combining brands and products so as to express their personality or style. The consumer is attracted by fashion offers, but does not simply accept them passively. This is the crucial point for understanding how the collapse of the *total look* happened. The *total look* is intended as women or men completely dressed by a single designer or brand down to the accessories. This phenomenon was an important one in the 1980s, and the clearest expression of the dependence of the consumer on the designer's taste and *diktat*.

Since the mid-1990s a move has been underway from the concept of fashion to the concept of style. Personal style is the manifestation of an individual identity (of values, lifestyle, and taste) that can be transversal to the seasonal fashion diktat. In other words, style can cross freely over different fashion offers, taking from each of them whatever serves to define a completely personal result. This view of style thus reflects the emotional and cultural need not to accept fashion passively, but neither to reject the opportunities offered by it. In this context the savvy consumer wants more variety and variability to be able to "mix and match". As a consequence, the global trend in not only clothing and leather goods, but also in industries such as eyewear and fragrances, has been towards the continuous increase in the number of collections shown and delivered to the point of sale during the year. In fact, the concept of the season has almost become redundant; instead we talk about "fast fashion" and "flow delivery". "Fast fashion" gives shoppers the latest styles just six weeks after they first appear on the catwalk at prices that allow them to wear an outfit once or twice and then replace it.

Some retail brands like H&M, Zara and Promod are structured so that they can design, produce and deliver new collections throughout the year following a model of flow delivery. These collections are destined to have very short sales, purchase and consumption periods. Changing stock frequently means customers come back to check what's new and that means added sales. The Zara shopper drops in 17 times a year, the High Street average is just four.

The fashion system has been speeding up its cycle for some time, making use of all the possible synergies such as the mass media and the star system to nurture it. High Street stores used to stock just two collections a year (Autumn/Winter and Spring/Summer) but now they are more likely to have something new every month. Instead of publicizing the new season of fashion trends twice a year, fashion magazines now advertise new trends every month or even every week, encouraging consumers to buy more and more.

There are positive and negative aspects related to fast fashion. On the positive side, it provides more choices and lower prices. Fast fashion also brings the designer look to Main Street, thanks to the collaboration of leading designers such as Viktor & Rolf, Karl Lagerfeld or Cavalli who have been working with the mass Swedish retailer Hennes & Mauritz since 2005. Fast fashion has proven that fashion does not have to be elitist and that designers are as capable of creating cheap chic as ready-to-wear. On the negative side, on the one hand, more and more consumers are saturated by the massive amount of products on the shelves and are therefore moving toward new product categories. On the other hand, consumers are becoming sensitive to the issue of how the ultra-cheap clothes can be manufactured. Growing concerns about environment and ethics are shaping values against excess, waste and concern for labour conditions. Will this fast fashion last?

1.4 The fashion pipeline

The fashion system is so large and complex that it can be considered a cluster of closely interconnected industries. Often attention is focused only on the end products (apparel, knitwear, hosiery, accessories, etc.), but these are the result of a long and developed chain of stages and activities whose interaction is largely responsible for the product's final success on the market. A fashionable suit is much more than the creative effort of the designer. It is the result of innovative fibers that have been woven by specialized machines into fabrics of the colors and shapes that the fashion system has presented through its trade fairs and expert operators, such as the Bureau de Style. Nor is this enough. The role of distribution in choosing from the various offers is fundamental in affirming a fashion trend, as is the critical opinion of fashion editors.

A fundamental concept for understanding the fashion system, intended as an interrelated system made up of different stages, is the concept of the fashion pipeline. Sometimes defined as a supply chain, the pipeline identifies the vertical system that starts from the production stages of raw materials (fibers from the agricultural or chemical industries) down to the manufacturing and distributive stages of the textile and clothing industries. The fashion pipeline is thus made up of different sectors (fiber, textile, clothing, accessories, etc.) that can be further segmented according to product categories and end-uses (knitwear, hosiery, menswear, womenswear, sportswear) and price ranges. Therefore the fashion pipeline is unusually long – fiber to yarn, yarn to fabric, fabric to garment and retailing with an enormous variety of end-products. Industries that are not part of the vertical production cycle, but which support the whole system, are also part of the fashion pipeline. These include the textile machinery industry and various sections of the service industry (fashion publishing, fashion trade fairs, advertising and communication agencies, design studios, and so on).

Developing a competitive advantage within several stages of the fashion pipeline is important for a country in achieving international leadership through its finished products. The success of "Made in Italy" in fashion has always been linked to control of the entire textile and leather pipelines, from yarn to distribution, and a very high level of innovation and technology. Fashion firms, at different stages, work together like a large workshop in the creation and manufacture of a wide and innovative range of products. Physical proximity is not the only factor supporting innovation; the average firm dimension counts as well: the average size of Italian textile firms is lower than that of European producers as a whole. This results in advantages in flexibility, an increase in the variety of semi-finished products, and a shorter product life cycle. The greater flexibility of Italian textile and clothing firms is also related to the development of sub-contracting, the so-called *façon*, focusing on CMT (cut, make and trimming). CMT is a production contract where the producer mainly undertakes cut, make and trim activities. The production process and quality control are often monitored by the buyer. All front-end (designed materials, components) and back-end (distribution, marketing) activities are provided by buyers. This is encouraged by the presence of industrial districts made up of small firms that specialize in a single stage of the manufacturing process rather than in product technology or in a particular raw material. Firms' success in the Italian fashion system is strongly connected to their competitiveness in all the stages of the pipeline. Partnership, co-operation, co-marketing and co-design are the keywords for understanding the nature of the collaborative and competitive relationship among fashion companies.

FIGURE 1.4 THE FASHION PIPELINE

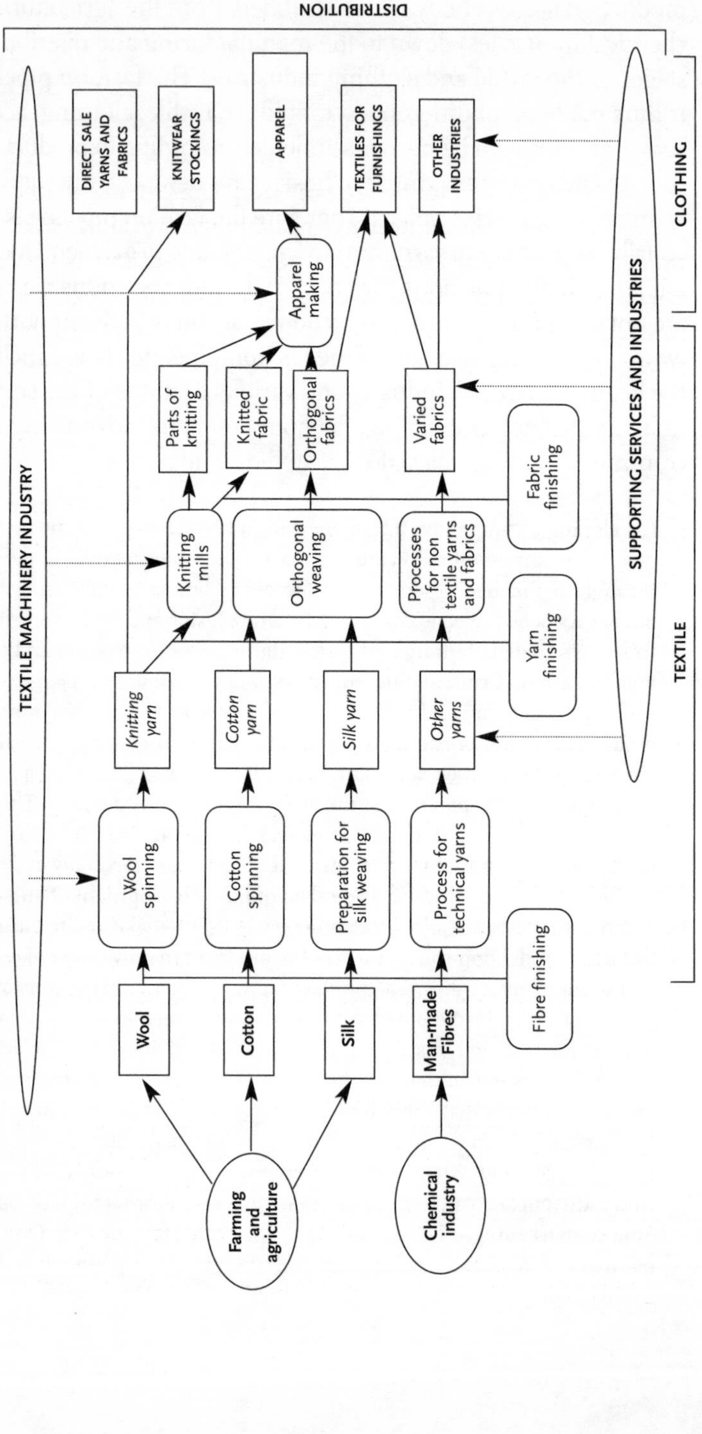

Figure 1.4 shows the different stages of the fashion textile/clothing pipeline, from raw materials to the fibers, yarns, fabrics, enduses and distribution of the final product. The textile machinery industry and supporting services work transversally to the entire pipeline.

Each stage of the pipeline has different characteristics in terms of capital versus labor intensity, profitability, prevailing business model, and growth outlook. While the fiber industry is very capital intensive and research-driven, apparel making is highly labour intensive and receives much of its innovation from the upstream phases (textile and fibres). Worth noting is the role of the pipeline in setting the timing of the fashion cycle and defining new trends, above all in terms of new materials (see *Chapter 11* on stylistic identity and product strategy).

When analyzing the evolution of the whole fashion pipeline in the last decades, two phenomena stand out: the development of synthetic fibers and their fundamental role in product innovation, and the loss of bargaining power of the manufacturing sector (textile and apparel making) to the advantage of retailers.

Fibers and innovation

The fiber is the smallest component in a fabric but, as we all know, it is also the one that gives the fabric its color, weight, solidity and "hand" (the so-called touch and feel). The fiber industry, particularly the man-made fiber industry, is the part of the textile pipeline where the most important innovations in terms of new functions and materials take place. Fibers can be natural or man-made, depending on the type of product being offered[4]. The diverse nature and structure of fibers implies differences in

---

4. Natural fibers fall into two main groups: protein fibers, which come from animals (such as wool, alpaca, mohair, cashmere, silk, etc.), and vegetable fibers which come from plants (cotton, linen, hemp, jute, etc.). There are two broad categories of man-made fibers: artificial and synthetic. Artificial fibers are natural raw materials that have been chemically treated, like cellulose from wood and linters from cotton. They generally have similar properties to natural fibers. Synthetic fibers have their origin in different polymers (oil derivates) that have been obtained through chemical treatments. Man-made fibers also include some inorganic fibers such as glassfiber and ceramic-fiber.

characteristics of the final garment in terms of comfort, stretch, touch and feel, weight, transpirancy, and easy care. Cotton has long been the world's major textile fiber. However, over the past 20 years, synthetic fibers have shown strong long-term growth, while production of cellulosic man-made fibers has decreased throughout the world. Synthetics now account for more than 90% of worldwide man-made fiber production. Growth in synthetic fiber production has resulted in a major shift in production from North America and Europe to Asia.

The real advantage of man-made fibers over natural ones is that they can be "made to measure" to suit particular applications. Thus we can have fibers that are brilliant or opaque, elastic or rigid, very soft or hard, delicate or super-resistant, or coloured or transparent, according to the needs of fashion. As they are made in the laboratory, there are many more man-made fibers than natural ones. Since there is not any constraint to the availability of raw materials (unlike with natural fibers), it is possible to continually increase volumes while reducing prices. Synthetic fibers such as polyester and nylon have literally invaded all areas of our everyday life, from jeans, to hosiery, underwear, and sportswear. To further improve the qualities of manufactured fibers, they are often combined with natural fibers. The blending technique combines all the qualities and feel of natural fibres together with the durability, elasticity and easy care of manufactured fibres. As a consequence most of the fabric composition in clothing nowadays is a blend.

From the supply chain to the buyer chain

In recent years, the textile and clothing industry has seen a shift in the balance of power, from upstream (industry) to downstream (retail), with the diffusion of supply chains based on "vertical systems". In such systems, retailers take on increasing responsibility for upstream activities such as textile procurement, product design and logistics. This is accompanied by a depletion of the range of activities required from industrial suppliers, who are often relegated to the role of mere providers of production capacity. Large, cost-conscious retailers are introducing changes in the organization and the implementation of purchasing activities (streamlining of the suppliers' portfolio, international centralization of procurement, high rotation of buyers, adoption of online auctions, etc.) aimed at systematically reducing purchasing costs. Manufacturers' responses to this trend range from enriching the assortment of services offered to their clients to extending downstream activities such as branding and retailing.

Outsourcing to cut costs has become the industry's mantra. But how much do production costs actually impact the final price the consumer pays? Very little. In the fashion industry, compared to the 2.5 mark up from wholesale to retail, the weight of industrial costs (materials and labor) rarely exceeds 15% of the final sales price. Choosing poor quality fabrics (a lining in polyester as opposed to viscose, for instance) considerably lowers the quality of the finished garment (albeit not in any readily perceptible way). Yet this amounts to a cost savings for the producer more than the consumer. In actual fact, distribution is what controls most of the value created by the supply chain, with rising investments in rents, key money to enter a store, store design and personnel. As a result, consumers buy goods which are high in price, yet low on tangible content, while being more and more standardized and undifferentiated, even when such items should belong in the most exclusive product range.

The entire supply chain (to include distribution, which is often the most inadequate) should instead make every effort to create a product culture in the minds of consumers that enables them attribute value to what they're buying. Quality is everything, but it is an asset that should be explained, emphasized, made to emerge – the risk being, otherwise, that what can't be perceived doesn't exist.

The Albini Group is one of the largest European companies specializing in the production of fine shirting fabrics. Founded in 1876 in Northern Italy, the company has always been a family business and it is still managed by the fifth generation of the founding family. The company employs more than 1.400 workers. The total turnover in 2007 was equal to € 69 millions with a production of 20 millions meters of fabrics. The Group, through its brands Cotonificio Albini, Thomas Mason, David & John Anderson, Albiate 1830, offers various fabrics collections targeted to the most important fashion designers, shirt makers, leading department stores and retailers all over the world. The company is present, directly or through its agents, in over 60 foreign countries.

Corporate culture focuses on the concept of total quality, which is assured by the high level of specialization (cotton and linen fabrics for high-end men's shirts, both for shirt specialists and total look designer brands) and service orientation. The company has always invested in technological innovation and is characterized by the newest and most modern production processes. The Group's size has significantly increased in recent years through a process of acquisitions, giving the company access to the historical archives and top clients of the acquired companies. In the year 2000, a manufacturing company was acquired to extend the offer to the retailer segment.

Albini has been able to maintain its competitive advantage as supplier of retail and industrial clients thanks to a mix of factors: its Italian heritage, creativity and quality, branding and service. The service dimension is becoming more and more relevant. In fact, along with the traditional make-to-order collections, the company has added a so-called stock service which has evolved from the original basic offer to a stock of highly fashionable and complex items. The Group is investing more and more in cultural and artistic events in order to convey the magic of the Italian lifestyle to its clients. In the meantime, Albini is establishing co-branded promotional activities with its best clients and is working to create and diffuse the culture of natural fabrics. The aim is to make final customers more and more aware of the importance of the "fabric ingredient" as a distinctive sign of product quality.

2.1 What is luxury?

While the concept of fashion has to do with something that changes, the concept of luxury pertains to something expensive, hard to obtain, extravagant, an indulgence rather than a necessity. Fashion is forward looking; luxury is timeless and well grounded in the past. Luxury has to do with one or few market segments, as defined by price, while fashion has to do with the evolution of styles across different market segments, from top to mass. Neither luxury nor fashion defines one single industry or one product category; instead they identify a wider concept applicable to heterogeneous product categories. But while fashion and luxury used to be two different concepts and markets, nowadays the boundaries between the two territories seem to blur.

Fashion companies such as Armani, Versace, and Prada are moving into luxury, offering exclusive, timeless and custom made lines. At the same time luxury brands such as Louis Vuitton and Hermès are entering into fashion apparel and accessories selling seasonal collections with the collaboration of fashion designers. In this chapter we will try to provide a definition of luxury first and then we will discuss how luxury and fashion are becoming more and more mixed.

Colloquially, we think of luxury goods as high quality, expensive, branded items that connote opulence. Sociologically, luxury items may be used to signal wealth and are emblematic of an upscale, lavish lifestyle. An economist defines a luxury item as one for which demand increases disproportionately to income. In addition, some luxury goods have positive price convexity (people's desire to purchase the item increases with cost). Brand managers would define a luxury good as one that retains its differentiation premium over commodity products. Another definition for a luxury good is an item that individuals do not need as an essential element of a reasonable quality of life. None of these definitions contradict one another, and each one informs our conception of luxury. Etymologically, the word luxury (_luxe_ in French and _lusso_ in Italian) has been used with its contemporary meaning only since the 17th century. It originates from the Latin word _luxus_, which means exuberance of vegetation, metaphorically the abundance of delicious things. But the word is also similar to the Greek term _lox-os_ which means "growing in a twisted way (not straight), oblique" from which "growing too much" and, more generally, excess. From _luxus_ comes _luxuria_, which describes any intense desire or craving for self gratification. From the same etymology therefore two different meanings seems to derive: the first is positive, _luxus_ as in splendour; the second, _luxuria_, is a negative association with the idea of sin and decadence. What emerges from all this is that luxury is always associated with opposite meanings of useful and superfluous, magnificent and wicked, splendour and extravagance.

Hermès bags are by far the most expensive and prestigious bags on the market. But they are not just bags, not just a piece of merchandise anyone with money can buy. Along with beautifully handcrafted, status-rich, stylish goods, Hermès clients are buying a myth, the keys to another world: the World of Hermès. That is, buildings in Paris and Tokyo, on Madison Avenue and Rodeo Drive, smaller shops in dozens of cities, duty-free outlets at airports, more than 4.600 employees, the craftsmen in Lyons and Limoges. It's a world that includes that alluring, sensual, aristocratic French lifestyle representing a staple in the collective cultures in many different countries.

If we analyze the meaning of luxury over the centuries we notice how the concept has evolved from a value associated with the public sphere to one more and more related to individual experiences. From ancient times to the Middle Ages the concept of luxury was associated with splendour and identified the sacred marks of princes and gods. Luxuries were the goods offered to divinities.[1] With King Louis IV of France, luxury become something profane, symbolic of ostentation, *grandeur*, the French Court. From then on luxury was connoted with concept of un-necessary, superfluous but also conspicuous, affluent, refined. People's desire for wealth, status and social recognition is ultimately the end product that is consumed with luxury goods. Projecting status was the original mission of luxury goods, and still today this is the main driver of luxury consumption in emerging markets. In more sophisticated markets, instead, luxury has become more about expressing oneself, about being and enjoying, and less about owning and displaying. Conspicuous consumption is much more important when people are not far removed from poverty. In developed countries status is always there, but the shift in the balance is towards enjoyment and individual pleasure, such as buying a private plane to avoid the queues at airports security checks. The ultimate luxury for trendsetting (and value-driven) luxury clients in Europe are items which are truly discreet, that no one can quite identify, things that shows how confident you are rather than how much money you have. In the words of Lipovetsky, in modern times luxury helps support an individual image rather then a social image[2].

Today, luxury is a multi-dimensional concept that means different things to different people. A study[3] recently carried out

---

1. G. Lipovetsky, E. Roux, *Le luxe éternel. De l'âge du sacré au temps des marques*, Gallimard, 2003, p. 59.
2. G. Lipovetsky, E. Roux, *op. cit.*
3. B. Dubois, G. Laurent and S. Czellar, "Consumer Rapport to Luxury: Analyzing Complex and Ambivalent Attitudes", *Cahier de Recherche du Groupe HEC*, n. 736, 2001. This study is based on open and in-depth interviews with a sample of men and women of various ages and occupations, each of whom had bought at least one product which he or she considered luxury.

in France analyzed the associations of different individuals to the word luxury. It found, once again, many different dimensions: excellence in terms of quality (reliability, durability, made to last), a very high price as a consequence of high quality, scarcity, aesthetic value and a heritage that becomes a myth, a legend. This study comes to the conclusion that even within a group of consumers of the same nationality (France), there are still many different visions and ambiguous attitudes and opinions related to the word luxury.

Therefore we may conclude that the definitions of "luxury", taking for granted a few fundamental principles (high quality, high price and scarcity), are highly subjective and should be interpreted in different ways according to age and ethnicity, at the least.

- *Age* is still an important factor in understanding luxury consumption, but only if combined with the nationality (country of origin) of the consumer. For instance in the United States, unlike France, the definition of luxury is often democratic – an object or service, which represents "an accomplishment," a "prize or reward" or "delicacy or elegance". The idea of luxury has been shaped along with the identity of the United States itself. Whereas in other countries, luxury is associated with the privilege of high birth, in America luxury can be earned. In addition, in the United States and in Europe baby boomers appear to be the most important age group for luxury consumption in the future while in markets such as China young people buy more than seniors. The youth in Europe "cherry pick" from the choices available and are not addicted to luxury brands – mainly because such brands are not tailored to them. Young consumers are not loyal; they feel that luxury brands don't represent them, and they don't like the experience in the store because it's a bit old and tailored more to senior tourists.
- *Emerging vs. mature markets.* Even if consumer behaviour differs in the two groups of countries, companies should still carefully consider local tastes, macroeconomics, and demographics when approaching mature or emerging countries. There are some patterns in emerging countries that are similar (men buy more readily than women; hard luxury items

such as watches and writing instruments are a status symbol). However, consumers will not all behave in the same way. Comparing China and Russia, for example, though the two countries are similar in terms of the existence of a top tier of consumers, in China there is a huge middle class who purchases luxury goods, while in Russia this is not yet the case.

2.2 Old and new luxuries

Luxury goods have traditionally been items associated with the individual, they represent objects with high intrinsic value (cars, jewellery and watches, clothing and accessories, some foodstuffs such as caviar, truffles, and vintage champagne). The segments that customarily make up the luxury system are the following.

- *Accessories* (leather goods, shoes, silk items). This segment has seen notable growth in recent years both in terms of market value and impact on corporate turnover. Accessories offer high margins, and enable companies to shore up both the mature apparel business as well as emerging businesses. Though accessories were originally offered by companies as an initial purchase for new customers who were getting acquainted with a given brand, today the accessories market is hyper-segmented. As a result, alongside accessible items earmarked for wide diffusion, very exclusive articles have been introduced in the form of limited editions and custom made goods. The term "accessorization" is used to acknowledge the fact that today's accessory is no longer a complement – it creates a look. Accessories have taken on apparel's fashion connotation. The sector is relatively concentrated with the top four global brands carrying a large market share (Louis Vuitton, Coach, Gucci, Richemont, Hermès).
- *Apparel.* The segments considered luxury in terms of apparel traditionally relate to *haute couture* and ready-to-wear. The

two have blended, and as a result *couture* is the most exclusive range of a ready-to-wear, which has become more and more expensive in order to stand out among voracious accessible luxury. Today clothing is losing ground in terms of its contribution to sales and corporate profits. Due to the intense seasonality and relatively high price tags (in addition perhaps to the lack of any major innovation), the apparel sector has not been able to ride the wave of trading up, which has had the greatest impact on accessories. Clothing is still the framework in which designers can best express their creativity and present a lifestyle. That is, if there are any designers left who are creative as well as commercial, and if clothing can succeed in communicating desirable lifestyles[4].

- *Perfumes and Cosmetics.* Over the years this category has been utilized by historical luxury brands as well as new ones with an eye to attracting young consumers, breaking into new markets, and consolidating brand awareness by means of wider distribution with respect to the core businesses of accessories and apparel. Through licensing agreements with leading companies in the sector (first and foremost the L'Oréal-Luxury and Estée Lauder Groups), in particular in the fragrance category, brands have been able to count on continuous, worldwide launches, promoted by famous celebrities and capillary distribution. For brands like Chanel, Dior, and Giorgio Armani, by now perfumes and cosmetics account for a significant portion of turnover.

- *Jewellery and Watches.* A category historically considered luxury, based on the concept of eternity and preciousness. This segment experienced hard times in the early 2000s, but later saw consolidation. Recent years have brought on a recovery driven by new markets and new product concepts. In particular, innovation in design and the fashion effect have contaminated this segment as well, where one finds the most

---

4. These are the questions posed by the English journalist Suzy Menkes in "Who's Next in Fashion? No One. A Designer Century Comes to a Close, with New Talents Caught Between Corporate Pressure and Fast Fashion", *International Herald Tribune*, October 2, 2006.

exclusive lines alongside new products which are relatively more accessible and "fast," both in jewellery and in watches. This sector is very concentrated, with the top three players dominating the market at a global level (Richemont, Rolex, and Tiffany).

Today the sector has expanded to include any product which, though it may not be directly linked to the individual, is nonetheless a component of a *luxurious* lifestyle – i.e. sailing, home furnishings, spas and technology, and more and more often food. But the most noteworthy trend in recent years is the progressive shift of consumer interest and spending toward luxurious experiences rather than luxurious products. Expert senior customers in particular want to have memorable and unique experiences, after having had luxury in the form of objects. What's happening in the food industry is interesting from this perspective: food is becoming more and more strongly associated with the value of uniqueness, and consumption is experience. In fact, wine- and food-related consumption is emerging as the new frontier in luxury. The search for experiences, therefore, is broadening the perimeter of the luxury sector still further, from objects to services and spaces:

- Exclusive services for saving what is considered the greatest luxury of all – time (banking and investment services, insurance, frequent flyers, doctors, personal shoppers, membership in private clubs, etc.).
- Luxury retail (concept stores such as Colette in Paris, luxury malls such as Plaza 66 in Shanghai, in addition to the upward repositioning of historic department stores (like la Rinascente in Milan, Printemps in Paris, Selfridges in London, etc.).
- Luxury real estate and hospitality (restaurants, bars, hotels, apartments, offices, etc.).

2.3 Defining the luxury brand

We conclude this chapter with our own definition of luxury brands that attempts to encompass the previous discussion, while adding some aspects that we believe are essential for the purposes of this analysis. Though the essence of luxury remains the same (excessive, elitist, lavish, and in these respects luxury is *eternal*[5]), the way luxury materializes through brands calls for new perspectives and new forms of expression.

We define a luxury brand as a "coherent system of excellence". Regardless of the product category, luxury brands have certain distinguishing traits, *all of which they share*. This is what sets them apart from the mass market, which can only take on some of these characteristics, such as *aspirational* advertising. According to this viewpoint, luxury is a perfectly calibrated system of attributes, a harmoniously orchestrated universe of values, never a single trait, a total brand experience as indicated in *Figure 2.1*.

- *Association with a powerful imaginary*. All but mythological, both desirable and exciting. Some authors call this the *dream factor*. Behind many luxury brands there is a celebrated creator, mysterious production processes, secret formulas – all legends that create an aura of mystery and respect.
- *High price*. A dream nurtures desire, but if the desire is easily satisfied, there is no dream. In a world of excess production capacity and distribution, and media hype surrounding almost every product category, we can say that luxury brands are those that produce, distribute, and communicate less than market demand. Luxury is hard to attain; it requires effort and sacrifice, overcoming ordinary and standardized.
- *Originality associated with creativity and innovation*. A luxury brand sets its own bar and does not follow fashion or consumer demand. The brand reflects a capacity for leadership, uniqueness and exceptionality, which brings together

---

5. G. Lipovetsky, E. Roux, *op. cit.*

FIGURE 2.1   **THE LUXURY BRAND EXPERIENCE**

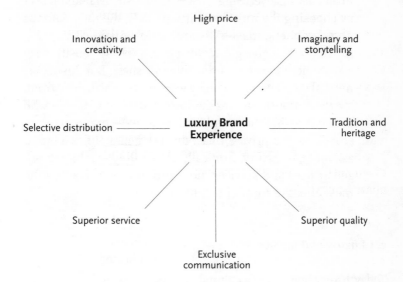

the work of artists and creative minds. The brand challenges its customers, their knowledge, taste, and discernment.
The brand creates a strong, virtually authoritarian culture,
where there is attention to detail and a sense of mission.

- *Superior quality, no compromises.* A guarantee that lasts a lifetime. Since quality in the mass market improves quickly,
luxury has to offer beyond-standard quality, continuously
raising the bar, also by rediscovering age-old knowledge relating to artisan skill and specific places. For example, the
concept of *supply chain traceability*, used in the food industry, could and should find widespread application in the
luxury sector as well.

- *Selective distribution.* Distribution positioning has become
crucial, perhaps the number one factor in determining
whether or not a brand is luxury. Exclusivity and selectivity
are two key words which, juxtaposed with accessibility, set
the boundaries of the luxury domain. In a market where
everything is available everywhere, unavailability breeds
desire.

- *Elite advertising.* Luxury builds dreams by creating a strong imaginary in advertising. Luxury demonstrates brand power by choosing the most beautiful models, the most famous photographers, maxi-billboards in international airports, the most exclusive glossy magazines (always positioning ads on the first pages of the biggest issues). But this aspect must always be integrated by work on the exclusivity front. Word of mouth among opinion leaders, the people who count choosing the brand, and finding the brand in exclusive clubs and private villas: this is what qualifies a brand as authentic luxury. Ironically, to sell the most highly prized articles and services, no communication is often the most effective form of communication.

2.4 Luxury and fashion

Today, luxury brands are a cultural presence. The big brands make culture; they convey their own culture. They interpret contemporary culture – they are contemporary culture. In a world where visual stimulation is ever more predominant, where value systems (of which brands are a representation) need a constant influx of new meanings, the lines between luxury and fashion tend to blur. This overlap is found in reports by financial analysts, in the language of the mass media, in flagship stores where historical and iconic brand goods mix with highly trendy items. Is it right, indeed does it even make sense to refer to ironclad definitions of luxury and fashion today? We believe the answer is no. The task of researchers should be to seek to rationalize complexity, keeping clearly in mind that schematization should serve to further our understanding of what is real, and not vice versa.

In our opinion, instead, more germane is an analysis of the multidimensionality of the concept of time in the consumption of luxury goods. This consumption, in fact, is marked by the dichotomy between *permanence*, meaning the inalterability of codes, and *fashion* as a continual and planned transformation of these very codes. In traditional luxury, products lasted over time (they did not go out of fashion), and needed time to earn a solid rep-

utation and build relationships with their custome
this sense, which can still be found in brands suc
and Cartier, represents a series of signs that mal
transcend the present toward eternity. Today, however, anouier
form of luxury co-exists with this one: pleasure, excess, super-
fluousness of people who have it all and can afford the luxury of
treating luxury goods like fashion items. Young people in particular demand that brands reinvent themselves, that they mod-
ernize their past and in so doing expose it.

This is what Vuitton did with reinterpretations of the Speedy model. The
celebrated monogrammed Keepall travel bag created in the 1920s, the perfect bag for Audrey Hepburn and Sophia Loren, and today it's more cult
than ever. Stephen Sprouse presented the Graffiti version in 2001, and
the eccentric Japanese artist Takashi Murakami made it Multicolor in 2003,
and even adorned it with smiling red cherries for the Cherry Blossom Pattern Collection in 2005.

The idea of luxury for Prada means a solid amalgamation of creativity,
quality and exclusivity. It is a dynamic concept that eludes the constric-
tions of a sterile, repetitive status quo and embraces the challenge of taste
that has to be able to renew and reinvent itself, anticipating and dictating
new trends, new sensibilities, and new parameters for what is contemporary. Underneath it all lies creativity. This is the very essence of fashion
and its connotations both from a cultural standpoint and a social and industrial one. The idea is not simply the functional act of creating: creativity
represents the synthesis of thought, culture, and experience which constitutes the true heritage of a brand and the precondition for creating channels of communication with diverse sensibilities and lifestyles the world
over. It is this intellectual capacity for continual renewal, the ability to
break new ground in "aspirationality" which generates the prime opportunity for a brand to be a true interpreter of luxury. But this is not enough.
Creativity has to be consolidated by a true obsession for quality. In order
for an object to be labelled luxury, quality must be total. In other words,
we must find quality in every stage in the process: from choice of materials to production, from commercialization to distribution and communication. Naturally, every element must be perfectly and coherently integrated with the design and the project, which underpin every single product. Lastly, luxury evokes exclusivity, that sense of uniqueness that one
must feel for the product. And it's not about price: a luxury item might
be expensive, yet it will never be considered "dear". Exclusivity, instead, is
an attitude by which customers, in recognizing and appreciating the features of luxury products, identify something personal and unique in their

form of expression, their need for self-representation, their desire to communicate. Therefore, the relationship with the buying experience takes on primary importance in every single phase as well: the window display, the shop, personnel, trying on the product, and packaging. Likewise, these are all aspects of a brand's exclusivity, with the product as protagonist and service as confirmation of this exclusivity. Creativity, quality, and exclusivity, then, are dimensions of luxury, never an end in themselves. Instead, these three aspects aim to establish a relationship with sensibility, culture, and communication at a global level. From this standpoint, luxury also becomes synonymous with belonging, with historical coherence, and cultural perception of one's own time. These are values that reside in the object, in the person who created it, and in the person who is able to identify and appreciate its quality.

Luxury for the Italian brand Tod's is about a contemporary, refined and impeccable taste combined with an enviable quality. The original idea of the signature shoe was born in the late 1970s when the entrepreneur Mr. Diego Della Valle understood that people needed a beautiful, well made shoe that could be worn in a professional, elegant or casual environment. The first successful Tod's item turned out to be the JP Tod's driving shoes that featured 133 pebbles along the soles. Since then the company expanded its collection introducing bags, accessories and capsule collection of ready to wear all categories supported by a clear vision: Tod's product must be recognisable even without its logo and there must be a great clarity as to the function the product will serve for the consumer. Giving the customer a special product with a strong and contemporary image is what makes the difference in luxury.

That is why luxury brands have to fulfill both of these needs: projecting the present into the future, creating iconic, readily recognizable products associated with their genetic code, and "eternalizing" the present by challenging codes with radical creativity, beyond all expectations. We will explore this topic further in the chapters to follow.

PART TWO

Country models

3 Country models

3.1 About country branding

Every nation has a legacy of symbols, values, and traditions that make up its intangible heritage. Generally, each country is associated with a particular moment in history: Italy with the Marine Republics and the Renaissance, France with the magnificence of the Empire, Great Britain with Shakespeare and colonialism. Often these images risk becoming stereotypes. Today, wearing a tartan has more to do with Sir Walter Scott than with authentic English life. Despite this, the kilt was re-launched by Vivienne Westwood and the corset by Jean Paul Gaultier. History shows that national symbols are constantly revisited and their significance reinvented. And fashion, more than any other form of artistic expression, has made contamination its credo, taking inspiration and meaning from history and transposing it into a context that transcends time.

Country branding is based on the history, culture, and values of a particular country. As a brand helps build consumer confidence, it in turn becomes the basis for the desire to buy. Associating the concept of brand to the identity of a nation can augment the consumption of products or services which originate in that particular country. A commercial brand can convey the image of a country. For example, ad campaigns by Coco Chanel and Yves Saint Laurent Rive Gauche, choosing sophisticated, romantic models who are also arrogant and haughty, brings the idea of "old French money" to life.

In the same way, the positive image of a nation can enhance the commercial perception of a brand. Country branding takes on even greater significance because it cannot be imitated; in this way it becomes the take off point for differentiating a company's products and services in the arena of global competition.

A research has shown that in acquiring "problematic" goods such as cars and luxury merchandise, the country of origin effect plays a larger role than it does for commodity goods, where brand provides a guarantee of product attributes and benefits. For this reason, there is an ever greater need for fashion companies to remember the tie with their *genius loci* (spirit of the place). Armani celebrates the Milanese fog with his grey jackets, Cavalli the signs of Florentine opulence, Versace the symbolism of Mediterranean classicism, and Dolce & Gabbana the religious rites of Sicily. Products, communication, and distribution format are winning elements when they reflect that particular alchemy of history, trades, and people which distinguishes one place from another. More enlightened companies recognize the need to strike a balance between preserving the personality of their brands and integrating the variety and change intrinsically linked to fashion. From this viewpoint, not only are flagship stores differentiated, in seeking a more intimate experience of the local context, but merchandise is also varied, in the belief that to attract luxury clients who move among the capital cities of the world, a company must offer diverse collections. At the same time, in an attempt to legitimize premium price, more often than not firms operating in the high-end of the market proudly claim their ties with their country of origin, echoing national codes in their ad campaigns. Some of the best examples of this are Paul Smith and England, Tod's and Italy, Hermès and France.

The country of origin effect

The *Made in* label has historically played two different roles. On one hand, it has allowed unknown brands to earn recognition in foreign markets due to a validation effect of certain qualities intrinsically linked to products that come from a certain place. On the other hand, this label is utilized with a protectionist/patriotic slant to encourage buying on the domestic market. This use of country of origin as an "access key" to foreign markets has become particularly essential for countries such as France and Italy that can't depend solely on their national clientele to sustain growth. In the second case, the "Made in" concept, in contrast to the globalization of French and Italian companies, is used in a protectionist vein. The *Made in USA* label, in particular, speaks to the patriotic sentiment of Americans. The objective is to guard against the threat of French and Italian fashion imports (the home country phenomenon). Moreover, due to the growth in international outsourcing, over time the meaning of *Made in* has been extended to the point of having very little relation to the country where a product is actually made. The majority of Geox shoes are manufactured in Romania, just as most Max Mara production is delocalized. Yet the perception of these brands is still *Made in Italy*. Gradually, as production is freed from geographical boundaries, and as the factory is substituted by branding (according to the paradigm "the product is born in the factory but what the client buys is the brand"[1], the definition of *Made in* is becoming more amorphous for end customers. In this context, the broad meaning of "country of origin", intended as the country the consumer associates with the place a certain product or brand comes from (despite where it was actually manufactured) takes on greater relevance. Nike sneakers, even though they are produced in South East Asia, are identified as American. In fact, because of advertising and retailing strategies, these shoes are strongly associated with the desire to emerge and the individualism typical of the American culture. Lastly, consider the fact that at present there is no global legislation or consensus on what *Made in* means. Each country has its own laws regarding the percentage of components of a product which must be manufactured internally in order to utilize such a label. Moreover, depending on the level of internal production, goods can be labeled *Made in...*, *Assembled in...*, *Styled in...*, *Designed in...*, *Dyed and Printed in...*, *Fashioned in...*, *Crafted in...*, *Created in...*, causing no small amount of confusion for the final consumer. What's more, often the same product can carry a different label depending on its market destination. The degree of domestic production necessary to be labeled "Made in" varies not only in the same country or sector, but, for example, in the fashion system sphere within different sub-sectors.

---

1. N. Klein, *No Logo*, Flamingo, 2001.

3.2 The French model: from *haute couture* to luxury conglomerates

Haute couture, or high fashion, began in France. Until the 1950s, Paris was the centre of the fashion world. This was where nearly all the fashion houses, the so-called *maisons*, had their headquarters. France's avant-garde position in fashion can be attributed to several factors.

Firstly, the relationship between pure and applied art has always been a very close one, and Paris has always been a workshop for the arts and culture. The role of the institutions and actors within the fashion world was also fundamental. Even today, the co-operation of designers, institutions, the media and opinion leaders make Paris fashion shows a powerful communication event, centered on fashion, culture and national pride. The French attitude toward fashion has always featured a luxurious, prestigious and exclusive character. This has made French fashion essentially an élite phenomenon.

Haute couture refers to the craftsmanship of the French fashion houses, whose designer-tailors create and present their own seasonal collections. These consist of unique creations that are made to measure for individual customers; very high prices reflect the excellence of service, workmanship, originality of a unique design and superb materials of the finest quality[2]. The terms *haute couture* and *couture création* are legally protected descriptions. The Paris Chambre Syndicale de la Couture Parisienne sets out the conditions that *haute couture* houses have to meet, and thus regulates the industry[3].

---

2. The manual labor needed to produce a *haute couture* garment takes between 100-150 hours for a suit and up to 1.000 hours for an embellished evening dress. Such a gown might have thousands of hand sewn beads. The fabrics available to the couture house are very luxurious and include the latest novelty fabrics and expensive silks, fine wools, cashmeres, cottons, linens, leather, suede, other skins or furs. In the case of a famous design house, the design and color of a cloth, may be exclusively reserved for that maison.

3. *Couture*'s strict admittance rules, which had been laid down in 1945, were finally relaxed in 1992. Before then, designers had to have at least 20 permanent members of staff working in their workshop, and their *salons* had to have sufficient capacity for twice-yearly shows featuring a minimum of 50 hand-sewn garments. Be-

The English-born Parisian tailor Charles Frederick Worth (1825-1895) opened what is generally regarded as the first *haute couture* house in Paris in the 1860s. Worth was the first to see how to attain star status, which he did quite simply by adopting the practice of signing his garments as if they were works of art. He also presented a new collection every year, and this introduced into fashion the constant factor of change, a pioneering innovation. However, it was only in the 1900s that the development of *couture* really took off. The Universal Exhibition arrived in Paris in 1900. Here all the fashion houses showed their collections to foreign customers, and buyers from all over the world came to Paris to see the exhibition. If Worth was the founder of *haute couture*, Paul Poiret (1879) is considered the first designer. He wanted to liberate women from corsets and the heavy fashion of the new century. So Poiret opened a small studio where, for the first time, simpler gowns were shown that did away with the underskirts and busts of the past. He was the first to use real women as models, and to tour Europe in order to "exhibit" his work. Poiret, who also became the first real designer of the 20th century, left his aesthetic mark on everything around him and on everything he could sell, from accessories to interior design.

In the 1920s, Coco Chanel made her entry in fashion history.

Chanel embodied the essence of the modern working woman, and her style is still contemporary. She invented sportswear: comfortable jersey trousers, summer clothes with very light lines, stripped pullovers, blazers in flannel, the first tailleurs, bright colors. She gave birth to the "uniform" for a new woman: the little black dress in *crepe-de-Chine* which *Vogue* dubbed "the Ford of fashion" for its democratic functionality. The hallmarks of her design were quality, comfort, proportions, simplicity, distinction. The menswear influence played a very important role: jersey[4] and tweed, uniform buttons and edging, cardigan jackets without collars and perfume in small square bottles. She was also the first to give bijoux a soul. For her fortieth birthday she launched Chanel N° 5: created in 1921,

cause 8 *couture* houses were forced to close down in ten years' time, and the remaining 15 had to fight for survival, rules were further relaxed in 1997 to facilitate entry to *couture*.

4. Chanel introduced in luxury clothing the use of jersey, which had been previously considered a basic fabric. Chanel jerseys were luxury items, and were rapidly copied so that the Chanel style became less exclusive.

it is still ranked the number one-selling perfume worldwide. By the mid-1920s, Coco had established her "Chanel look" consisting of a wool jersey suit with a straight, collarless jacket. Overall, Coco Chanel's clothing styles embodied much more than appearance in that they also contained a message: she celebrated women and their freedom, equality, and ability to express themselves through dress.

The fashion market came to a halt during the Second World War. It was only the first Christian Dior collection of 1947 that re-established French leadership in *couture*. The Corolle line, as Dior called it, became the New Look[5] that would define fashion for the next decade. In over eleven years of his reign, Christian Dior was the king of *haute couture*, dictating fashion not only to his clients but to all women who asked their tailors to reproduce the models. He was the first to transform the catwalk into a fashion show. He was also one of the first designers to understand the potential that lay in the commercial exploitation of a *couture* name and to invent the copyright. In 1948 he signed the first licensing deal in fashion history.

Up to 1940, the *haute couture* product was a luxury product, and it was only available to a small élite. Later, workshops and small firms began to reproduce high fashion items for a wider segment of the market. Dior made the first moves towards an international ready-to-wear industry in 1949, by opening a New York office for the sale of clothing to American department stores. This was also the era when American ready-to-wear clothing began to spread. Designers such as Traina-Norell, Hattie Carnegie, Claire McCardle, Adrian and others, showed clothes in very small but expensive series for their European customers. It was similar to *couture*, but did not require fitting and measuring. Ready-to-wear clothing manufacturing was based on the development of standardized sizes. French fashion continued to offer *couture* and luxury ready-to-wear items during the 1950s. At the same

---

5. In fact, Christian Dior is the man who revolutionized fashion by restoring turn-of-the-century virtues. The New Look meant soft, sloping shoulders, round hips, very thin waists and bell skirts in luxurious fabrics with embroidered flowers. According to many, it was a real restoration that brought women directly back to the past, to pre-war elegance and femininity (Seeling 1999).

time, from the United States leisurewear was becoming popular, supported by the image of the Hollywood movie star Lana Turner, the "girl in the pullover".

It was Italy, however, that led the way in knitwear. Italian jumpers were elegant and well made, and they ousted the dull products designed for informal occasions. The growing ready-to-wear market in Italy had its base in Florence, with Palazzo Pitti for the fashion shows and Palazzo Strozzi for commercial activities. Rome was the centre of Italian *couture*, with fashion houses like Valentino, and Emilio Pucci. It was in accessories, however, that Italian fashion was particularly strong during this period – Salvatore Ferragamo's made-to-measure shoes were legendary for Hollywood actresses and European princesses.

New names appeared in French *couture* in the 1950s and 1960s, including Guy Laroche, Hubert De Givenchy, Pierre Cardin and Yves Saint Laurent. The new *couturiers* interpreted the new woman with inspiration and imagination – Yves Saint Laurent has forever changed feminine fashion with the trouser tailleur, the motorcycle jacket, the Saharan, the nude look, the feminine tuxedo, and Pop Art dresses.

Above all, these were the years when licensing of the great French names in perfumes and accessories began. Cardin and Saint Laurent promoted a phenomenon that was later to allow all the *couturiers* to leave the *couture* niche and create brands with strong market power designed for the (fairly affluent) masses. In fact, ready-to-wear was the most important innovation of the 1960s, and all the couturiers contributed to it by creating secondary/young lines, each one progressively cheaper and aimed at a younger market than the *haute couture* collections were.

Pierre Cardin, "the man who became a label", was one of the first to recognize the power of the press and had an intuitive understanding of PR. He was the first big designer who saw no shame in working for Printemps Department stores and he was the first to establish commercial relationships with China and Japan as well. He also invented the first unisex line. In 1959 he was the first to present a collection as a *prêt-à-porter*, even before this word existed in the French language; as a result he was thrown out of the Chambre Syndicale. In the same year he was the first *couturier* to sign a licensing deal for off-the-rack dresses. Although his fashion star was declining by the late 1960s, licensing went from strong to stronger: Cardin found that his name could sell pretty much anything from chocolate to carpets.

It was the cultural revolution which marked the progressive loss of importance of the demiurge tailor. Paris wasn't able to interpret street fashion, where it lost ground to England and the United States, nor was France able to translate creative concepts of *couture* into industrial terms, enabling a *prêt-à-porter* to emerge, as Italian fashion did.

In the 1960s, the world of casual wear and youth clothing exploded. England had Mary Quant's mini-skirt revolution and "swinging" London, and the USA had James Dean and jeans. The English spirit was closer to young people, and new market segments for young people's clothing began to develop in these years. The current English supremacy in streetwear and the American dominance in sportswear had their origins in this period.

Italian ready-to-wear won international leadership in the 1970s. Until that time, Italian designers tended to be anonymous and it was the manufacturer's name that was on the label. Giorgio Armani, who was supported by a licensing agreement with the Gruppo Finanziario Tessile (GFT), appeared with his first collection in 1978. It was dedicated to the working woman, and focused on refined and feminine jackets. Versace also appeared in the same year, with his more feminine and seductive lines.

In March of 1980, the *International Herald Tribune* commented: "The competition between Milan and Paris is in full force, and Milan is clearly winning. Paris provides the inspiration and the direction, and Milan interprets and manufactures ... France earns glory, but the Italians are much better at earning money". In 1982, *Time* magazine gave Armani international status by putting him on the front cover. Italy definitively conquered the fashion world in the autumn of 1985, when Milano Collezioni became a seasonal appointment for international buyers.

The success of Italian ready-to-wear is closely related to a profound change in society, and the new, modern and accessible fashion was able to respond to this change. Further, although it was disadvantaged because it lacked the institutional protection and consensus that sustained the French industry, Italy showed that it could reach the same level of success thanks to high standards of workmanship and a superior textile industry. France went on offering inspiration and eccentricity in *couture*.

Today, only about 3.000 women or so worldwide can actually afford to buy clothes at the highest level, and fewer than 1.000 buy regularly[6]; there were 20.000 in the 1950s, the last big decade for *haute couture*. The profits from *haute couture* activity are negligible, or sometimes even represent a loss. However, the fashion shows attract huge media attention and gain enormous publicity for the *couture* houses. They sell a dream of the intangible, a dream of chic cachet, of beauty, desirability and exclusiveness that the ordinary person can buy into. If a consumer can afford the bottle of perfume, the scarf, the bag of the season, the *couture*-name cosmetics or the ready-to-wear "designer label" products, she convince herself that she is as exclusive as the celebrities who wear *haute couture* on the red carpet. Rather than a business, *couture* has to be considered a communication investment: the launch pad for the wider and more profitable business of perfumes and accessories.

Though names like Chanel, Dior, and Hermès have managed to outlive their past, today many of the once-famous *maisons* (Grès, Balmain, Patou, for example) have closed down, or survive on the memory of times past, covered by the dust of the present. Nowadays, luxury conglomerates have taken the place of the historical *couturiers*. Collecting new brands has become the core business for these companies, as they search for multiple identities to keep growing. In fact, they have grown through a process of acquisitions, inheriting fashion houses that were no longer able to sustain the investment needed to preserve their brand identity. The current French model of luxury conglomerates seems biased towards wines, perfumes and cosmetics.

LVMH came into existence in 1987, following the merger of Moët Hennessy and Louis Vuitton, and is one of the world's most profitable companies in the fashion industry. LVMH also takes on the title of world leader

---

6. A *couture* house like Chanel for example will have about 150 regular clients who buy *couture* and a house like Dior will make about 20 *couture* bridal gowns a year.

in luxury goods. The Group consists of over 60 brands and companies ranging from clothing (among them: Dior, Givenchy, Fendi, Marc Jacobs), to accessories (Louis Vuitton, Loewe ...), cosmetics (Sephora), wines and spirits (Moët et Chandon, Dom Pérignon ...), a cruise line and the online retailer eLuxury. The Group regards itself as the ambassador of the "art of living" and of French luxury. With 16 billion euro of net sales in 2006, LVMH operates through five product divisions that control different designer brands, category leaders, and specialist distribution trademarks. The Group's philosophy for managing a wide portfolio of luxury brands can be summarized in three points: very tight control of production, large investments in communication, and large investments in direct distribution.

Although PPR (formerly Pinault-Printemps-Redoute) has become best known for its majority stake in the Gucci Group (among the various brands owned: Gucci, Bottega Veneta, Yves Saint Laurent, Stella McCartney), the retailer remains a multinational conglomerate of widely divergent interests (including the Fnac music and book chain and the Conforama household furnishing retailer; the Redcats mail-order business also belongs to the division, which includes Brylane in North America, and the La Redoute chain). In 2007, PPR's total sales reached € 19.6 billion. Over the past few years, the company has sold almost all of its business-to-business holdings to focus on higher-margin retail and luxury chains, and recently acquired 62% of stock owned in the Puma Company.

3.3 The American model: from workwear to vertically integrated chains

The United States is the birthplace of modern democracy. This fact has translated into clothing with a transversal approach to occasions for use (casualwear) and with an accent on accessibility (good value for money). Geographic isolation and, at the same time, a lack of aristocratic tradition have made the US a country best known for all things associated with the concept of "mass": mass production, mass consumption, mass marketing, mass media. "Made in USA" is synonymous with enormous volume, as well as wide open spaces and big dreams (the frontier). The American Dream has spread its magic all over the world via Hollywood and Disney. Made in USA clothing is characterized by mass consumption and an emphasis on performance.

The American clothing industry came into existence at the start of the 1800s for menswear. The first garment factory was built in Philadelphia in 1812 to manufacture uniforms for the army. Then some small East Coast tailoring businesses (New York, Boston and Philadelphia) had the idea of producing and selling low-price ready-to-wear clothing for the sailors who came ashore on leave and needed to replenish their wardrobe. These first tailor-shops were both producers and distributors. The market grew from there. A mass market within the middle class grew up during industrialization in the first half of the 1850s. One of the greatest and most famous retailers of modern menswear, Brooks Brothers, was also one of the first producers. Brooks Brothers was founded in 1818 as a tailor's shop, and by 1857 it already employed 75 tailors and 1.500 outside workers.

The Gold Rush of 1848 had a significant effect on the development of the menswear industry. A man called Levi Strauss, foreseeing that the prospectors would need tents, started in business in California. He had a certain quantity of a resistant textile from France – *de Nime*, which was later Americanized as *denim*. Levi Strauss decided to use this material, not for tents, but for work trousers with a large number of pockets that were strengthened by metal rivets. These trousers had considerable success and, together with work clothes for the pioneers, contributed to the development of the manufacturing industry.

Levi Strauss started as a small shop run by its founder. In these early days, Levi Strauss was able to develop a patent for rivet-reinforced pants that would change the future of clothing. Thanks to this unique patent, the company could charge premium prices and consequently make management and organizational decisions based on principles other than strictly costs. The patent separated Levi's pants from the rest of the market, and therefore brand identification became possible. In addition to the rivets, a V-shaped stitch was sewn into the back pockets of all the pants in an orange thread that was meant to match the color of the rivets.

After the Second World War, the US population was getting younger as a whole, largely because of the baby boomers. Levi's began to shift its advertising away from the "cowboy" and more towards the youth of American society. This also shifted the target sales area geographically. Most of America's youth lived in predominantly urban neighborhoods as opposed to the rural areas in which Levi's were most heavily marketed and sold. With the new urban market, the firm changed its distribution outlets. Levi's were now sold in large-scale department stores rather that in "mom and pop" stores. The 1950s and 1960s marked Levi's new image with American youth, its expansion into the European market, and the introduction of Sta-Prest jeans. Captivated by James Dean's and Marlon Brando's image, American teenagers clung to their uniform of T-shirts, boots, leather jackets, and most importantly, fitted, worn, blue jeans.

The strategy of Levi Strauss from the early 1980s was characterized by alternating periods of re-focus on core business and of diversification. Facing a major setback in its market at the beginning of the 1980s, the first response of Levi Strauss was to change its business focus from manufacturing to marketing, more precisely to marketing the core product: the 501 jeans. This particular type of jeans (buttonfly, shrink-to-fit), which today is the best known article of clothing in the world, is in fact Levi's great strength, the essence of its brand identity and reputation.

The main event that paved the way for ready-to-wear clothing on an industrial scale was Elias Howe's invention of the first sewing machine in 1845. This was adapted by Isaac Singer for industrial use. This invention, together with the abundant immigrant labor force, sustained the growth of the industry. With the increase in mass production came mass distribution. Department stores and specialty stores began to devote a large amount of space to the sale of clothing.

The origin of ready-to-wear clothing in the USA was thus very democratic, right from the start. The American industry came into existence because of the need for comfortable work clothing, which is known as workwear. Although the industry would lose this feature over time, it allowed firms to develop native products, superior production methods and mass distribution channels. The firms themselves grew with a strong market orientation and integrated production and distribution roles from the outset. This feature helps to explain the current American model based on the centrality of vertical chains, department stores, and a strong marketing orientation.

Up to the second half of the 19th century, ready-to-wear clothing and women's fashion did not exist in America. In fact, most women made their own clothes. The few who could afford to do so imported clothes from France. Womenswear began to grow only at the end of the century. The 1920s saw the emergence of three major women's fashion magazines: *Vogue, The Queen,* and *Harper's Bazaar. Vogue* was first published in 1892, but its up-to-date fashion information did not have a marked impact on women's desire for fashionable garments until the 1920s. These magazines provided mass exposure for popular styles and fashions. Washable, easy-care fabrics were introduced in the US during this decade.

The first openly synthetic fibers were developed in the 1930s. Prior to this, manufactured fibers had been developed to emulate natural fibers. In 1935, the DuPont de Nemours Company successfully synthesized nylon. This fiber was introduced in stockings during 1939, but its use in fashion was interrupted by World War II. Widespread use of nylon didn't come about until after the war. The 1930s also saw many improvements in mass production techniques, which meant that a wider range of women now had access to well-made clothes. The American company Warner created the first bra with different cup sizes.

Retailers played a particularly important role in the development of American industry. They were the ones who, from the beginning, applied "suggestions" from Paris to their products. Nowadays, large department stores and vertical chains still make up the backbone of the American model. Today, they are in a position to teach their prestigious European "suppliers" how to deal with service, deliveries and merchandising.

In the early 20th century, specialty stores emerged with new retailing approaches and offered their customers high fashion merchandise. Bergdorf Goodman and Saks Fifth Avenue in New York City and Neiman Markus in Dallas concentrated on the highest fashion and customer service. And while great retailing establishments were growing in the big cities, chain stores selling lower priced merchandise were taking hold elsewhere, becoming a national phenomenon.

In the 1920s, every large city already had its department stores and speciality stores, and ready-to-wear fashion was also available through catalogues. The industry and large department stores still looked to Paris for their inspiration. Buyers and owners attended the haute couture presentations twice a year, and then turned these into mass items. The expression "Paris inspired" was the key to promoting fascinating apparel.

It was only after the Second World War that the first American designers began to appear on the scene. It was Dorothy Shaver, the president of Lord & Taylor, who promoted American designers for the first time in her shops – Elizabeth Hawes, Clare Potter, Vera Maxwell, and the woman considered by many to have been the first real sportswear designer, Claire McCardle. The development of the great American designers, who now battle against the Europeans for the world fashion market, took place in the 1960s.

Finally, the invention of "casualwear" and superior marketing management, above all in the mass market, allowed the American model to enter the international markets by building competitive positions which European competitors found hard to imitate.

The post World War II Baby Boom had created 70 million teenagers for the 1960s: now young people were not merely revolting, they were devising a counter-culture of their own and marketing this so fervently that it became omnipresent. The young market was supplied by young people who became rich thanks to young people's interests (fashion, discos, underground magazines and, above all, music). London was the new center of gravity which inspired fashion: Mary Quant (or was it André Courrèges?) invented the miniskirt; Twiggy was the first model ever to have mass appeal; young people discovered India and the hippy Flower Power movement; bell-bottom trousers and worn velvet clothes were the fashion "must-haves". Whereas the 1960s are remembered as the great period of youth revolts, the 1970s were an intensely tumultuous time, with various cultures and subcultures coming out into the open. Everything was allowed: fashion no longer had any rules. The 1970s was the decade of lifestyle jeans (which proudly bore the labels of designers like Fiorucci and Calvin Klein), the unisex trend and glam-rock, people crazy for kitsch, the punks. For the first time what was beautiful was questionable. In the 1980s, hip hop, rap and break dance gave voice to the black culture, which would become very influential from a fashion point of view (Seeling 1999).

The apparel industry in the US, as well as in most developed countries, faced a major crisis in the 1970s. Cost increases and changes in consumption patterns coupled with the competition of labor costs in developing countries: the apparel industry in US lost almost half its employees in 20 years. The disinvestment from the apparel industry, job losses and off-shore production occurred in all the major industrialized countries, except for Italy.

Nowadays there are two types of big players in the American apparel market: retailers and marketers. Retailers, who used to be apparel manufacturers' main customers, are now becoming their competitors. As competition is progressively more price-driven, retailers have increasingly turned to imports. Private labels, merchandise made for specific retailers and sold exclusively in their stores, are now a large part of American retail business.

Gap was born in 1969 in San Francisco, and was the result of the efforts of Donald Fisher. Gap was a specialist jeans shop that sold all sizes. The business grew from one shop into a chain, at first in California and then throughout the US. From 1974 onwards, other merchandise was introduced with the Gap label. In 1976, Gap was listed on the Stock Exchange, and in 1983 the company purchased Banana Republic, a chain store specializing in travel clothes, when it already had 550 specialist shops throughout the whole country. In 1985, Gap decided to enter the children's market as well, and did this by developing new lines and opening the first Gap Kids' Store the following year. Gap began its international development in 1987 by opening its first shop in London. In 1992, it created a new division for family clothes, Old Navy Clothing. This had a lower price positioning than earlier lines. Gap now employs 50.000 people and has a vertically integrated structure. The company is directly involved in the entire supply chain, from product development up to visual merchandising in the sales point. The retail network is owned by the company. There are five divisions: The Gap, Gap Kids, Banana Republic, Old Navy and Gap International. The Group is able to segment its casual clothing offer effectively. In fact, Banana Republic satisfies customers who are looking for items that are sophisticated from the point of view of quality and image, while Old Navy offers lower-price items that are still fashionable. Within the USA, the Gap is seen as a "social passport", in the sense that everyone, from children up to adults, owns at least one Gap item. The style has been defined as "modern American classic with a twist", and the brand evokes informal values, style and fun.

Marketers are companies such as Liz Claiborne, Donna Karan, Ralph Lauren, Tommy Hilfiger and Nike which established most of their sourcing overseas while they fortified their activities in the high value-added marketing and retailing segments of the apparel chain. Where creativity was once the main ingredient, marketing now guaranteed a brand's success. American designers were the first to understand this fact, becoming giants of marketing and making immense profits.

After establishing his reputation as a designer, Calvin Klein was able to exploit it by diversifying into low cost/high profit products such as jeans, underwear and perfume. His advertising campaigns have always played a primary role. The 1979 communication campaign with Brooke Shields declaring that "Nothing comes between me and my Calvin's" introduced the use of overt sensuality in the promotion of fashion and helped to generate designer jeans sales. His advertising has continued to be sexy, controversial and cutting edge. The strategy for the 1985 introduction of Obsession (a carpet-bombing TV advertising campaign) changed the way the entire industry launches fragrances, introducing the idea of ambisexuality, and using the word smell in the ads instead of aroma or scent. CK one gave life to a new market segment: unisex.

Calvin Klein was among the first to embody fashion market globalization – all over America, Asia, and Europe. He developed fashion, fragrances, cosmetics, accessories and home collections. Nevertheless, the excessive dilution of the brand versus the mass market made it difficult to market the top line in Europe and depreciated the value of the brand, which was sold in 2002 to PVH (Phillips-Van Heusen, also Klein's men's shirt licensee) at half of the amount initially requested. Since Phillips-Van Heusen bought Calvin Klein in 2002, the focus has been on the hugely successful jeans, underwear and fragrances, which are all global operations.

Americans are more inclined to buy a style rather than a production method. The concept of product origin has been substituted by brand origin. What counts is not so much artistic/creative superiority (as is the case with France) or production excellence (as with Italy), but consistency with respect to the values that inspire the American dream. The greatest American designers in the past thirty years have understood this lifestyle perfectly, and transformed the simplicity and taste of "casual" into clothing that works for every occasion. Bill Blass, Anne Klein, Halston, Calvin Klein, Donna Karan, Michael Kors, Marc Jacobs, Narciso Rodriguez and many others have created an American stylistic identity, each with his or her own look but with certain elements that all their lines have in common: clean lines, neutral color tones, and few prints – accessible, casual, comfort-oriented fashion.

Ralph Lauren "makes new wealth look old"[7], combining the idea of the freedom of the American West with refined, timeless elegance of Old England tradition. Taken alone, cowboys are neither rich much less aristocratic, but the artificial mix has become real. Rather than using his own name, he developed Polo to evoke an image of understated elegance and sophistication. In collaboration with the photographer Bruce Weber he established the advertising tradition that celebrates the entire spectrum of the American experience: continuing in the spirit of the Polo philosophy that individual clothes are not as important as the lifestyle and the world they reflect, Polo pioneers advertising with little or no text, and a sweeping, cinematic scope.

Ralph Lauren himself is the personification of the American Dream: from the Bronx to English polo fields, he is the living example that old money and class are something that people can aspire to.

3.4 The Italian model: from designers to vertical integration*

Many reasons lay behind the development of the "Made in Italy" and the Italian fashion system over last 20 years. The competitive advantage compared to other countries (e.g France, the US and Germany) has been the simultaneous presence of the following three conditions: Italian designers, Italian entrepreneurs, and the textile industry.

We can divide the history of the Italian apparel industry in at least four cycles of approximately 10-15 years each.

The development of industrial production from the 1950s to mid-1960s

After the Second World War, in Italy for the first time there was a surge in growth of the mass market for apparel. Apparel technology was imported from the US. At an industrial level, "sizing" was

---

7. F. Davis, *Fashion, Culture and Identity*, The University of Chicago Press, 1992, p. 63.
* This paragraph, with the exception of pages 55-59, was adapted from Saviolo S., Testa S., *Strategic Management in the Fashion Companies*, Etas, 2002, chapter 4, par. 4.4.

an issue and Gruppo Finanziario Tessile (GFT) was the first company to measure a wide sample of the Italian population, creating a single national sizing system. The high-end of the market was still tailor made, and female ready to wear was in its infancy. The final consumer was looking for functional, durable, good quality garments. Fashionability was not important at that time; it was only a need of the High Society, inspired by French *couturiers*. The business model of Italian manufacturing firms started in the 1950s and was characterized by big plants, economies of scale and strong specialization (menswear; womenswear).

Companies also competed abroad on price/quality. Manufacturers were few and the industry was quite concentrated, especially in menswear; major players were GFT, Marzotto, and Lebole.

The possibility of an Italian Look in fashion was conceived for the first time in 1951 in the magic of the White Room (*Sala Bianca*) of Palazzo Pitti in Florence, where Gian Battista Giorgini organized a show for some Italian fashion houses with a very innovative look in comparison to Parisian fashion. Unlike *haute couture*, which is presented in January and July to a generally small, select circle in private salons, from then on designers were able to show their *prêt-à-porter* lines in March and October before a larger, though still select, audience which included the press, buyers and celebrities. Success was immediate and American buyers celebrated the rise of the Italian style.

The crisis and the reaction of the Italian apparel system from the mid-1960s to the mid-1970s

Major economic and social events occurred from the end of the 1960s to the early 1970s: the "global revolution" of the young generation; major social and union conflicts; dramatic increases in labor costs; the surge of apparel imports from developing countries; the oil crisis; the internal economic crisis (negative GNP). New values and new lifestyles spread in the society, determining a new market segmentation: people were asking for more informal wear, and new trends were no longer driven by *haute couture*. All of these changes meant the end of the mass market, and big industry was caught unprepared. The difficulties of large firms were also due to stagnation and rapid changes in demand, which prompted the production of smaller product series. Smaller firms showed that they had strategic advantages in terms of flexibility and product innovation (fashionability). After the first stage of development, small firms found it increasingly difficult to enter final market and distribution. Market orientation required considerable communication investments and sales management techniques. Only a few companies managed to make the quality leap to become "industrial fashion-oriented firms", differentiating themselves from the mass production of large traditional firms. The others, however, maintained their role as subcontractors, and in doing so supported the decentralization of productivity that was being carried out by the large firms.

The development of subcontracting among large, medium and small firms was further supported by another specific feature of the Italian fashion system – the distribution and concentration of the productive units in specific industrial areas specialized in textiles or leather production (such as Biella, Prato, Bergamo, Carpi, Firenze, Ancona, etc.). Industrial districts share some characteristic elements: specialization in a manufacturing sector, the division of work between companies, high entrepreneurial levels and permeation between social and economic life[8].

Industrial districts provided a stimulus which benefited large firms as far as subcontracting and small firms in terms of growth. All this helped increase the specialization and innovation of the industrial structure and at the same time ensured the advantages of large size (economies of scale) and small size (flexibility) at a district level.

This development of the industrial system would not have been a sufficient element of competitive advantage if it had not

---

8. Each firm in the textile industrial districts specializes in a particular stage of production or a certain type of product or material. Physical proximity, cultural homogeneity and social and personal relationships encourage communication and the containment of logistics costs. Above all, these factors encourage the development of a very advanced know-how that acts as a lever on strong partnership and imitation processes. Thanks to the availability of labor and qualified personnel throughout a specific area, the districts make up a wide and continuous basin for the birth of new firms. These, in turn, contribute to reinforcing the stimuli for further improvement in productivity and product throughout the whole system.

been accompanied by two important and closely-related factors for change. These were the birth and establishment of designers and the revitalization of demand.

The close relationship between designers and the industry is an additional feature of the Italian model. Up to the 1960s, some designers were unknown external contributors to the manufacturer's product office. Other designers were used to producing made-to-measure garments for the élite (*haute couture*, as described in *Section 3.2*). This was the case of Valentino Garavani, who opened his own maison in Rome in 1959. His dream was to disseminate a new style for elegant and feminine women: Valentino achieved world success thanks to the concept of the suit as a work of art, as the expression of the designer's greatest creativity. This suit should be made to measure and was thus destined for a very restricted public – the aristocracy and movie stars. Based on these assumptions, it is evident that *couture* had long been regarded, and perceived itself, as quite separate from the clothing industry. This was particularly true at a time when the clothing industry was offering mass production based on a strategy of low prices and high volumes.

The distance between the two worlds of *couture* and industry finally disappeared thanks to the youth revolution and the increasing emancipation of women. All this took place in Western societies in the 1960s and then was definitively consolidated in the second half of the 1970s (see also *Section 3.2*). *Couture* thus lost its attractive and distinctive role, and Milan took the place of Paris in the ready-to-wear industry. Industrial firms like Krizia, Mila Schön, Missoni, Genny and Basile developed in the Milan area. The shift of European and world fashion to a new center of gravity in Milan seems to evidence a widespread desire among operators in the industry to have greater links with industry, efficiency and organization. Although the preconditions for a profound change were already in place in the early years of the 1970s, the process itself could not move forward because of the economic crisis of 1974-75. The middle years of the 1970s saw a radical change in the economics and value system of industry. This was due to the inversion of the economic cycle, growth in income, and greater social/political stability. There was more interest in the private dimension rather than the collective one, with a search for the daily pleasures of life. Middle- to upper-class women were the first consumer segment to give in to the unprecedented scale of consumption.

The most developed firms, starting with Gruppo Finanziario Tessile (GFT) realized that it would be easier and faster to seize the new opportunities that were emerging from demand if they had a new relationship with designers.

The 1980s: the boom of "Made in Italy"

The Gruppo Finanziario Tessile was a clothing manufacturing company located close to Turin, in Nothern Italy, which had a fundamental role in the development of "Made in Italy". In 1978, GFT proposed a consulting agreement to a young Giorgio Armani aimed at bringing an innovative technical and stylistic know-how to the Group's industrial culture. Armani declined the simple consulting agreement, and proposed a licensing agreement instead for the production of a line under his own name; the accord also set down a clear-cut division of tasks between the two parties. The Armani case, with all its peculiarities, became the model on which the relation between industry and creativity was built in Italy. The experience of Gianni Versace in Genny and Giorgio Armani and Valentino in GFT during the second half of the 1970s made the large firms aware of the complementarities of the industry/designer skills and the need for a genuine partnership with designers. Thanks to the large firms' financial and commercial resources, designers could rely on wider diffusion of their products on both the national and international markets. New relationships between industry and designers were established: from "contractual relationships" to partnerships. Licensing became a way to extend the designer names into new product categories (sportswear, kidswear, fragrances, homewear, eyewear). And firms moved from product specialization to multi-product capabilities.

The connection between designer and industry requirements was fully realized in Armani's experience, first with GFT and then with smaller firms. Armani succeeded for the first time in going beyond the exclusive ambit of high-end ready-to-wear to reach a much wider target. The diffusion collections (intended as the designer's second and third lines in terms of price points, after *couture* and ready-to-wear) started here. Armani was able to maintain his stylistic identity in the new lines as well, such as the Emporio Armani line. The pieces in this collection were Made in sufficient number to be produced in series, but they had features that differentiated them from ready-to-wear.

The revitalization of the product that follows from this partnership provided a further stimulus to the growth of demand. The same article of informal clothing could be casual and sporty without competing against formal apparel, but instead integrating the offer for different use occasions (free time, the weekend, travel and holidays, and so on). In this way it was possible to create a new market space enlarging the target of reference from just young people to new "yuppies" and youthful adults.

Although licensing has been an important money-spinner in the fashion business for several decades, ostentatious use of brand names and logos only really came into its own in the 1980s, the total-look designers' decade par excellence. It was acceptable not only to spend, but also to advertise the fact that you did. For those who couldn't afford ready-to-wear, there were plenty of products on offer that carried a designer name, designer cachet and a suitably inflated designer price. Designer jeans, t-shirts, sunglasses, handbags, belts and perfumes meant that almost anybody could buy into the dream and announce to the world that they had.

The internationalization process brought Italian brands on the world markets; the Italian style was gaining consensus especially in US. The drive toward exports by Italian firms developed from the early 1980s onwards, after the first signs of a slowdown in internal demand. Italian currency devaluation made Italian exports more competitive abroad. However, the internationalization process of Italian clothing and fashion firms reflected an orientation towards the export model instead of direct investments. The focalization on the product and the lack of marketing orientation prompted Italian firms to rely on importers and distributors rather than creating their own commercial structures. Noteworthy exceptions to this are GFT and Benetton. The former began to build its own subsidiaries in the most advanced countries (Germany, France and the US). The latter, thanks to its know-how in franchising and its global vision, spread its own distributive formula first in Europe and then in the US.

Made in Italy

Made in Italy is not a label of origin that can be applied indiscriminately to every product manufactured in Italy, such is the case for *Made in China* or *Made in Taiwan*. It is, instead, an abstract concept, a signature that defines products that Italy actually specializes in, and where there is a distinctive advantage in terms of innovation, style, service, and price. *Made in Italy* is:

- A blend of creativity and functionality.
- Craftsmanship and small scale production that guarantee product quality.
- Districts and small family-run businesses that give rise to a model based on flexibility, specialization and continuity.
- Control of the entire textile production process, from yarns to distribution, and that of leather/footwear/accessories which, with the support of the mechanical/textile and advanced tertiary industries, orient the system toward continual innovation.
- The Renaissance effect, a consequence of living in the world's biggest open-air museum, which influences the aesthetic sensibilities of all Italians. Italian consumers are the most demanding in the world, though they are also willing to pay a premium price for quality and design. Italians buy products *Made in Italy*, not out of patriotism like the Americans, but out of an appreciation for beauty; this has allowed companies to continually raise the quality of the products they offer.

Italian products are not revered as works of art; rather they are valued for their usability and functionality, for their capacity to give an aesthetic dimension to daily routine.[9]
Made in Italy evokes harmony – not the perfect one-of-a-kind item, but garments that can be worn with elegance, matched with just the

(continue)

---

9. "Tod's shoes with rubber pebbles were created with an eye to the consumer who wanted to be elegant and relaxed at the same time. I wanted a product that was warm, comfortable (in place of those terribly uncomfortable winter shoes) that wouldn't slip, with a transversal aesthetic appearance" (Diego Della Valle, CEO Tod's).

right pieces, which separately do not give a sense of elegance or beauty. For this reason *Made in Italy* is identified with certain products (like clothing, shoes, bags, home décor, marble and tile, cars, food, coffee, and wine) but not with any specific fashion style. From Gianni Versace's rock-n-roll sensuality to the sartorial minimalism of Giorgio Armani, from high-tech rigor of Prada to Roberto Cavalli's wild exuberance, *Made in Italy* is, with respect to *Made in USA* or *Made in France*, a much more complex concept because it finds as many expressions as there are ways to interpret beauty.

For foreigners, *Made in Italy* reads *la dolce vita*, great food, a beautiful landscape.

The most representative *Made in Italy* brands make this imagery their fundamental element: Ferrari red symbolizes the Italian pleasure of driving sports cars, and Riva yachts evoke the beauty of Italian coasts and beaches. In fashion advertising, many symbols and geographical references characterize *Made in Italy*: Versace's villas, Roberto Cavalli's beaches, the Sicilian piazzas of Dolce & Gabbana, the scenic Roman panorama by Laura Biagiotti.

The center of gravity for *Made in Italy* leans decisively toward manufacturing. Italy controls the production processes (from raw materials to finished products) of most goods that are defined as high intensity from a symbolic viewpoint (clothing, accessories, home décor). Though there are charismatic entrepreneurs (Giorgio Armani, Renzo Rosso, Luciano Benetton), Italian excellence remains production excellence. The quality of a Gucci bag or a pair of Salvatore Ferragamo shoes has its origins in the tanneries of the Santa Croce district and culminates in the extraordinary leatherwear tradition of Scandicci.

The new century: toward the integration of the system

In the 1990s, the environment changed dramatically: fashion was no longer seen as a status symbol (yuppies, dress for success) and logos were no longer the purchase driver (except for accessories). While the 1980s were the period of the total look, the 1990s saw the emergence of mix and match: being fashionable meant being yourself. In keeping with the spirit of the time, the fashion decade's hallmarks were: sales and basics; anti-fashion and grunge (everything that's not fashionable is trendy); *less is more* and minimalism elegance concepts; the spread of street fashion and sneakers (Puma-Jill Sander and Adidas-Yamamoto brought activewear and technical fibers into fashion); self-expression and cheap and chic; the growth of the men's fashion segment.

Although the work of Hanae Mori, Junko Shimada, Issey Miyake, Rei Kawakubo, Junko Koshino and Yohji Yamamoto had been appearing on the catwalks of Paris ever since the 1970s and 1980s (Kenzo was the first Japanese designer to establish himself in the French capital), they definitely became a reference point for the fashion community in the 1990s. Though they never attained significant market success, the Japanese enchanted the fashion world for their ability in cutting and their philosophical approach to clothing. In contrast to their Western colleagues' obsession with exposing the female form in ever tighter and more transparent designs, the Asians exhibited an aesthetic of concealment which borrowed heavily from the geometric forms of the kimono. While Westerners try to transform the body into a masterpiece, Japanese create dresses that are masterpieces.

In the new century, luxury is not necessarily synonymous with logo; instead it is more closely related to exclusivity, creativity, craftsmanship.

Italian designers have entered a new cycle of growth based on vertical integration of their core business, both upstream and downstream, while they have strengthened strategic partnerships with licenses in cash-cow sectors such as fragrances and eyewear.

At the end of the 1990s, Dolce & Gabbana decided to turn itself from a fashion house into a vertically integrated brand. The Group organization integrates two different structures. The chief production company is Dolce & Gabbana Industria which controls the two manufacturing facilities in Legnano (clothes) and Incisa Val D'Arno (shoes and leather accessories), and a number of companies that provide support services. DGS S.p.A., instead, controls the Italian own-store network. International marketing operations are headed by the two wholly owned subsidiaries in the US (NY) and in Japan (Tokyo). The own stores in Europe and China are managed by local companies, which are also wholly owned by Dolce & Gabbana (the first Italian fashion company to obtain a license to directly operate its stores in China without a local partner).
The company decided not to renew the license to produce the second line – D&G line – with Ittierre (in-house production since Spring/Summer 2007); the remaining major licensees are fragrances (Procter & Gamble), eyewear (Luxottica) and watches (Binda).

With the new century, the fashion system has experienced dramatic evolution. First, the fashion context is becoming more and more global in geographical scope: evolution is increasingly affecting Italian firms as well as French and American ones. New players are coming on the field (i.e. luxury groups into fashion), new market segments are being created (i.e. upper bridge), entry barriers are getting higher (higher investments in advertising and retail), and new formulas are developing in retailing (experiential shopping is becoming the new communication tool). The growth of multibrand and multi business fashion groups has moved the competition from clothing to total living.

Many companies are now listed on the Stock Exchange; among the Italians are Gucci, Bulgari, IT Holding, Tod's, and Mariella Burani. The acquisition and repositioning of brands with a heritage is becoming a must for luxury conglomerates. More and more *couture* houses are attempting to relaunch under the helm of another hot name. Most examples come from France: Karl Lagerfeld, who has been designing Chanel for 20 years, continues to win accolades for his modern interpretations of the house's signature style. The same is true with Christian Dior, overhauled by John Galliano, Yves Saint Laurent first with Tom Ford and then Stefano Pilati, Riccardo Tisci at Givenchy, Antonio Marras at Kenzo among many others. Also in Italy the designers-for-hire syndrome now represents an established career path. Italian labels have carried on after the death or retirement of their founders as well, like Moschino, Ferragamo, Trussardi, Versace, Gucci and Ferré. Companies still led by their founders are also facing the succession issue, given the high average age of designers.

Four groups of players dominate the competitive system:

- *Industrial companies*: acquire brands (mostly previous licensors), launch own brands or develop retail strategies (Aeffe/Moschino, Ittierre/Ferré, Max Mara, Zegna).
- *Designers/entrepreneurs*: control production and distribution processes, very few licenses, purchase plants (Armani, Dolce & Gabbana, Versace).
- *Multibrand groups*: conglomerates, acquire brands and designer companies, especially at a luxury level (Gucci Group, Prada Group).
- *Pure designers*: sell the companies to industrial or multibrand groups (Valentino).

In an industry which today is global, there is no longer one single country leader: British, French, Italian, Japanese, Belgian and soon Chinese designers are all legitimated to make their statements. Consumers are mixing and matching different designers, different occasions of use, and different price ranges. Fashion is more than ever a way to express your own individuality.

3.5 The Asian model: from outsourcing to integrated production networks and vertical retailers

For a long time, East Asia was exclusively an area for low-cost production by Western firms. The countries of the region have shown themselves capable of astonishing growth levels in the last decades, however. This has stimulated local consumption and promoted the development of new countries and actors in world textile and clothing industries. It is thus impossible to consider the analysis of national models complete without examining the case of East Asia. This region promises to be the largest growth engine of the new century.

Industrial business models
Before analyzing industrial models in the Asian clothing industry, it would be useful to make some general comments about the economic models and growth routes that have been taken in this area. The purpose is to clarify the industrial realities as part of a wider economic analysis. Recent empirical studies have shown that the *economic proximity* of countries in the region has increased as a result of strong growth in the 1980s in trade and direct intra-regional investment flows.

The *flying geese* model has been used to examine trade and intra-regional investment flows in the case of textile and clothing. This theory concentrates on the relationship between changes in the stage of industrialization and the comparative advantage of countries. According to the theory, the spread of technology is transferred through direct investment by leader country to follower country. Firms from the leader country move their production to the follower country in an attempt to exploit their ownership advantages and to take advantage of lower cost factors. The combination of direct investment and relatively cheaper factors of production helps to increase competitiveness on world markets and leads to a rise in the follower country's exports. The expected result of this process is the decline of the leader country's comparative advantage in a particular product, following the de-localization of production, and an increase in the follower country's comparative advantage in the same product.

There is some empirical evidence that countries in the Asian region have been pursuing the flying geese model since the 1950s with regard to international specialization in textiles/clothing. The so-called "first migration"[10] of production took place in the 1950s and 1960s. This entailed moving the production of textiles and clothing from industrialized countries (mainly Japan, the US and Germany) to the "big three" Asian producers: Hong Kong, Taiwan and South Korea. Large Western firms, generally competing in the mass market, tended to transfer the most basic and labor intensive productions to Asia. Over time, technology and controls for ensuring respect of qualitative standards were transferred; as a result local producers moved up the learning curve. They became increasingly focused on products and activities of greater added value, and also increased their share of production destined for export. The combined share of Hong Kong, Taiwan and South Korea was 10.3% of world textile and clothing exports in 1980, but this jumped by 18.6% in 1990. Hong Kong was the leader of the three countries, and its exports over the same ten-year period grew by 365%[11].

The three countries progressively lost their attractiveness as production sites at the end of the 1980s as a result of the increased cost of labor and the lack of export shares. Instead, they became logistic and service centers heading new productive networks and encouraging the growth of new producers in the area – China, Thailand, Malaysia, the Philippines and Vietnam. The strong develop-

---

10. S.R. Khanna, "Structural Changes in Asian Textile and Clothing Industries: The Second Migration of Production", Textile Outlook International, Economist Intelligence Unit, September, 1993.

11. GATT, International Trade, 1992.

ment of textile trading companies[12] from Japan, Hong Kong and Taiwan in emerging areas suggested that these nations were forming regional networks organized on the flying geese model. These changes have been called a "second migration" of production in the textile-clothing industry, with migration being taken to mean the transfer of the production of the three large producers (Hong Kong, South Korea and Taiwan) towards new areas within the region. China seems to be the main beneficiary of this secondary migration of production. It has been also the largest beneficiary of the end of the *Multifiber Agreement* and the liberalization of exchanges in the industry at the global level. Since 1997, the return of Hong Kong to China has caused exports from both countries to increase rapidly. China today is the strongest world producer, while Hong Kong is taking the role of a regional financial and services center in addition to representing an affluent market for fashion consumptions. China is one of the main textile producers in the world with particular regard to natural fibers (wool and silk). Silk, for example, is one of the few sectors in which China has a world monopoly, with its exports of raw silk accounting for more than 85% of world production. China is also one of the few Asian countries with an integrated textile pipeline that includes raw materials and manufacturing.

China and the shifting center of gravity for global clothing manufacturing

The dynamics of global clothing imports reveal a complex process of relocation and concentration of production which have led China to become the world's largest clothing supplier, out-performing all other producers.
China's higher labor productivity compensate for its wages, which are much higher in China's garment sector than those, for example, in

(continue)

---

12. The trading company or *shosha* is one of the principal actors in the Asian clothing market. Its origins are in Japan, and it performs the functions of a central commercial office for the sale and purchase of various types of merchandise, both nationally and internationally. It offers the retailer and the producer a vast range of services including finance, technical assistance and the direct management of the sales network.

Bangladesh, Cambodia, India, Indonesia and Vietnam. A high degree of vertical integration also contributes to lower garment assembly time and costs. China has long been set up for full-package production, making it relatively easy for US, European and Japanese companies to source reliably completed garments from Chinese factories. In addition, solid infrastructure permits fast transport and quick turnaround of containers and ships in ports in China and Hong Kong. It has been reported that suppliers increasingly use air transportation for fashionable items. As a result, China can produce almost any textiles and clothing product at any quality level and at a competitive price both for major retail groups and brand-name marketers. Large retailers characteristically have large volume requirements, which lead them to consider only large producers (more than 1.000 workers) as potential suppliers.

In addition, since the mid-1980s there has been a move towards "lean retailing", particularly in the United States but also in Europe and Japan. This favors producers who can provide quick turn-around – either because they are geographically close to their principal markets (e.g. Mexico, Central America and the Caribbean countries to the United States; Turkey and Eastern Europe to the EU) or because they can quickly and efficiently organize the entire supply chain. The latter favors producers in Hong Kong (China), Taiwan, and the Republic of Korea which are well positioned to manage manufacturing in the global clothing industry.[13] The elimination of quotas facilitates a further geographical concentration of production.

Yet, there are signals that could challenge the future role of China as a global supplier of clothing[14].

---

13. UNCTAD, "TNCs and the Removal of Textiles and Clothing Quotas", UNCTAD/ITE/IIA/2005/1.

14. Many sources, such as UNCTAD, provide evidence that the future role of China as a global supplier of clothing could be challenged. Here are the reasons why. Firstly, power shortages and emerging bottlenecks in the transport and distribution of oil and coal in China have already disrupted textiles and clothing production in 2003. The second uncertainty is China's status as a "non-market economy" at the World Trade Organisation for 15 years (or to 2016). This means that anti-dumping duties on textiles and clothing products from China can be higher than those from other market-economy members of WTO. Indeed, government subsidies are a contentious issue. According to the Organisation for Economic Cooperation and Development, state enterprises in China account for 35.7% of textiles output, 6.7% of garment production, and 32.8% of manufactured textiles and clothing machinery. However, state enterprise losses are equivalent to 1.8%-3.7% of the outputs in those three sectors. The third uncertainty relates to the textiles safeguard provision (effective until the end of 2008) and the transitional product-specific safeguard provision (valid until December 2013). These provisions form part of China's WTO acces-

Large Asian transnational corporations are likely to play an increasing role in shaping the future global production chains in textile and clothing, both as buyer and as suppliers. The sourcing strategies of a small number of large retailing companies are relying more and more on few global supply chain orchestrators (such as Li & Fung from Hong Kong) for fashionable items requiring specific competences in terms of merchandising. For basic items, retailers will increasingly adopt a direct approach to procurement, sourcing at large factories mainly in China, India and Pakistan (examples of large and integrated manufacturers are the TAL Group or the Esquel Group, both from Hong Kong). Therefore concentration of production within fewer, vertically integrated factories is expected to rise in less developed countries. As they become more important at the procurement and production stage, the bargaining power of both Asian large manufacturers and supply chain orchestrators will increase vis-à-vis retailers in developed countries.

Market structure

Consumer markets have been subject to intense development in East Asia. After a first stage (from 1980 to 1995) of high growth in purchasing power and consumption on the one hand (South Korea, Japan, Hong Kong and Singapore), and market transition or the end of the subsistence economy on the other (China and Indonesia), the East Asian market is now converging towards a polarization in branded clothing consumption.

- The growth and success of imported brands (Italian and French) in the very high-end of the market; this segment is obviously well consolidated in Japan, South Korea and Singapore and still emerging in China, Thailand and Indonesia.
- The spread of local brands or international ones produced on licence in the medium to low price range for a rising middle class. Global vertical retailers and local brands fiercely compete in this territory.

---

sion. How often these two safeguards are used by WTO members is an open question. Price competition, lack of marketing know how and strategic vision, together with quality issues view will keep destroying value and deteriorating output of Chinese factories.

Compared with Europe, distribution in Asia is very concentrated. The Philippines, Indonesia and Thailand have adopted the American model of the shopping mall hosting shop-in-shop formats. Nowadays, Japan, Korea and Hong Kong and China as well make more balanced use of the street shop, the department store and the speciality shop. Japanese operators have the widest distributive base in Asia through trademarks like Sogo, Takashimaya, Yaohan and Isetan. The large high-end Asian importers (Japanese, Taiwanese and South Korean) choose the best *concepts* (a mixture of product, image, distributive layout, accessories and fair price) that can attract their customers. The historic French brands (Lanvin, Dior, Cardin, Yves Saint Laurent) were the first to import their own labels through production and/or distribution licenses. This became the model for other countries as well, such as Italy. Italian luxury brands developed a strong presence, particularly in Japan.

The typical entry mode used to be partnerships with trading companies (such as Mitsui) for Japan or importers (Joyce, Blue-Bell) for Hong Kong; then importers distributed the product through mono-brand boutiques or corners inside department stores. Recently, most global brands have decided to serve the main East Asian markets directly (Japan, South Korea, China) through commercial branches and a directly controlled network of boutiques. In the luxury segment, prices are very high as they incorporate mark-ups related to the length of the channel (such as in Japan) and/or steep import taxes and duties (such as in China). Rich Japanese and Chinese prefer to shop when they travel to Europe, to Hong Kong or to Macau to benefit from lower prices. Still, what has proved to be important is to open stores in these countries to build awareness and image for the brand.

There is very strong local competition in the medium and low market segments. Hong Kong producers like Toppy (Episode, Toppy and Colour Eighteen brands) Theme, Bossini and Giordano are "American inspired" vertical chains.

They have an aggressive approach to the market, offer good fashion content in line with European trends, make large advertising and brand investments, and use very careful visual merchandising and information systems in the store. In recent years European fast retailers such as H&M and Zara have also entered East Asian countries bringing European flavor in more affordable price ranges and cashing in on the fast rise of young, fashion conscious customers. We will discuss this further in the following chapters about India and China.

4   India strategy for fashion and luxury brands[*]

In collaboration with *Leandré D'Souza*[**]

4.1. Introduction to India

In 1947, at the stroke of midnight, India shook off its fetters and awakened as its new self when Jawaharlal Nehru delivered his "Tryst with Destiny" speech to the country's midnight children with the following words: "A moment comes, which comes but rarely in history, when we step out from the old to the new, when an age ends, and when the soul of a nation, long suppressed, finds utterance".

Over sixty years later, it is still one nation and is now celebrating a turn in its history: a contemporary "India that is proactive, fast-paced, conscious of its identity yet open to change and ready to challenge the Chinese tiger with its disorganised democ-

---

[*]   This chapter is the result of research undertaken by SDA Bocconi "Perspectives for luxury firms in the Indian market" by the two authors in 2007, conducted with an analysis of available literature (articles and studies) and a series of interviews and discussions with senior entrepreneurs, Indians and expatriates with experience and knowledge in the Indian luxury sector.

[**]   Leandré D'Souza is of Indian origin and is Area Officer, India, at Bocconi University's International Relations Office. She has even worked as a journalist for *The Indian Express* and *The Asian Age*, Mumbai, India.

racy, chaotic change and all the contrasts that render it so diverse from its Asian neighbours"[1].

India is, above all, a complex country. It is a country of over a billion people spread across 28 states, a multilingual people that converse in 17 languages and 22.000 dialects. Its geographical landscape ranges from the snow-peaked Himalayan ranges to the scorching deserts of Rajasthan. With the worlds' religions at its doorstep, every imaginable faith is present in this pluralistic nation from the Hindu majority to the large Muslim minority that also includes Christians, Buddhists, Sikhs and Jains. In spite of sporadic tumult in this "unnatural" country, India is one of the world's biggest democracies. However, its cultural politics is based on a "vision of democracy which too often means not the will of the majority but the will of organised minorities — landowners, powerful castes, farmers, government unions and local thugs"[2]. This peculiar rendition apropos democracy has taken several shades over the years as the country shifted from socialism to liberalism.

The India that somersaulted from an agricultural to a services industry is still riding high and advancing rapidly: Goldman Sachs estimated that by 2050, India will be the world's third largest economy while today it rests at twelfth position[3].

Despite the buzz, if one looks beyond the surface, the fissures reveal that there exist two faces of this new India – an urban and a rural side. This is because all the action is currently centred in the main metropolitan cities of Mumbai, Delhi, Bangalore, Kolkata, Hyderabad and Chennai.

Strangely though, with respect to other emerging countries, the actual percentage of the urban population is rather limited (28% as opposed to 41% in China and 73% in Russia). And unfortunately for rural India, most development has been concentrated in the big cities thus largely neglecting this integral part of "shining India". Incidentally, rural India accounts for 20% of the country's GDP.

1. Z. Fareed, "India Rising", *Newsweek*, March 6, 2006, p. 34.
2. *Ibidem*, p. 35.
3. D. Wilson, R. Pusushothaman, "Dreaming with BRICs: The Path to 2050", *Global Economics Papers*, n. 99, October 1, 2003.

Colossal disparities in wealth continue to be a cause of grave concern as India is still home to more than half of the world's hungry that comprise about 800 million living (on less than $2 a day) below the poverty line[4]. As a result, while urban India is rapidly embracing modernity, a large portion of the country is being left in the shadows. And class and caste differences are so rigid that they still determine one's right to access basic amenities like education, food, water, electricity and also determine one's right to climb the social and corporate ladder.

So what is it that makes India so hot? Its success is in its private sector. It is home to industrial families that have revolutionised economic history: the Tata's, the Birla's, the Godrej's and the Mittal's are today large conglomerates that produce everything from automobiles to steel. Other home grown companies like Infosys, Wipro, Satyam Technologies, redefined the production and distribution of information and communication technology: over 125 *Fortune 500* firms have R&D bases in India.

The government too can revel in its creation centres of excellence like the famous Indian Institutes of Technology and Indian Institutes of Management that churn out over 350.000 graduates annually. This also signals the large size of skilled labour qualified internationally, for positions in prestigious multinationals, banks and consulting firms[5].

Gone are the days when the country's finest minds would race off to the US; the tide has turned with an estimated 25 million people of Indian origin having returned home[6]. Finally, India is a young country where 65% of the population (thrice that of Europe) are under 25 years[7]. For Indians, the key to success is English and the Internet: there are, in fact, 200 million English speakers[8] and 11,6 million Internet users[9].

---

4. Z. Fareed, *art. cit.*, p. 35.
5. R. Kakkar, Secretary General – Indian Chamber of Commerce in Italy, "Summit Made in Italy", November 16, 2006.
6. J. Sudworth, "Indians Head Home in 'Brain Gain'", BBC Delhi, August 27, 2006.
7. A. Populier, Agre International, "Summit Made in Italy", November 16, 2006.
8. C.P. Ravindranathan, "English – advantage India", *The Hindu Business Line*, May 12, 2007.
9. Internet and Mobile Association of India, "32 per cent Active Internet Users Rely

New Silicon Valley, hub of low-cost labour with both skills and age to their advantage and even a country with a refined creativity that has imposed its products on the West (India is the world's largest producer of films and Bollywood, its mainstream cinema, has in recent years, gained recognition internationally)[10].

In spite of this, gleaming flaws still exist: adult literacy is at a shameful 61%[11]. Metropolitan cities are so crammed that the concept of personal space is alien to Indians (by 2026, the population of its metropolis will total 122,8 million inhabitants)[12]. Bureaucracy is a nightmarish affair and foreign companies eager to enter the country are stalled for months with paperwork and rigid laws. Despite obstacles posed by bureaucracy and outdated norms, foreign direct investment is encouraged through incentives to export for those with an equity share in Indian companies. In comparison to other developed economies, India's growth has been less linear: its version of democracy implies endless hours spent in negotiation among opposing party leaders in order to put forth different interests. However, one must not belittle this unlikely democracy, which guarantees more solid development in the long term because it is based on the principle of equity, redistribution of resources and environmental sustainability.

And thus, the coexistence of realities that are vastly different, the impossibility of finding a common denominator among these contradictory factors, sets India apart from the rest of the world. It is a market that can offer grand opportunities to luxury brands (skilled labour at low cost, affluent and sophisticated consumers, a strong aesthetic culture) willing to invest time and resources to learn and understand its nuances first and then to decide and react.

---

on the Internet as the Primary Source of Information and for Research", Press Release, October 10, 2006.
10. CII-KPMG, "Indian Entertainment Industry Focus 2010: Dreams to Reality", Report, 2005.
11. C. Murphy, "India the Superpower? Think Again", February 9, 2007, money.cnn.com.
12. A. Populier, "Summit Made in Italy", cit.

4.2 Luxury consumption in India

An overestimated boom

According to the book *The Cult of the Luxury Brand: Inside Asia's Love Affair with Luxury,* by Radha Chadha and Paul Husband (Penguin, 2007), the Asian consumer evolves in a five-stage process as it absorbs luxury into its way of life. While Japan is already at stage 5 where luxury has now become a "way of life", China is at the "show-off" stage at phase 3 and India, at the bottom of the pyramid has embarked from stage one of "stupor" and is infiltrating towards stage 2, that of "acceptance"[13]. This passage from the first to the second phase implies a transformation in the Indian mindset, from *self-denial* to *self-indulgence.* Earlier, Indians would put all their wealth in investments or basic needs such as education. Today, young Indians with substantial wealth want to spend. But how many consumers can actually afford luxury products?

What clearly emerges is the existence of a segment of consumers with a high purchasing power[14]. However, the real number of luxury consumers could be less than the optimistic forecasts given by analysts. This for various reasons: not all wealthy consumers buy luxury brands and adopt Western attitudes; Indian consumers that buy international labels do so at international shopping destinations – Singapore, Hong Kong, Dubai, New York, London – which means that these clients have a refined knowledge of luxury and are more demanding in terms of quality and service. This further complicates the entry of foreign brands in India, already affected by hefty duties that end in higher pricing. In order to permeate this market, companies require heavy investments to create prestige and to develop the brand's

---

13. "Hindustan Times Luxury Conference", 2007.
14. With reference to the upper classes, Altagamma revealed that there were 83.000 High Net Worth Individuals (HNWI) in India with at least $1 million in net financial assets as opposed to 320.000 HNWI in China. This number is growing by 10.000 per year. For McKinsey & Company, the size of the luxury market in India has surged at an annual rate of 20% and in 2004 reached $454 million. Similarly, the *KSA Technopak Study* evaluated the market at $444 million. According to other sources, the actual dimension of the luxury market oscillates between $326 and $435 million with a growth rate of 15-20% annually.

retail presence. It would certainly be difficult for enterprises to breakeven not only in the short term but also in the medium or long-term.

Indian designers themselves have not understood the sheer immensity of the industry and have yet to pervade the market as today they hold only 1% share of the market[15]. Does the market exist? It definitely does. Is it overestimated? Probably yes. The critical issue is not whether luxury brands will gain success in India but how to convince Indians to buy locally.

A nascent market

The luxury market in India is nascent, and it is merely an infant precisely because, until recently, international luxury brands were reluctant to set foot in the country. Until 1991, the economy was closed to foreign investment: the only international brands present were Bata, Fiat and Benetton. At their time of entry, India was considered a place to direct old stocks left over from other markets. What's more, the majority of Indian consumers were convinced that Benetton was a local producer of t-shirts.

Thus, it is only after the end of the 1990s that one witnessed a filtering of international brands into the country and into collective mindset of the Indian people. And it is only recently that Indians themselves have started to buy branded clothes.

Tommy Hilfiger launched his first store in April 2004 in collaboration with NY-based Murjani Group. A few years later, the company had flagship stores in Mumbai, Gurgaon, Bangalore, Hyderabad, Chandigarh, Kolkata and Chennai. When it first made its foray into the country, it priced its jeans at $100 — about as much as two months' salary for most Indians, with a 2.000 square foot store that sold the same products, atmosphere and prices consumers would find in stores in New York and Chicago. Today, Tommy Hilfiger is a brand of international success. Being one of the first players in the market, the brand enjoyed a greater visibility whereby consumers, mostly belonging to the upper-middle class, perceived it as a luxury brand (with a higher positioning than what it enjoys in Europe). In the future, the brand plans to transfer its manufacturing base to India

---

15. A. Giriharadas, "Global Goals for Indian Designers", *International Herald Tribune*, May 5, 2005; A. Giriharadas, "Indian Designers Look to Export Their Heritage", *International Herald Tribune*, February 22, 2007.

and to introduce a range of evening gowns made of sarees exclusively for Hollywood stars[16].

Louis Vuitton, part of LVMH Moët Hennessey Louis Vuitton SA, began its affair with India since its inception in 1854, with the Maharajahs who were their most loyal "special order"clients. However, it was only in 2003 that the company set up its first flagship store in Delhi at the Oberoi Hotel through a distribution agreement with LV Trading Private Limited India. Following its positive performance, it extended its presence to Mumbai at the Taj Mahal Hotel, which coincided with the brand's 150-year celebrations. In 2006, Louis Vuitton Malletier became one of the first brands to own a majority stake in its Indian distributor. With the majority stake of 51%, the company announced initial plans to invest $13 million for its Louis Vuitton and Fendi units[17].
LVMH is also present through a number of brands that include Tag Heuer, Christian Dior and Fendi that function as separate and independent entities.

Tag Heuer has been greatly successful in India. The company has set its sights high with the aim to become the main luxury watch retailer in India and has expanded its presence in major cities such as Kolkata, Ahmedabad and Hyderabad at leading retail chains – Reliance, Shopper's Stop, Pantaloons and DLF. Under the LVMH flagship, plans also include the setting up of luxury malls to launch other brands.

With a firm belief in design and marketing capabilities in India, the Luxottica Group, which bought the Eyeware division of Bausch & Lomb in 2000, established RayBan Sun Optics India Ltd. and was quoted in the Indian market. While the diffusion of branded sunglasses is still limited because of complex distribution channels and because of the impossibility for the multibrand to directly own its distribution, Luxottica has turned heads with its recent ventures. It partnered with real estate giant DLF. The Milan-based luxury group would open 100 stores of its retail brand Sunglass Hut at DLF's upcoming shopping malls[18].

A market still partly closed
Luxury imported goods are subjected to stiff tariffs (customs and excise reach an average of 33%). This poses a dilemma to firms

---

16. T. Tandon, H. Sengupta, "Brands ready to rock India", May 4, 2007, moneycontrol.com.
17. R. Chandran, J. Kirpalani, "Luxury Brands Take Baby Steps in India", June 16, 2006, moneycontrol.com.
18. "DLF ties up with Luxottica; to launch first store in November", November 4, 2008, *The Economic Times*, http://economictimes.indiatimes.com/.

who have to decide the best pricing strategy: renounce the option of placing the burden on the Indian consumer and maintain a coherent international positioning but with a major setback to margins or consider all the necessary additional costs, although this would arouse disappointment in those clients used to purchasing brands abroad and who are already aware of the actual price?

Companies have also urged for more coherent bureaucratic procedures that still remain uncertain and slow[19].

On the other hand in recent years these taxes have been drastically reduced. In 2005, the government enforced a 12.5% VAT on a national scale to stabilise investments and to clear the path to foreign investments. In the end, the government allowed the entry of foreign direct investment in retail, confronting the critical retail knot. On 15 February 2006, a law was approved allowing monobrands collaborating with a local partner, a 51% majority stake (while investments for multibrands like Luxottica remain at a standstill). This is of significant relevance as luxury brands finally have direct control of their own distribution. Similarly, the opening of shopping malls has also been encouraged in order to provide the right context for these products.

To keep control over the business it is imperative for fashion and luxury companies to safeguard the company's identity and brands, but in India this becomes a mandatory choice, given the paucity of Indian partners with actual knowledge of how to market fashion brands[20].

One must also underline the presence of big industrial families in India like the Tata's (Lakme, now part of Unilever, was one of the brands launched by them) and the Wadia's with diverse interests – from cars to textiles, mechanics, hotels etc. These

---

19. For instance, the law pervades that every color on textiles have to be carefully scrutinised. But each color takes no less than a week to be analysed. As a result, a design by Missoni with 16 diverse shades is likely to be held up in customs for as many as four months, in G. Ferré, "Altagamma sbarca a Mumbai" (Altagamma enters Mumbai), *Corriere Economia*, June 5, 2006.

20. A few are present – like Mafatlal Luxury, partner for Valentino Fashion Group; TSG International Marketing which introduced Moschino in India; the NY-based Murjani Group, former distributor of Gucci, Bottega Veneta (these brands have joined with Genesis Colors in Delhi) and La Perla (now partnering with Reliance Brands); Mohit Diamonds that distributes Piaget, Chopard, Vacheron Constantin and Bulgari.

families have a profound knowledge of the market and command a strong reputation in India.

Prior to imports barriers and partner selection, other obstacles to foreign investment exist such as the absence of adequate infrastructure (roads, airports, railway lines and telecommunication facilities), bureaucratic inefficiency and corruption.

Not the consumer but Indian consumers

To understand the Indian consumer one has to take into account the paradox prevalent in terms of religion, region, values, lifestyles, cultures, buying habits that vary between cities and rural areas; North versus South; women versus men; young versus old.

Even regional differences exist, as consumers in North, West, East and South are immensely diverse from each other. Traditionally, the South tends to be more conservative and as a result, consumers are not easily swayed by change. However, these factors like tradition and regional disparities are becoming less rigid as more Indians travel abroad and become more Western in their outlook.

Differences still linger in the consumption patterns of men and women: the evening wear category has more potential for men than for women as the latter still prefer the *saree, kurta, lehenga* during ceremonies. Women are more prone to buying accessories – footwear and bags to match traditional outfits. And while other Asian markets respect fashion codes and are more inclined to buying of closed footwear, in India it is considered sexy for women to buy open shoes like sandals or stilettos. What's more, the more conservative kind are likely to shy away from low necklines or short skirts.

In the sportswear category, brands must make reference to the most popular sports played in the country thereby evoking styles associated to games like cricket, golf and polo. In India, a class of nouveau riche is also present. This new bourgeoisie is ostentatious, prone to splurging and what's more, is still unable to tell the difference between a Chanel and a Tommy Hilfiger and is inclined to extravagance to show off his professional and social success. And despite the embryonic stage of luxury in India, what makes it diverse from other emerging markets is the existence of the luxury consumer. These are clients that prefer a Bottega Veneta to a Gucci, who love status symbols but refuse to be driven by them. They have an intrinsic knowledge of luxury and the brands they love and belong to the foreign educated class. They have a refined aesthetic and are familiar with the origin, heritage and value of brands and the elaborate level of quality attached to luxury products.

Accustomed to buying all the latest designs at the world's shopping capitals, they have a higher expectation when it comes to service. Thus, particular attention has to be invested in the training of sales personnel on the characteristics of the product and also the ability to convey the brand's ideology to existing and new clients. Wealthy Indians love to spend but like all great business minds, they also need to be reassured of their value for money.

Indians, designers of the future?

India has always had a rich clothing and textile heritage. One that has continuously infatuated and inspired international designers. If in the past, only a few turned their products into brands, today there is a growing stress on design (and not solely on embroidery and embellishment of products), communication (even towards the choice of brand name as in the case of clothing brand "Stanza" where the Italian name induces an importance to quality) and distribution (opening of monobrand stores) to develop not just products but also concepts. Several Indian companies are also aware that ties with recognised international firms constitute a strategic move[21].

The Indian fashion arena can still not be defined as an industry[22]. The "phenomena" of fashion is still absent – that where a designer is capable of capturing an international audience. However, in the future, with a style that is distinctly Indian yet distilled to capture an international audience, Indian brands will be able to make a mark globally. They will also attain an added advantage within the local market as it imbibes the taste and quality inherent in international luxury. They would also be able

---

21. Raymond launched a joint venture with Italian textile companies of the upper-middle class bracket like Grotto S.p.A, Zambiati and Lanificio Fedora, in T.A. Deshpande, "Textile Sector Shops for Italian Brands", *Business Standard*, February 1, 2007.
22. Reports by the Associated Chambers of Commerce and Industry reveal that Indian designers sold just $45 million worth of clothing in 2006 and sales were principally domestic and the figure, a fraction of the global industry.

to offer consumers internationalised collections, fabrics and finishing of fine quality at a lesser price.

In order to harness this talent, the "Made in India" concept could be extended where the country could be developed into a supply base for luxury brands. If the collective imagination is one of manufacturing at low costs (manufacturing costs in India are 15 to 20 times less than in France), it is also true that at most fashion houses like Emanuel Ungaro, Cerruti, Romeo Gigli, Gianni Versace, Moschino, Genny, Louis Féraud, Rena Lange, much of their applied decoration has been done in India (and most of it by the Paris & Delhi-based house of Nina Gill)[23].

It was Dilip Kapur that transformed the Indian consumers' vision of leather. From being an industry confined primarily to decrepit mills, it was the Pondicherry-based guru that took leather goods, gave them a sensuous *je ne sais quoi* combined with refined craftsmanship and packaged them neatly into prestigious boutiques. That marked a drastic transition for the Indian leather industry that has since never looked back. As founder and President of HiDesign, Kapur is always reinventing his brand. With an already international presence in China, South Africa, Russia, the US and the Middle East, Hidesign is the most prominent leather manufacturer in India. It is no wonder that Louis Vuitton aroused the curiosity in international fashion houses in 2007, when it bought a stake in the company. As part of the alliance, the French brand will develop its first factory in Asia. In addition, both companies will develop manufacturing facilities alongside that will produce select components for Louis Vuitton products in Europe. While HiDesign has been selected due to its technical expertise in industrial planning, designing and manufacturing of leather goods, it will not be an outsourcing destination for Louis Vuitton. Naturally, the acquisition will ensure that HiDesign remains the foremost Indian leather brand and Louis Vuitton might be able, in future to threaten market competitors like Coach with lower pricing strategies.

4.3 Brand building in India

Product: triumph of the glocal

India is open to all ethnicities, religions and cultures. It is also profoundly nationalistic, conscious and even proud of its uniqueness

---

23. K. Treacy, "Made in India: Western Brands Attracted, but Ironing Out Wrinkles", *International Herald Tribune*, October 6, 2005.

and strong customs. Unlike in China, where aesthetic sensibilities were erased during the Cultural Revolution, India has a strong visual culture. It has overshadowed Hollywood with its own cinematic formula and has besotted the West with its fashion, music, cuisine, colors. Thus, brands have to flex their muscles and project a strong global personality. In some cases, they might even need to scale down the *haute couture* image associated with their products, publicity and services to appeal to a wider clientele. The biggest challenge is to find a right blend of European and Indian tastes without however, risking one's own brand identity. This is because luxury in India is a symbol of financial power and social standing.

With the exception of the North, the rest of India has only three seasons: spring, summer and the monsoon. Autumn and winter don't exist and it remains hot for six months of the year. Despite this, the concept of hosting "fashion week" has recently taken shape: the Lakme India Fashion Week and Wills Lifestyle India Fashion Week are organized twice a year.

In order to create a successful model in India, brands have to work against their regular seasonal approach and have to learn how to work towards the logic of "flow delivery", pitching more than one main collection per season and churning out a continuous retail supply. Moreover, brands need to design collections that are wearable. And while the *belle du jour* of the West is leaning towards androgyny, the epitome of Indian femininity and beauty is strikingly diverse. Also, a large segment of the population strictly abides by traditional customs and beliefs.

There also exists garments and jewellery worn only in India such as the turban. These could offer interesting branding perspectives. Designers that could incorporate sarees or turbans into their collections are sure to garner clout.

Finally, the use of color, embroidery and accessories, the choice of fabric and materials are fundamental to Indians: the elite Indian is fascinated by the minimalist elegance of the West as well as baroque Indian designs, rich textiles and handcrafted goods.

Indians have always been fixated with fair skin. This is because culturally, fairness is associated with upward mobility, lifestyle, beauty and for women, the assurance of finding an eligible husband. The obsession with fair skin is so intrinsic to Indian culture that even matrimonial ads in newspapers will favour fairness over education. This "snow white" syndrome is indicative of the gargantuan size of the fairness cream industry as it sweeps through every social class.

Despite Chanel's dogmatic image of strictly adhering to international fashion codes, it entered the country in 2005 by pandering to Indian tastes with a make up line that consisted of shades of pink in order to suit the Indian complexion, the launch of which would be inadequate in its major markets of operation such as the US.

Besides what will occur and what could take place in other virgin markets, the exchange with India has been two-fold. Bollywood has taken over the ramp, is themed at lounge bars and inspires major advertising campaigns. In the same manner, Indians can be won over by our style. We have certainly been taken over by theirs.

The arrival of retail – soon

It is evident that there is a potential for luxury goods in India, but until recently, the main problem has been that of the right channels to market these products. Unlike China, India does not have luxury shopping malls[24]. With the inability to directly control distribution (but this limit, as stated earlier, is being reduced since 2006), brand presence is confined to shopping arcades of luxury hotels, without any possibility of external visibility. However, figures for the next few years projected the possibility of a luxury mall fever where the country would witness the building of over 600 malls[25] and estimates foresaw a growth in retail space of 30% in these new malls[26].

In an environment that is still not well-defined, *first movers* could garner better positioning by choosing the best location. However, this could be risky as even the most appropriate location might prove inadequate due to lack of infrastructure available as well as the number of visitors to the store which might tarnish the brand's exclusive image.

The shop-in-shop in a luxury mall is, however, not always the best alternative. India has a purchasing culture mutated by frag-

---

24. For a definition of shopping malls, please refer to footnote 2 in *Chapter 2*.
25. R.T. Sharma, "Luxury Malls to Hit India Soon", *Business Standard*, March 31, 2007.
26. luxuryculture.com, "India Captivating The Luxury World", April 25, 2007.

mented distribution patterns spread across the streets (similar to the purchasing behavior of Italian consumers). Attempts by distribution giant Tesco to enter the country were rejected by the government keen to protect the diversity of small and medium businesses. The opening of independent flagship stores were able to better address the buying habits of Indian consumers even if, in this case, a brand might find limitations such as inadequate retail space and an urban context that is not always in sync with the brand's aesthetics.

However, as long as luxury brands remain confined to hotels, it will be difficult to create that prestige essential for luxury brands and not just for exclusive products like headgear and accessories but even for relatively accessible luxury goods like perfumes, glasses, bags. As is said, "out of sight is out of mind".

Communicate to educate

Communication means brand visibility and such strategies in India must emerge from the assumption that a brand's awareness, even among the affluent segments, is still limited. Sure there are clients able to appreciate niche brands, but there is also a segment of Indians with the right purchasing power unable to distinguish between luxury brands, industrial brands and emerging brands. This is especially true of traditional fashion categories: clothing and accessories. The reason for this is because luxury in India is still perceived as 5-star hotels, fancy tourist destinations and high-powered cars. The attention paid to a brand's image as a vehicle of one's social status – for instance the importance given to the right tie coordinated with the right suit or shoes as important accessories – is a phenomenon that has to be nurtured.

> The satellite channel Fashion TV was launched in the 1990's. However, the channel has been frequently banned by the country's Information & Broadcasting Ministry as it supposedly denigrated Indian culture by revealing too much skin on air. To demonstrate its interest in Indian culture, the channel started featuring Indian fashion weeks, shows on culture and style on its global fashion segment[27].

---

27. Government of India – Press Information Bureau, "Satellite Channel FTV Banned", March 29, 2007.

With distribution channels still blocked, promotion becomes a paramount task: billboards to create awareness, publicity and editorials in magazine glossies that will sell new aspirations by pitching a new lifestyle, fashion shows, events and brand endorsers to generate hype.

While the country still has a few designers, it does have two fashion weeks which attract media publicity as well as international buyers. While the Wills Lifestyle India Fashion Week of Delhi has been affirmed and consolidated as the most prestigious platform for designers and for those with a classic sense of taste, the Lakme Fashion Week of Mumbai has positioned itself as the trampoline for emerging designers not only from India but also those from South East Asia. The recent entry of IMG (agency leader and international production house in sports marketing which manages fashion week in New York, Los Angeles, San Paolo, Melbourne and Singapore) in the organisation of events, could change the balance between the two Indian cities.

When India signalled the green light to *Cosmopolitan* it did so under one condition: that the magazine would only give young girls sound advice on gardening techniques. A few years later, women got bolder, their skirts got shorter and the men tagged along silently. Even Bollywood, the mirror of Indian Zeitgeist, did what it refused to do five years ago – depicted an on-screen kiss. Several lifestyle magazines spurned out the latest in fashion trends and for that extra treat, gave men more than a peak into the fantasies of naughty women. With *Elle* and *Cosmopolitan* came the big bang of fashion magazines like *Marie Claire*, *Verve*, *Vogue* and *GQ*[28].

---

28. *L'Officiel* is a bi-monthly launched in 2002, with a monthly distribution of 40.000 copies and a readership of 160.000; 81% of its readers reside in Mumbai and Delhi while 14% are from Bangalore, Kolkata and Chennai (*L'Officiel*, Sales & Marketing Department, Mumbai).
The first edition of *Verve* was published in 1997 and today it enjoys a distribution in all the principal cities with a readership of 80.000 people, majority of which are below 25 years of age (*Verve*, Marketing Department, Mumbai).
Marie Claire, launched in 2006 in the metropolitan cities of India, has a circulation of 60.000 copies with the average age of readers between 20 and 35 years. The monthly turnover is approximately 40.000 INR (€ 720) and the percentage of international publicity varies from 25 to 30% (*Marie Claire*, Marketing & Sales Department, Mumbai).
The monthly *Cosmopolitan*, launched in 1996, has a circulation of 97.000 copies, while *Elle*, present in the market since 1991, is a bi-monthly publication with a readership of 65.000 (Narendra Kumar, Designer and Founding Editor, *Elle*).

When Tag Heuer (one of Louis Vuitton Moët Hennessey's premium watch brands) launched its Link collection in India in 2003, it chose none other than Bollywood King himself – Shah Rukh Khan (aka SRK). While Khan joined the list of illustrious brand ambassadors for Tag Heuer, like Tiger Woods, Uma Thurman, Brad Pitt and Maria Sharapova, the company extended their association with him through in-film advertising and television campaigns showcasing the film star (the actor presents the Indian version of "Who Wants to be a Millionaire").

Media links are also imperative to brand building.

Hindustan Times, one of the most respected dailies in India endorsing the Indian good life, organised luxury conferences sponsored by Luxury Connexions and undertaken in collaboration with CNN-IBN with government support.

However, one's brand name is not sufficient. The brand must be associated with a series of product traits and expected benefits. Communication in a new market calls for visibility that serves to educate consumers – through billboards at international airports, in *Vogue* and *Verve*, by organising events that, besides the glam of the usual A-list crowd, inform consumers on the brand's heritage, celebrate its origins by demonstrating its refined craftsmanship, attention to detail and by expressing its values.

Louis Vuitton's communication strategies have been geared towards educating the media on luxury. Several projects in collaboration with key magazines like *L'Officiel*, *Elle*, *Verve* and publications such as the *Hindustan Times* are initiated in order to diffuse knowledge and information on luxury trends. And in order to reach out to India's one million lifestyle consumers, the brand chose the one thing closest to every Indian – the soppy Bollywood love story. It tied-up with director Karan Johar's film *Kabhi Alvida Naa Kehna* (Never Say Goodbye) with the lead actress Amisha Patel endorsing the brand. The film industry with Mumbai at its epicenter and the image and lifestyle portrayed in the film were in perfect sync with LV's ideology. Through cinema, Bollywood defines fashion trends that strongly influence consumer choice. With its fabulous cast and its unusual script for a Bollywood drama (the film narrates the heartbreaking tale of two lovers before marriage while in this case, the focus was on the ménage that follows soon after), the film conquered the hearts of even the super rich. It was on screens in the US in 2006 and was immediately successful, raking in over $1 million in the first week, while in the UK, it earned £750.000 in the first two days of projection becoming one of Bollywood's greatest success stories.

Finally, what is fundamental is the time factor. The so-called BRIC countries (Brazil, Russia, India and China) are at the height of investment strategies by luxury corporations and brands. However, for success in India, it is necessary to adopt a perspective that is not just financial. Time plays a very important role. It is not only a matter of finding the right process to create the right offer: dealing with bureaucracy, choosing a local partner, finding the right location and adapting the collection to the market. Also from the demand side, the history of one's brand can be elucidated (though this is not an easy task in an Indian boutique) but in order to understand it, the consumer has to experience it. In Europe, we have always known brands like Dior, Chanel, Armani, Versace: they are part of our imagination since our childhood, we have evolved with these brands, grown old and changed with its designers. In countries like India everything is new: the people, places, mythical elements of a brand's history arrive much after the it bag or the sexy perfume campaign. The ostentation, visibility and fashion impulse necessary in the short term to create awareness must be carefully calibrated and balanced by instruments like selective distribution, exclusive availability of the product, the importance of word-of-mouth. If one wants to build an iconic image that is both mythical and exclusive – and this is the vital point for the long-term sustainability of luxury brands' –, the growth of business must be rigidly linked to the profound growth in the knowledge of the brand.

In the past, luxury was the preserve of aristocratic élite. Today, it is still the hot pursuit of affluent social class, but the consumer groups that can afford it have broken through the old restrictions. In fact, it has become a global business and it is worth our notice that East Asia has become a powerful engine of growth for the luxury market. For example, it accounts for over 50% of the total sales of French conglomerate of luxury labels LVMH (Louis Vuitton Moët Hennessy) and 45% of the foreign sales of Gucci. In recent years, China, a new emerging market, has become the focus of attention for luxury companies. What luxury dreams is the Chinese dreaming? During the past years, we have studied the emerging luxury business in China in great depth. Our studies demonstrate that success and failure depends upon the understanding of the Chinese practice of luxury consumption and the serious and long-term commitment to a consistent brand building exercise.

---

*   This Chapter is adapted from S. Saviolo, "China Strategy for International Luxury Brands", *Harvard Business Review China*, June, 2007.

5.1 Luxury consumption in China

China is a complex consumer market comprising a collection of markets where consumers differ from one another in purchasing power, attitudes, lifestyles, media use and consumption patterns. For administrative purposes according to 2008 China Statistics yearbook China is divided into 656 cities, 2.860 country level regions in turn divided into 41.040 towns and township. The city is an administrative unit and it may comprise many towns and villages. Many companies use these administrative tiers as a starting point when devising their branding strategy. For example cities in the so-called "tier one" (Beijing, Shanghai, Guangzhou and Shenzhen) are the most important in terms of the size of their middle income to affluent population (defined as monthly household income higher than 5.000 RMB). The most critical issue of brand building is to define targeted customers and find out their needs and expectations.

The social and cultural background of consumers clearly influences their consumption preferences and brand selection, especially the type of symbolic value sought from luxury goods. Consumers in Beijing are interested in understanding what is behind a brand in terms of heritage and storytelling. So in Beijing an exhibition presenting the brand heritage could be the best way to build knowledge whereas in the most fashionable Shanghai a fashion show or a glamorous party or store opening with celebrities might work better. Understanding Chinese attitude to luxury and their practice of luxury consumption is therefore crucial to position the brand. Our analysis starts from the language since it plays a very important role in defining cultures.

Chinese use two different terms to translate the word luxury, *Haohua*, which means extraordinary, splendid, and prosperous with a positive association, while luxury goods is translated as *Shechi Pin*, meaning something extravagant, and offers a negative connotation of waste. Obviously, Chinese culture, which appreciates luxury as a symbol of status and modernity, seems to warn people from it at the same time. In spite of all these conflicts and contraries, the emerging consumer culture in large first and second tiers Chinese cities is rapidly evolving towards

Western consumption patterns. In this process, two characteristics of Chinese consumers are particularly relevant to the practice of luxury consumption: ownership and display and brand
consciousness with a low awareness.

The "bling factor": ownership and display

Conformity and status seeking are widely agreed to be key motivations for luxury consumptions, no matter the consumer age
or location. From our research, we found that the best sold items
in luxury stores are in-your-face luxury, such as, diamond-stud-
ded gold watches, big logo printed products and recognizable accessories. Luxury consumptions are item driven: the latest model
well visible in the store window or advertised in the street is the
most wanted. Besides, bold branded accessories are considered
particularly appropriate for gift giving as they are used to communicate the gift giver's status.

Chinese seem to place more emphasis on publicly visible pos-
session. This is consistent with the social definition of identity
in Chinese culture, which encourages the outward expression
of success. Western consumers are increasingly more concerned
with inner private self (consisting of emotions, desires, personal
values, etc), while Chinese consumers with outer public self
(based on social roles and the persona presented to others). In
Mainland China, luxury goods are supposed to project status and
a forward movement in life; therefore, their intrinsic and symbolic value should be easy to display.

Within a society where affluence is a new phenomenon, brands
should have distinctive signs and symbols of identity because
they are used to mark social categories. For Chinese consumers,
being trendy and fashionable has more to do with marking their
position in society than with making a statement about their personal taste. For instance, sales associates told us that women's
fashion consumptions are more driven by specific occasions of
use (i.e. ceremonies) and dressing codes (as imposed by the company) than by their personal taste and dressing style. The similar mentality is also reflect by the fashion preferences of Chinese
consumers: strong and bright colors are preferred to neutral
palettes; tight fittings are preferred to loose fittings; classic style

is preferred to fashionable style; and in accessories, expensive materials – such as leather – are preferred to what is perceived as a poor material such as cotton fabric or nylon. However, we have observed among young MBA students in Beijing and Shanghai that the notion of individual pleasure and the expression of "Enjoy Life" (take care of body, more health concern) are starting to gain importance. We have good reasons to believe that in the near future, luxury consumption in China will become more sophisticated, and will not merely be about projecting status, but also about projecting individual style or providing pleasure.

Brand conscious but low awareness

Chinese consumers consider a plus the brand international status and "Made in West" appeal. This attitude is common to other Asian countries such as India and Korea and could be explained by the fact that Westerners have maintained their power and wealth over the last few centuries, so "Made in West" embodies the culture and lifestyle behind the superior Western economy. The fact that people like to buy goods Made in West indicates their recognition of and intimacy with this culture. Chinese customers want the international flavour and the "real one": the same product they can find in Paris or Milan. While we observed major adaptations in Western products and brands targeted to the mass market, the Chinese affluent consumer is willing to buy products that are not available in China and represent the Western lifestyle. Even the seasonal collection and window display must be the same as they are in the West.

> This is what Giorgio Armani has exactly learned. When Giorgio Armani opened his Beijing store in 2001, he ordered the installation of a large red-lacquer door – a nod to motifs of traditional Chinese architecture – but Chinese patrons hated it and the door was later replaced with Armani's global store design. He finally understood that Chinese wanted his style, the Western style.

Although Chinese consumers think Western brands are cool, few could differentiate between US and European luxury brands (especially apparel), which reflects their low brand awareness. We also noticed during our research that even young executive MBA students couldn't differentiate between established brands and upstarts, traditional luxury and fast fashion brands. Mass market brands like Adidas or Benetton are even often taken as luxury. Due to the confusing market situation, people look to advertising for help in making buying decisions. The most advertised luxury brands are the most successful ones. This virgin market represents an opportunity since any European brand could virtually enter and be appealing with a huge investment into brand image building. In fact, some Chinese companies are registering their trademarks in Europe and opening stores in Italy and France in order to revalue their own brands.

However, this situation poses a threat to establish brands, because they cannot repeat their success in China by making full use of their global image. The wide availability of counterfeits in Mainland China is another indicator of the low brand awareness among Chinese consumers. Nevertheless, this situation should not impede makers of luxury goods as they help to build brand awareness. Further, since fakes are usually of a very low quality, consumers could be likely to upgrade to the genuine product when they can afford it.

5.2 Brand building in China

Understanding the consumption mentality and culture of Chinese consumers is only the start of brand building. One will truly occupy this market only after working hard and paying high cost. Managing luxury brands is as much an art as a science. Creating a demand for something very expensive which is not really needed it's an art while managing multiple products, markets, channels under one brand is a science. At current stage, the challenges facing international luxury brands on the Chinese market are about how to foster brand awareness, build noble brand image, and create pleasant retail experience for customers, grasp channel portfolio on a vast market, and conduct effective customer relationship management by using advances technologies. Concerning these issues, first movers of the Chinese luxury market have done many beneficial explorations. International luxury brands like Italian brand Ermenegildo Zegna and French brand Louis Vuitton entered China at the beginning of the 1990's. In the early days, they developed their business through agents. After Mainland China opened its retail market at the end of 2004, they have speeded up their expansion all over the country. After more than a decade's hard work, these brands have just started seeing returns on their investments.

Their experience on Chinese market uncovers some principles that most international luxury companies have embraced during their successful exploration on emerging markets:

1. build awareness through location;
2. build image through culture and lifestyle;
3. create brand experience through retailing;
4. control your shop portfolio development;
5. profile your client.

Build awareness through location

As we said before, Chinese consumers are brand conscious but there is low awareness concerning international brands. Therefore, establishing brand awareness in China has been for companies the first step to enter the market. Some luxury brands, including Burberry, Louis Vuitton and Chanel, have found that Chinese consumers already recognize their names and trademarks – in part because counterfeiters have been hawking their styles on the streets for years. But smaller and less globalized luxury labels, such as Tod's, Celine and Lanvin, have more work to do to make their products known. China's consumers are bombarded by brands like never before. Therefore in China, visibility must be extensive and impressive. In Western countries, advertising on top luxury and fashion magazines, such as *Vogue* or *Elle*, is the key tool to build awareness. In China, those magazines are developing but their diffusion is limited. Therefore, location is the first driver for visibility. By opening direct-operated stores, many companies hope to build brand recognition, so that they will become familiar names by the time China's luxury consumption starts to boom. In addition, a window display next to other top brands at a primary location which is extremely expensive is the best signal of prestige and distinctiveness.

Three on the Bund Armani flagship is a typical example of the massive effort the company is making to impress Chinese consumers. The Armani Group is one of the leading fashion and luxury goods groups in the world. Armani was a late comer into China compared to other brands, but the designer invested heavily into his brand visibility: he opened his 1.100 sqm flagship store in Shanghai in 2004 within the historic building Three on the Bund. Armani considers this place, which was built in 1916, the most prominent location in Shanghai and a vision of the future of Chinese luxury consumerism: a lifestyle destination converging contemporary fashion, art, dining, culture, and music. The company invested all the money required to set up a full-service luxury store with all the allure that the brand should have. The idea was not to make a quick return on investment but to build awareness by a location that any Chinese will notice.

Build image through culture and lifestyle

Brand image has to do with building of a lasting positive image in the consumer's mind. Many Chinese consumers may be aware of some international brand names but still unable to perceive differences in their positioning. How to build a brand image associated to status and prestige for the Chinese consumers? How to make them perceive the differences between Prada and Ports?

Since Chinese consumers perceive Western culture and lifestyle as the symbol of luxury, top luxury brands built their noble and distinct brand image by associating their brands with these two elements. We already underlined that Chinese luxury consumers have exceptionally good impression of the personal values and lifestyle of Western (especially European) noble class in old times. The heritage of luxury has to do with those practices that are handed down from the past by tradition, culture, and characteristics of past times. Therefore, it is an effective way to project one's noble status and prove the origin of one's image by organizing memorable events showing the history and heritage of luxury. In fact, this method has been widely used in Mainland China.

Louis Vuitton organized a touring exhibition on the history and heritage of luxury in late 1997, which pulled in 45.500 people in five cities. This spectacular event made Chinese people associate the name Vuitton to the history of Western luxury. Later in 1998, it organized the second event called the "Louis Vuitton Classic China Run", a 1.500 km rally featuring 48 vintage automobiles from around the world through the diverse landscape between Dalian and Beijing. For many Chinese, the sight of so many antique cars rolling through their villages was more than just a novelty; it was a huge and splendid event that associated the brand with the prestige, heritage and performance related to that rally. Even its competitors had to admit that these two events made significant contribution to reinforcing its leading position on the Chinese market. Richemont, the Swiss group owning top luxury brands such as Cartier and Mont Blanc, implemented the same strategy. The group used culture and tradition to inform the wider public about its luxury watches and then much focused PR strategies to support brand image of each individual brand. Its Beijing exhibition called "Watches & Wonders" portrayed the history of Western mechanical watch making, from its origins at the end of the Middle Ages to today. The exhibition also included a detailed presentation of the various artistic métiers that must come together in order to create a fine watch. The aim was to anchor the noble identity of the various brands in the collective consciousness of the Chinese consumers and, after that, the brands can take their own action to establish their differentiated brand image.

In addition to this kind of exhibitions, companies organized sumptuous fashion shows or parties at some special occasions. Pioneering events in this sense included the Italian designer Laura Biagiotti's fashion show at the Forbidden City in Beijing or Pierre Cardin's fashion show at the Temple of Heaven in Beijing. In China, openings of flagship stores often represent a unique occasion to publicize the brand. For example, Richemont iconic brand Cartier used grand flagship openings as memorable PR events to vigorously publicize its unique brand culture, which had obtained wide media coverage. Another practice worth recommendation is to organize activities with more definite themes for targeted customers, so as to leave them a clear impression about the brand image.

For example, both Louis Vuitton and Chanel organized luxury weekends for their special clients at 5-stars hotels. At the private fashion shows, people could experience the lifestyle contained in the brand in person, so that they would interpret the unique brand image in a more accurate and exquisite way. We should be aware of one thing that these clearly-positioned activities often have some commercial characteristics. For instance, customers can see and buy the latest models before they enter the street boutiques, which gives a direct spur to sales.

Create brand experience through retailing

Publicizing activities centred on culture and lifestyle can help consumers get a clear understanding of brand image, and the perception of customers more depends on their direct brand experience during the consumption process. And exactly because of this, all top luxury brands are making great efforts to create unique retail experience to make consumers understand their value proposition and develop intimacy with them. Choosing an appropriate retail format is the first step to creating retail experience, because it will decide the imagination space of retail experience. Large shopping malls, department stores and boutiques used to be the popular formats, but now, the space provided by large shopping malls is getting limited. Brands entering China now will find fewer spaces and higher fees to open their stores. Space is still available at the highest floors of large shopping malls, but for luxury brands, not locating at the street or first level is considered less prestigious. On the other hand, department stores located in major business districts are no longer the best choice, because competition on prices and promotions are becoming more intense, so it is difficult for luxury brands to find suitable locations for opening stores.

The French Group L'Oréal first introduced its luxury cosmetic brand Lancôme in Shanghai in 1997 by setting up retail outlets in large shopping malls and department stores. As the market kept growing, the company conducted in-depth analysis and examination of the retail experience that the brand offered to customers. According to its survey, space at crowded Chinese department stores was limited, so there was not always the possibility to welcome clients in "the French way", show the large variety of products, and establish a close relationship with customers, if it completely relied on these channels. Obviously, department stores, the traditional channel for luxury cosmetics, were not the right way to make consumers perceive the value proposition associated to the brand: French allure, expertise and wide range of products. Therefore, Lancôme decided to go into retail business in Greater China by developing a new concept store and using it to offer an innovative retail experience. The first boutique was opened in Hong Kong in 2004. After successful test of the concept, Lancôme launched the second boutique in Shanghai. After choosing an appropriate retail format, they should also elaborately design the services offered to customers at the retail link, so as to reflect their brand image in a better way. Designed to create all-round brand experience for customers, Lancôme's concept stores organize their products and services in four areas: skincare, perfume, diagnosis and make up. Apart from widest assortment of products, there are also products of limited editions that customers normally cannot find in other stores. The accessible and effective merchandising enables each customer to identify, choose and try the products she wants. These stores also provide "Diagnose Expert" service, which combines a high performance tool and a specially trained skincare expert. Inside the stores, there is a wellness centre equipped with latest technologies and treatments. Beauticians working in the centre have received training on the classical facial techniques of Lancôme in France. The impact of these concept stores has been substantial. At these stores, Chinese consumers can experience Lancôme's professionalism and French allure in person, and will then grow deep feelings for the brand. In China, Lancôme has become one of the leading brands on the Chinese luxury cosmetic market.

Reasonable retail formats and elaborately designed services are still not enough to guarantee a pleasant brand experience. As an interactive process, experience depends on the expertise and service standard of retail people. To ensure that their retail people can grasp rich knowledge, offer excellent services and accurately transfer the connotation of their brands, companies must provide them continuous training, which is especially the case with luxury goods. In fact, training for retail people is especially important in China. It is not only because China is an emerging luxury market, but also because outlets are one of the key factors to successful brand building on Chinese market. To conduct such training is also a challenge in China, because on the one hand, customer service is still a new concept in China, and on the other hand, it is impossible for retail people to grasp the professional knowledge on the history, craftsmanship and details of luxury brands without receiving intensive training. Luxury brands, such as Zegna, are making more investment in internal retail academies to educate their international sales people, especially those of emerging markets. Such training is focused on teaching retail people professional knowledge and how to properly treat customers, so that they can communicate the connotation of a luxury brand through customer experience.

Control your shop portfolio development

Apart from detailed management of the services of each retail end, luxury brands should also develop a proper channel portfolio on the vast Chinese market. Companies should adopt a consistent channel strategy, which will take into account both retail chains and wholesale chains, and both attention-grabbing first tier cities and fast-growing second tier cities, so that they can maximize their market coverage while reinforcing their brand image.

In China, with continuous market growth and after the opening of retail market, balancing the shop portfolio in terms of locations and retail formats has turned out to be a major issue for luxury brand development. To a large degree, distribution within the vast and diverse China is a trade-off between exclusivity and coverage. Opening a small number of exclusive flagship stores in first tier cities is vital for building brand awareness. But returns for some brands can be better in lesser-known cities, such as Chongqing, Harbin and Shenzhen, because costs in the major cities like Beijing and Shanghai are continuously rising, while in less-known cities, the sales per square foot might be the same, but operating costs will be much lower.

To decide their shop portfolio, they have to take comprehensive consideration of the development stages of their brand on the Chinese market as well as their own strategy. The Italian garment and accessory group Ermenegildo Zegna is engaged in integrated operations ranging from fabric to retail. The company was among the first European brands to enter into China in 1991. Right after its entering, it set up a large number of stores in many cities, which were mainly self-standing boutiques and shops in shops. So far, it has successfully opened 60 stores in over 25 cities. Thanks to its wide coverage, it has become one of the first European brands to achieve returns on investment. Zegna could have continued to grow pretty quickly with a very large number of boutiques, but it soon realized that converge was not anymore the point. Above all, in capital cities, Chinese customers were becoming more demanding and wanted to have more choices and better services. Small boutiques could not be the right format to satisfy these needs. Further, Zegna was willing to position itself in China as a luxury brand offering full-range of men's products:

not just menswear, but also leather goods, accessories and fragrances. In order to project this status, it was important to have prestigious flagships. Finally, new luxury competitors in men's wear were entering China to fight for the same clients and locations. Zegna needed to reinforce its leadership and occupy the best locations. The company decided to better balance its channel portfolio: it would maintain a reasonable growth speed in second and third tier cities by adding new boutiques, while keeping the number of flagships under certain limit in first tier cities, so as to improve its image and service quality. For the moment, it has 4 flagship stores in China, which includes the most recent addition of a 500 sqm store at Eighteen the Bund in Shanghai.

Profile your client

For the luxury sector, despite the huge population and amazing growth rate, there are few people that can afford the price and only a few customers contribute greatly to the brand turnover. Luxury companies must recognize each of these most important customers and offer them excellent services. Chinese affluent clients are normally willing to leave their personal information; they would feel honoured to be treated as VIP guests, invited at parties, openings and collection previews. As what happens on Western markets, an efficient integrated Customer Relationship Management (CRM) data system could help luxury companies in China to substantially understand the market and intimately connect with their customers. For example, Ermenegildo Zegna implemented also in China an advanced CRM system to measure retail performance and focus marketing activities. Information on retail traffic, customer retention, customer loyalty, new customer generation, cross selling helped the company to better know its local customers store by store, what they need and expect and how the brand can successfully meet their needs.

The company could customize the product mix by using these customer profiles: stores with more traditional clientele continued to be supplied with established products while new lines and innovative product categories were introduced in stores with a younger and trendier clientele. Customer databases enable Zegna to invite their consumers to attend collection previews, end-of-season sales and other events to reinforce customer relationship, and also ensure that even when salespeople leave, their knowledge is not lost.

The rationale behind the evidence is that establishing brand awareness and image in China is an expensive and long-term venture: entering China is first-time launch even for the most established luxury brands. Every profit made needs to be reinvested right away in boutiques, in advertising, in looking for talent and creating a culture for luxury goods. So far only the biggest and strongest players are most likely to benefit from this promising clientele. But the market is growing fast: key factors are a promising demography (consumers of luxury items are considerably younger than those in US and Europe), a huge middle class and a rising Chinese traveller. Many international brands could establish a profitable positioning in the next future if they commit themselves to a consistent brand building strategy and they always question themselves about the future. Luxury brands on Chinese market should always remember: doing business in China is an ever learning journey.

PART THREE

Industry segments, business models and drivers for consumption

6 Industry segmentation

6.1 About industry segmentation

A successful strategy differentiates the firm from its competitors, providing it with a unique positioning. This uniqueness is tied to the firm's ability to offer a specific segment of customers a particular set of benefits. Each strategy imposes choices. A firm cannot offer the whole range of benefits that the market might desire. It has to focus on just some, and to offer them in a unique way. It often happens that firms' inability to make choices leads them to compete for the same customers through the same offers. Industry segmentation forces the firm to identify its own competitive positioning within the industry. In nearly every industry there are distinct product varieties, multiple distribution channels and several types of consumers.

Segments are important because they have differing needs: an unadvertised basic shirt and a designer shirt are both shirts, but are sold to different buyers at very different prices through different distribution channels. Understanding the particular environment in which the firm operates is thus the first step to analyzing the firm and the brand positioning.

Industry segmentation analysis is not the same as identifying and analyzing market segments. Market segmentation is focused on identifying buyer needs, purchasing preferences, and marketing activities in a value chain. Industry segmentation combines market segment information with other significant variables that define where the firm should compete, the so-called competitive scope. It answers the question: *What segments of the industry should we serve and how best should we serve them?* Industry segments differ in structural attractiveness and also in what is required to gain and sustain competitive advantage.

The fashion system is made up of many industries (textiles, clothing, knitwear, leather, accessories). Luxury is a segment defined by price within the fashion system but also in other industries such as jewels, watches, cars, yachts. These industries in turn can be further sub-divided into different competitive segments. Each firm has to decide how to compete, or position itself, within each industry segment. Therefore, within competitive strategies there is, first, a process of industry segmentation aiming at defining the segment in which the firm competes.

What follows is then an *internal* process aiming at delineating the single firm's competitive space within the segment. In this chapter we will be concerned, above all, with the structural segmentation of the clothing industry. This is the most important and complex industry, and most of what will be said can be applied to other industries in the fashion system, such as leather goods, shoes, and eyewear.

6.2 Segmenting the fashion industry

We segment the clothing industry by grouping three macro-criteria together – product end-uses, groups of clients and price. Further criteria can be defined within these macro-criteria as we'll see in the following.

Product end-uses
End-uses describe a product's functions and final destination. In clothing, for instance, the main categories of end-uses are ex-

ternal clothing, underwear and beachwear. Materials, shapes, structures and finishing processes can vary according to different product end-uses; in this sense there is a strong relation between a certain end-use and a given technology/manufacturing process. In the beauty industry, products end-uses are makeup and cosmetics; within makeup, the business of lipsticks is different from that of mascara in terms of technology. End-uses might be different from the occasions of use, which is a very important category in fashion. Unlike end-uses based on product performance and functional attributes, occasions of use is a market-oriented criterion becoming increasingly important for segmenting the offer. Formal occasions of use are thus distinguished from casual; workwear is different from sportswear. As demand becomes progressively sophisticated, occasions of use are further segmented. Formal occasions include both moments in the working-day and evening ceremonies. Informal occasions encompass urban free time and leisurewear for weekends, while sports occasions involve both leisure and active sports. Segmenting the industry by product occasion of use, we may obtain segments such as sportswear or swimwear.

The sportswear product is usually made for specific occasions of use (active sport, outdoor, leisure) with special fabrics and treatments (i.e. waterproof, breathable); therefore the suppliers and manufacturers along the pipeline are selected according to their competencies. The segment is characterized by a high level of globalization and is very concentrated. A few players such as Nike, Adidas and Puma enjoy strong brand awareness and have large market shares. Companies differentiate through marketing, research and innovation and the competition is often "cut-throat". Most of the production is outsourced in Asian sites. Communication and brand building activities (such as athletes' endorsement and event sponsorship) are also crucial to compete in this business.

Clients

The industry can be segmented on the basis of client groups: intermediate clients (trade channels) and end customers.

- *Intermediate clients.* The first criterion for segmenting distribution is the distinction between direct/retail and indirect/wholesale channel. The former creates a direct relation between the industry and the end consumer without any commercial intermediation. Sales are managed through monobrand stores/boutiques, company outlets and electronic commerce. The latter includes specialized distributors and retailers in commercial intermediation, such as multibrand boutiques and department stores. The wholesalers distribute the final product and offer various types of services. As we will see in *Chapter 12*, companies depending mainly on the retail channel are different from business models relying on a wholesale channel in terms of the way the supply chain is structured and organized (deliveries, mark-ups, etc.).

- *End consumers*. Consumers can be segmented on the basis of several variables. These include the traditional demographics (age, gender), geographical (area of residence), socio-economic factors (social class, income), or psychographics (segmentation based on people's lifestyles). Segmenting the industry according to end consumer characteristics, we may obtain businesses such as kidswear, menswear or womenswear.

A traditional segmentation approach in the fashion system mingles end-uses (external formalwear) and client groups (gender), obtaining as a result two large segments: menswear and womenswear. Menswear is characterized by little product differentiation, limited fashion content, and the importance of service. Margins are lower than in womenswear; therefore companies usually implement volume strategies. In womenswear, on the contrary, fashion content (and thus product seasonality) is a key element. Womenswear is the most important segment of the fashion industry in terms of size. Industrial firms sub-contract to specialized suppliers to increase flexibility and reduce time-to-market. Profitability can be very high due to the fact that firms can differentiate their products according to several dimensions. Where menswear is dominated by medium to large vertically integrated firms, womenswear, at least in Europe, is a very fragmented business, with a variety of competitors from large to small specialized firms and ready-to-wear designers.

Price

Price is the most common way to segment markets in any industry. In fashion, five price segments are commonly recognized:

FIGURE 6.1   SEGMENTING BY PRICE (WOMENSWEAR MARKET)

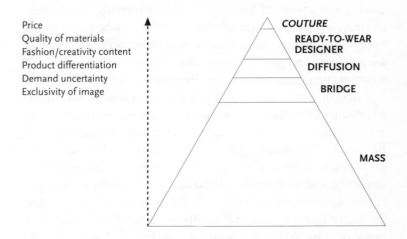

Price
Quality of materials
Fashion/creativity content
Product differentiation
Demand uncertainty
Exclusivity of image

COUTURE
READY-TO-WEAR
DESIGNER
DIFFUSION
BRIDGE
MASS

couture, ready-to-wear/designer, diffusion, bridge and mass (*Figure 6.1*). This segmentation particularly applies to the womenswear market. The menswear market follows the same pattern, although it is divided into slightly different segments. The various price segments are defined as multiples of the average market price level for a certain product. This type of segmentation goes beyond simple price value to the point of designing within each segment different business models with specific key success factors. Moving from the ready-to-wear segment to the mass market, the importance of elements such as stylistic creativity, product innovation and the "dream factor" decreases in favor of aspects such as the price, volumes, efficiency of the supply chain.

6.3 Description of fashion segments

Couture, originally referring to the work of Englishman Charles Frederick Worth, was born in Paris in the mid-19th century as "made to measure" clothing. In modern France, *haute couture* is a "protected name" that can be used only by firms that meet certain well-defined standards in terms of product and branding strategies. The final price is not comparable to any market price, as this is more craftsmanship than business and each dress is considered a piece of art. *Couture* is less important nowadays compared to the past. Nonetheless, it still offers beautiful made-to-measure clothes addressed to very selective, international customers (not more than a few hundred of the upper tier of super-wealthy customers worldwide). Prestigious *couturiers* with tailoring skills rarely exist any more. The entrepreneurial model has moved from the *"couture maison"* centered on the great couturier to the branded multibusiness company competing in the high-end of the market. These companies consider *couture* as a creative laboratory and communication medium for supporting the wider and more profitable business of perfumes and accessories. As observed by the great British journalist Suzie Menkez, the major threat to *couture* is not the cheapness of "fast fashion" but time. The new generation of women will not wait six weeks for an outfit. And also for the designers it is not easy to see where *couture* can fit into their packed schedule of pre-collections, ready-to-wear and global travel for store openings and promotions.

If *couture* has lost its allure (also because clients refuse to wear clothes that they see worn by celebrities for free on the red carpets), ready-to-wear, on the other hand, is repositioning itself on a higher price/creativity segment compared to the past[1].

The press calls this new segment *demi couture*.

Industrial *prêt-à-porter* meets traditional *haute couture*: this is *demi couture*. Made entirely by hand, it is winning shares in the most challenging market segment – the high-end – which reproaches traditional *haute couture*, even more than for the prices, for the protracting fitting and waiting time for a garment. Representatives of this new wave, among others, are names such as Olivier Theyskens for Rochas, Alber Elbaz for Lanvin, the Italians Giambattista Valli (produced by Gilmar), Stefano Pilati (Yves Saint Laurent), Riccardo Tisci (Givenchy), in accessories Bruno Frisoni (Roger Vivier)

---

1. Pierre Bergé (Yves Saint Laurent's business partner) declared to the press on May 2004: "The *couture* has lost its raison d'être. *Couture* isn't art. It's not meant to be hung in a closet like a painting. The women who wore *couture* no longer exist, the art de vivre that spawned *couture* has died. If houses such as Chanel and Dior one day get proof that they can sell as many bags and fragrances without a *couture* show, they'll stop *couture*, too".

and Tomas Meier from Bottega Veneta (PPR), in the US Rodarte (Kate and Laura Mulleavely) and Zac Posen. But consolidated brands have their own take on this new phenomenon: Isaac Mizrahi, Dolce & Gabbana, Chanel, Oscar de la Renta, Escada. They are the creators and interpreters of this avant-garde, which achieves superlative levels of quality with regard to creativity, lines, cuts, and details. The prices are higher than normal *prêt-à-porter*, but much lower than a high fashion garment (around one-tenth of the price of *couture*). *Demi couture* means uniting the timing and prices of today's market while preserving uniqueness.

Ready-to-wear, also called *prêt-à-porter* is a segment whose average price is between three to five times higher than that of the average market price. The ready-to-wear business had its origins in the 1970s in Italy as a result of the partnership between designers and manufacturing firms. Its distinguishing characteristic is the presence of a designer who manages the creation and development of the collection and controls the communication strategy. Also competing within the segment are a few small premium brands, very creative and exclusive, that are perceived as fashion houses even if they do not have a designer. Ready-to-wear collections are sold at a high price and offer strong creative content according to the designer's taste. It is a seasonal business, showing at least two main collections a year plus the pre-collections, the cruise collection and flash collections. (We will explain these terms in *Chapter 11*). The segment is becoming global in terms of actors, channels, targets; the key success factor for competing is the designer's reputation, which is a mix of creativity, image, opinion makers, marketing and good relations with international store buyers and international fashion editors. Investments in communication are much higher than in other segments: getting press recognition is central for the designer's success. The main channel of communication is the *fashion show*, a very expensive means of promotion held during the traditional fashion events. Another successful way to gain media attention is lending out clothes to celebrities.

Considering the high-end of the market, it is important to distinguish between the ready-to-wear segment and the *luxury* segment. Ready-to-wear is essentially "fashion" clothing – i.e. a seasonal product strongly related to its time. Luxury goods, instead, are timeless items, mainly accessories (jewellery, accessories, pens, perfumes), very exclusive and unique. The business press, reporting on market shares, profitability and price-earnings is used to considering fashion brands and luxury brands as competing in the same business. This vision has been driven by the fact that the luxury market, once a very specialized market niche, mainly local and exclusive, has now become transversal to product categories; luxury is global and more accessible than in the past, also as a consequence of corporate diversification and globalization strategies. Yet it is important to note that the core business of luxury brands is, or used to be, activities and products other than fashion clothing. Many luxury firms, above all French ones, (Hermès, Chanel, Louis Vuitton, Cartier) established their own offer of products with a very high level of prestige and image that are still classic and timeless. Their entrance into fashion ready-to-wear can be interpreted as an attempt to use the communicative potential of seasonal clothing collections to renew and update their brand image.

Diffusion (priced two or three times higher than the market average). The second and third lines of designers are positioned here, as well as some collections from prestigious industrial firms. They can be managed through licensees or, as soon as the designer brand reaches a sufficient size, be vertically integrated. Diffusion lines are characterized by a prevalence of wholesale. (Worth noting here is the development of multibrand DOS in which the licensee puts together the various lines in its portfolio). This segment is one that offers a more affordable brand label with a balance between a good product (trendy, fashion) and a good price (economies of scale).

Key success factors used to be style and image consistency with ready-to-wear (strong association with first lines, values reinforcement), since diffusion came into existence as the designer's brand extension to wider market segments, traditionally occupied by industrial brands. In order to offer critical mass to designer brands, most of the diffusion lines have been stretched into fragrances, eyewear, watches, kidswear and sportswear chic. For many *maisons* over the years, young lines have grown into an enormous business, which often brings in double or more the turnover of so-called first lines. However, if in the past young lines used to represent the more affordable version of the first lines, offering young people the possibility to buy into a designer experience, now this market segment is facing a deep evolution. In fact, lines such as Miu Miu, Versus and Emporio Armani have become autonomous lines with a strong creative personality and their own target audience, consumers who choose these collections because they can identify with the style these lines propose, not because they cost less.

In fact, both the pricing system and the clientele have changed, the latter being much more mature and sophisticated today. Gone is the principle of graduated pricing, by which second lines cost from 30 to 40% less than first lines, and sportswear and jeans followed. In the meantime the age criterion, the reason for the widely-used "young line"[2] label, has disappeared as well. Identifying the personality of these lines is crucial, also to avoid the risk that when these collections are big hits, they cannibalize the first line and products become interchangeable.

Bridge (priced one and a half to two times higher than the market average). The bridge is a segment that came into existence in the American market as an initiative by department stores to offer a product that would act as a "bridge" between the mass market and the first and second lines of European designers. Premium industrial brands compete against each other, as well as the younger designer lines. The critical success factors are related to the ability to serve the market at the right time with the right style. Image and time to market are more important than creativity. As opposed to the global niche of the high-end and the increasing globalization of mass retailers, bridge is characterized by many local competitors.

Squeezed in the middle, between the attack of the mass retailers (which are upgrading creativity and image) and the higher segment (which is upgrading service and trading down with more

2. Giancarlo Di Risio, CEO of Versace, stated "if you call them young lines, you implicitly make the first line old and too institutional, while the word 'second' infers inferior quality". "Non chiamatele più seconde linee", *Corriere Economia*, January 16, 2006.

entry-priced products), companies in this segment are trying to reposition themselves in the diffusion range by achieving the strong brand identity needed to become a global brand. In addition, these competitors are innovating their business models in the direction of service (to retail and to the consumer).

Within the bridge segment, the Italian brand Patrizia Pepe Firenze made its market debut in 1993 and closed 2008 with a turnover of more than 120 million euro. The key to the success is a seemingly simple concept – sell by making trade sell – and an innovative business model: advanced quick fashion.

In the early 1990s, the company started opening directly owned showrooms in the main Italian cities. By developing a network of local diffusion showrooms, Patrizia Pepe gave retailers the chance to make limited purchases even during off times (like November). In doing so, stores could continually come up with new window displays for their clientele without running the risk of being stuck with unsold stock. (With traditional make-to-order, retailers had to choose what to buy "in the dark," six months prior to the season in question, which meant there was not yet any market feedback on actual trends). The company, in return, had the advantage of constant production. Moreover, there was a significant financial gain: the company gave retailers the opportunity to defer payments (i.e. to pay once goods were sold), and in exchange Patrizia Pepe collected after just 30 days (in contrast with the Italian industry average which can run up to 120 days). In order to fill store shelves frequently, on the top of make-to-order main collections, Patrizia Pepe developed a total of 40 weekly mini-collections produced and delivered in a very short time with a made-to-order logic. These collections are on display every week in the company's diffusion showrooms where retailers can visit to make new purchases and replenish merchandise. This is also an opportunity for consulting on products, mixing and matching, visual merchandising, and training sales staff. Continuous collaboration is the basis for a good sell-out, and consequently growth for the store and the company.

Nonetheless, the formula for traditional quick fashion – small frequent purchases – is not sufficient to explain Patrizia Pepe's success. To beat the competition Patrizia Pepe had to focus on distinctive creativity. This is a fashionable brand where trends are always filtered to be consistent with Patrizia Pepe's target: a modern, elegant woman who wants to enhance her femininity, not flaunt it. Certain elements define the Patrizia Pepe style, first and foremost wearability, along with flowing and elasticized fabrics, long garments to make up for what's lacking in width, simplicity and ease in mixing and matching that tends toward minimalism.

In order to enhance brand identity, direct distribution was initiated in 2000; a few years later the group had flagships and shop-in-shops in 19 countries (with a strong presence in Russia and China). The firm was then ready to aspire to greater visibility: advertising investments increased with a focus on high-end printed magazines. The company also sponsored cultural events and shows for charity, to convey the brand in an institutional setting[3].

Mass (below the average market price). As one moves down the price ranges, products become increasingly basic and less differentiated. Differentiation is based on elements such as the price-quality ratio, retailing and communication. Volumes matter, and therefore retail traffic is fundamental. Unlike other fashion segments, the mass market follows the competitive patterns of other consumer goods – only communication follows the logic of seasonal fashion. The more affordable branded lines compete in this segment, as well as retailer's private labels and unbranded goods.

Price segmentation allows us to clarify the different business logics on the fashion market. We must point out that in the last two decades many new players have entered the fashion and luxury business. What's more, business models of actors competing within specific price segments have changed a great deal from their original structure. Consequently in the same market range we now have heterogeneous players with differences in terms of:

- market positioning (i.e. Japanese designers creative niche *vs.* American mass fashion);
- growth strategies (i.e. Armani top down diffusion *vs.* Calvin Klein bottom up development; French focus strategy on first lines only and diversification in fragrances and accessories vs. Ralph Lauren portfolio of lines);
- level of integration and control of the business (i.e. Dolce & Gabbana vertical integration *vs.* Cavalli "maison" model);
- different level of business complexity (i.e. Belgian "evolved tailor's shops " *vs.* French luxury conglomerates);
- models of conglomerates (i.e. Gucci Group industrial capacity *vs.* LVMH financial assets);

---

3. "Patrizia Pepe – Advanced Quick Fashion", E. Corbellini, SDA Bocconi, 2005, ECCH Case Collection.

- ways of raising new designers (Valentino now: internal, unknown designers; John Galliano: rising star in a traditional brand; Stella McCartney/ McQueen at Gucci Group: joint ventures with emerging talents).

6.4 Segmenting the luxury industry

Just as we proposed a segmentation of the fashion market, we now do the same with the market of goods considered "luxury".

In recent years, in fact, a great deal of confusion has arisen surrounding the concept of luxury because two opposite yet convergent phenomena have crossed paths. On one hand, historical luxury brands have traded down – i.e. extending their offering to include a wider range of customers, with products priced for greater accessibility (from perfumes to eyewear to chocolates). On the other hand, more recently the mass market has been qualified through trading up strategies, essentially based on appropriating the design, communication, and marketing environment of luxury products, minus the exceptional products and services.

Luxury leaders are further segmenting their offering according to exclusive, selective, and accessible categories (the concepts of supreme luxury, luxury and accessible luxury) within the same brand, with an eye to maximizing growth opportunities. On the other end of the spectrum, some brands and sectors which were once considered commodities have managed to escape from the "price trap" by transitioning from the logic of convenience into the arena of symbolic competition (so-called masstige). High-end and mass market brands alike have grown into segments that previously did not exist.

Imagine the market of luxury products as a pyramid. At the apex, we find supreme luxury, consisting of unique, ultra-expensive pieces and very few brands. Positioned at the next level is the contemporary luxury of the foremost *griffe*, which are expanding production to draw in a larger number of customers. Then comes accessible luxury, made up of good products, though without a spokesperson, or workshop, or the authority of a powerful advertising image. Here we also find very high-profile brands

FIGURE 6.2   **THE LUXURY PYRAMID AND THE MASSTIGE**

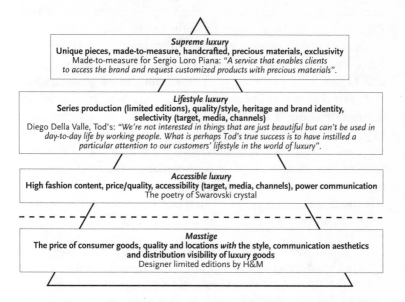

Supreme luxury
Unique pieces, made-to-measure, handcrafted, precious materials, exclusivity
Made-to-measure for Sergio Loro Piana: *"A service that enables clients
to access the brand and request customized products with precious materials".*

Lifestyle luxury
**Series production (limited editions), quality/style, heritage and brand identity,
selectivity (target, media, channels)**
Diego Della Valle, Tod's: *"We're not interested in things that are just beautiful but can't be used in
day-to-day life by working people. What is perhaps Tod's true success is to have instilled a
particular attention to our customers' lifestyle in the world of luxury".*

Accessible luxury
High fashion content, price/quality, accessibility (target, media, channels), power communication
The poetry of Swarovski crystal

Masstige
**The price of consumer goods, quality and locations *with* the style, communication aesthetics
and distribution visibility of luxury goods**
Designer limited editions by H&M

that operate in young segments (jeanswear, sportswear, technology). *Figure 6.2* provides an illustration of this new segmentation of the luxury offering.

As we can see, the concept of luxury applies to super-exclusive, ultra-expensive goods and services that are unknown to the general public. Yet luxury likewise refers to more accessible status symbols, objects that take on this connotation because they are shared by a whole host of people. In some cases, supreme luxury, luxury and accessible luxury are driven by different brands (jewelled sandals by René Caovilla *vs.* sport shoes by Hogan). In others circumstances, supreme luxury brands compete with a part of their offering in the more accessible segment as well, for instance by selling eyewear or perfumes. (Bulgari, for example, created a hugely popular fragrance line, and in jewellery the Boɪ model ring – industrially manufactured, very young and contemporary as far as styles and occasions of use).

In any case, there are two differences between truly luxury brands and premium brands. The first is that luxury brands enter product/service categories and more accessible price ranges while preserving their recognizability in terms of codes in products (and packaging) and in communication (advertising and PR), both in visuals and service in the point of sale. The second difference is that as the accessible offering expands, the historical core product is repositioned even higher, at times a great deal higher, to ensure that the "dream factor" remains unchanged. *Supreme luxury* is the response of luxury brands to growing democratization. It identifies uncompromised luxury, exclusive beyond imagination, where one does not sell, one has private receptions; the product is not displayed, it is unveiled with a gesture art that follows a precise ceremonial protocol. Attention to detail is fanatical, and uniqueness – even before customization – is the dogma. This is luxury that can be opulent or more discrete. Whatever the case, it is not for everyone.

Today, 700 to 800 private jets are manufactured a year and over 70 are owned by private individuals who spend up to 60 million dollars to have one. For such rich customers, some who even request solid gold washbasins, spending 10 million euro on personalized designer décor is a triviality. This is the starting point of the agreement between Gianni Versace S.p.A. and the Tag Group, world leader in the preparation, technical realization, and management of large private jets. This goes to show that the Versace brand is more and more synonymous with exclusive luxury in every field[4].

With historical *prêt-à-porter* brands trading up, the distinction is disappearing between luxury logic (timeless items) from fashion logic (shorter product life cycles).

Giorgio Armani has often said he doesn't care for the word luxury because of its connotations with waste and ostentatious consumption, which is far removed from his elegant and contemporary style. Nevertheless, no one can claim that his Privé line, with its superb creations, unique and infinitely precious, does not represent the most exquisite dimension of luxury.

Thus the concepts of uniqueness, personalization, and limitation are expanded. An interesting example is the limited edition.

---

4. Exerpts from E. Desiderio, "Versace 'vestirà' i jet privati e gli alberghi di lusso", *Italian National Daily*, April 7, 2006.

Once exclusive domain of luxury, these product series were the fruit of production restrictions due to short supply of raw materials and qualified craftsmen. This is still true for some accessories, like Bottega Veneta's Cabat bag; just one takes two working days to make, meaning that only 500 pieces can be produced in a year. Today, however, limited editions are also utilized by the mass market (from ice cream to clothing, to mobile phones, to perfumes) as a marketing strategy to enhance the desirability of a brand by commercializing one-off production that can't be repeated in the future. In the high-end, running limited editions on special items is usually done in conjunction with certain events (fundraising for Ralph Lauren or anniversaries for Gucci) or places (store openings or new markets).

Personalization of the offering is also done at various levels today: from one-of-a-kind items like certain pieces of jewellery or tailored garments, to made-to-measure articles which are not based on a unique model, but are instead a unique combination of stylistic options such as colors, materials, and details.

Made-to-measure has always typified the highest range of the menswear market, till today exclusive territory of the most prestigious tailor brands (such as Caraceni Kiton, Borrelli, Brioni, Zegna, Loro Piana, Savile Row tailors in London). Nonetheless, recently leading designers seem to have realized that personalization is the access key to the wardrobe of men who are more and more willing to spend, who are competent and demanding.

After Armani Privé, the *haute couture* women's collection realized entirely by hand, Giorgio Armani created a line of men's clothing called "Hand Made to Measure". It isn't a collection, but actually an exclusive service available only in a few select Armani boutiques. The customer can select the fabric, the buttons, the lining, the position of the pockets, and the line of the jacket and trousers[5]. The label carries the Armani name, and the name of the client. Once the suit is finished, the model is saved, so customers can place new orders without having to go to the shop.

5. "The tailoring is created exclusively for the customer, who is involved in the choice of style, cut, details, fabric, lining and buttons and is handmade to fit him perfectly". Interview with Giorgio Armani, *Esquire*, September, 2006.

6.5 The masstige

In a society of wide-spread well-being, the desire for luxury crosses the confines of people who can afford a Hermès bag or Gucci moccasins. Well-being becomes the individual gratification people get from treating themselves to little daily pleasures, expensive – but not inaccessible – emotions, such as a Nespresso coffee, a Swarovski charm, or a San Pellegrino water. This makes more room for penetration by products that were once considered generic in the super premium world of luxury products[6]. It is an enormous market, very different from the restricted luxury market as we traditionally understand it. What distinguishes this new market is the choice of a series of goods and services that are connoted with an all-encompassing idea of well-being: cosmetics and spas, high-tech items, food, water and wine, and travel.

Hence the word masstige, that is, mass business logic takes on prestige connotations, used to refer to:

- a retail category that includes brands and products that have high-end, prestigious characteristics but with prices and locations that make them accessible to a mass consumer audience;
- the blurring of the distinction between the prestige and the mass end of the market across many elements of the marketing mix;
- a fashion statement that mixes both mass-produced and prestigious clothes (so-called *mix and match*).

Consumption choices are more and more personal, and difficult to slot into traditional demographic and psycho-graphic categories for reasons explained in *Chapter 8*. Evolved, refined consumers, in search of an individual look, move towards purchase behaviors such as mix and match, rocketing and conspicuous austerity, blurring the traditional boundaries of the industry.

For aspirational consumers, downgrading on certain product categories is the obligatory trade-off for upgrading in others,

6. M.J. Silverstein, N. Fiske, *Trading up*, Portfolio, 2003.

while the super-rich mix consumption to express their individualism, paying full price and discount prices, saving here (for ethical reasons if not for economic need) only to overspend there. The middle range disappears because consumption is polarized between the high-end and lowest price. However, just as the word luxury encompasses a wide variety of different positionings, the mass market is progressively more segmented. Below we've listed some of the more current concepts in the context of masstige:

- *Entry lux*: consists of the lowest-priced models from a manufacturer or line normally associated with luxury. Examples are the city cars by BMW and Lexus.
- *Populux*: low-cost consumer goods that are also perceived as being stylish or fashionable. Chains such as Target, Kmart, Top Shop, H&M and Zara have not only made their mark with a trendy yet inexpensive offering, have not only chosen the maximum-impact locations, often opposite the same luxury brands they imitate in style and exceed in service, have not only blanketed cities with top models in sexy and accessible negligee (the famous H&M campaigns with Claudia Schiffer, Angie Everheart, Naomi Campbell and Daniela Pestava), but recently they've even proven they are capable not only of following, but actually dictating style: Martha Steward for Kmart, Isaac Mzrahi for Target, Kate Moss for Top Shop, and the amazing success of H&M's limited editions.

In the beginning it was Karl Lagerfeld, the designer symbol of Chanel, who created a clothing collection for Fall/Winter 2004 for H&M, with a fragrance developed by Unilever to mark the occasion. This was a limited edition because it could not be repeated in the future, and was distributed in only half the Swedish chain's stores. Priced from 15 to 149 euro maximum, the line covered everything from womenswear and menswear to a fragrance and accessories. In the first two hours after the collection went on sale in Milan, 4.000 garments and 2.000 accessories were snatched up; many of these items were sold a few hours later on eBay at inflated prices. A PR initiative without precedent for H&M, but also an unexpectedly exceptional opportunity for Chanel, which saw sales jump because the partnership shored up the designer's "cool quotient".

- *Commodity chic*: once an undifferentiated product, now an expression of taste. This identifies the art of making something special out a product that was considered indistinct, in a bid to make design a critical selling point. The phenomenon is particularly apparent in the food industry – chocolate, bread, water, and yogurt – variety gone wild. Today products focus on appealing to all the senses: superior taste, the fruit of the best raw materials (the excellence of the illy supply chain), gratification for the eyes (the colors and packaging of Godiva chocolates, the espresso cups by illy's artists), smell (the fragrance of Starbuck's bread fresh from the oven), sound (the sensuality of the sound of biting into a Magnum ice cream).

From the fjords of Scandinavia comes one of the purest and most crystalline waters in the world: Voss. The name means "cascade" in Norwegian, which calls to mind the water's key attributes of freshness and unspoiled purity. (It contains the lowest percentage of dissolved solids of any mineral water in the world). Voss's cylindrical bottle was designed by an ex art director at Calvin Klein and Ralph Lauren. Voss mineral water is now served in the most exclusive restaurants, clubs, and hotels the world over, such as the Trafalgar Hotel in London, the Ritz-Carlton in Manhattan, and the Bulgari Hotel in Milan.

Summing up, then, the mass market is no longer a monolithic category, because its communication has moved into the same territory as prestige goods (image), and because part of the offering has traded up on quality and creativity. (For example, the different labels for Zara and portfolio segmentation at the Inditex Group, which makes Massimo Dutti a higher level brand than Zara). As a result, products can be created with a sizeable price premium, even in categories and market segments that have never existed before. Though this expands market potential considerably, by the same token it can also set a trap which is difficult to escape from.

This is what happens in the cosmetics sector, in particular with makeup, where it's practically impossible for the consumer to distinguish between two beauty products (such as mascara), one destined for the mass market and the other for a selective channel, without the respective packaging and brand name. The premium price applied to luxury cosmetics is far superior to the quality differential that these products offer with respect to mass brands. The basic similarities from a quality standpoint are compensated by the symbolic value associated with high-end products thanks to marketing practices. However, it is extremely difficult to establish an ongoing relationship between products, consumers and points of sale due to the rapid acceleration of the rate of product innovation in cosmetics (which makes it a challenge to invent iconic products), ever shorter lifecycles, and brands' cannibalization of their very own creations.

The situation is further complicated by the characteristics of selective distribution in cosmetics (multibrands, with few levers for direct management by brands, and overcrowding of brands and products) and increasingly aggressive communication strategies by mass brands that steal celebrity testimonials and media visibility from the high segment.

The key then is: how can a product become unique and exclusive in the eyes of the consumer (even though this is not actually the case)? And how can this uniqueness, this exclusivity be so convincing as to justify a longstanding relationship with the brand (which the product is an expression of)?

As compared to true luxury, masstige brands compete primarily through communication, elevating product status with the signature of designers and celebrities, choosing top models for testimonials in ad campaigns, creating (artificially) limited editions, occupying high-traffic locations, investing in huge retail space as a sign of visibility. But these brands are not luxury because they offer a "mass" experience, one which is not unique. In addition, they focus entirely on aspirationality, in other words, the implicit distance between the world they represent in their communication and the product their consumers can actually afford to buy. In other words, they don't engage the super-rich. In fact, the people who already are "jet society" have no desire to belong to the world of masstige. The "happy few" seek exclusivity.

Masstige brands can achieve differentiation by focusing on a single feature, but they can not afford to offer a luxury system, in other words, to act on all fronts simultaneously and synergetically.

7.1 About business models

Business model is a term that applies to a broad range of informal and formal descriptions used by enterprises to represent various aspects of their business (purpose, offerings, strategies, infrastructure, organizational structures, operational processes and policies). Like all models, it is a simplified description and representation of a complex real-world object, so we can define a business model as a simplified description of how a company does business and makes money without having to go into the details of all its strategies and processes. The business model concept is a particularly helpful unit of strategic analysis. In fact, executives as well as entrepreneurs can increase their capacity to manage continuous change and constantly adapt to rapidly changing business environments by injecting new ideas into their business model.

There are a variety of business models in fashion and luxury industries. This is because there are many options for differentiation in terms of value proposition, market segments, distribution channels and organization of key activities. As seen in previous chapters, companies have different origins (manufacturing, a designer workshop, a retail activity) but during years of intense organic and external growth, most competitors become something very different from what they used to be. Since the term business model is also closely related to innovation, it is only natural that over the years, business models in fashion and luxury have become much more sophisticated.

We define a business model in fashion and luxury as consisting of four building blocks:

1. The value proposition of what is offered to the market.
2. The segment(s) of clients that are targeted by the value proposition.
3. The communication and distribution channels to reach clients and offer them the value proposition.
4. The way the value chain is organized (degree of vertical integration).

In this chapter, we will discuss the business models of branded companies; we will not refer to companies that simply act as production partners. Combining the four factors above, we define four business models:

1. Fashion griffe.
2. Luxury brands.
3. Premium brands.
4. Fast fashion retailers.

It is important to note that a brand name such as Armani or Zegna may use different business models to compete in different market segments. For instance, the Armani Group competes among the fashion griffes with Giorgio Armani, and with Emporio Armani among the premium brands. In luxury, Zegna competes with its Ermenegildo Zegna line, and with Zegna among premium brands.

7.2 Fashion designers

This group is made up of actors competing in the high segment of the fashion market (*couture*, ready-to-wear, diffusion and upper bridge) with a strong finely-honed competence in fashion clothing. The value proposition is therefore related to the prestige and image of the designer name, but also the high exceptional quality and accentuated seasonal product fashionability. Everything started with a small designer workshop and an original sketch of a garment. Thanks to the originality and success of their own style, designers such as Giorgio Armani, Gianni Versace, Valentino Garavani, have created global fashion empires under their own names. French designers started first; Italians followed in the 1970s; American designers entered the fashion system in the 1980s. Nowadays their names are associated with a wide range of products, from accessories to cosmetics and home textiles – often far-removed from the original core business of clothing. But clothing, the fashion show and the seasonal renewal of the collection still represent the core of the company's offering. A famous designer taking a bow on the catwalk after the show to garner applause: this is still needed to create the dream behind the brand. Communication entails using the catwalk, celebrities, and product placement and is always very connected with aspirational and contemporary lifestyles. Today designers are involved not only in style, but also in selecting materials and accessories, in merchandising, communication and store design. They are at the heart and the soul of the company.

Fashion designers are usually more product- than market-oriented. Historically they have been supported by specialized industrial partners who produce and distribute the clothing collections and above all the extended product categories (eyewear, fragrances, and accessories) on the designers' behalf. The rapid changes in fashion and the need for high and reliable quality requires sourcing each season from different companies with different specializations in terms of fabrics, treatments, and product categories. In the last few decades some designers (mainly Italians) have acquired majority stakes in their licensing companies in order to gain tighter control over the entire value chain, mainly in the core business of apparel. Both Armani and Dolce & Gabbana, for instance, decided to acquire/build their manufacturing companies. Likewise, most of the fashion houses decided to go retail, opening directly operated boutiques in order to create a better image of the brand on the market and display more product categories. Another specificity of this model is that fashion houses usually undertake line extensions to develop their creativity and stylistic concept in more accessible or younger product lines. Here we can cite the examples of Armani with Emporio Armani and Armani exchange, Dolce&Gabbana with D&G, Valentino with Valentino Red or Prada with Miu Miu.

The great Italian designer Gianni Versace was born in 1946 Reggio Calabria in Southern Italy. In the early days, his mother supported the family with her small seamstress shop, where a young Gianni could get a feel for the world of fabrics and hand-made tailoring. At the age of 25, he moved to Milan and started working as a fashion designer, collaborating with well-established Italian *prêt-à-porter* brands. In 1978, he presented the first womenswear collection signed with his own name and started a fortunate collaboration with the American photographer Richard Avedon. Versace opened his first boutique in Milan's Via della Spiga. Soon, with the growing popularity of the Versace style, boutiques started to spread across the globe. The Gianni Versace Company has always been very centered on the designer's vision and personality. Versace's interpretation of fashion was original, somewhat exhibitionist and brightly colored. He believed that fashion is a form of art, and he was the first to start professional collaboration with internationally renowned photographers (such as Avedon, Newton, Penn, Weber, Barbieri, Gastel, etc.) and art directors (Robert Wilson, Maurice Béjart, Roland Petit, and Twyla Tharp) to design costumes for the opera and the ballet.

Versace paid special attention to promoting the image of his name, also by using the top fashion models for his ads. The same models strutted down the runway during his fashion shows, for which he was the first to use dramatic klieg lighting instead of the traditional overhead lights.

Versace liked to consider himself a tailor rather than a designer. He knew how to cut and sew the clothes he made. He tried on the men's collections personally and had his sister Donatella try on the women's clothes. He paid careful attention to the male and female body. The Versace look of the young, aggressive and sexy woman is well-known. In fact, he liked to create sexy clothes for his women: skin-tight with low cut necklines and high slits on the skirts. Versace was among the first to revive the cat suit, to bring back the mini skirt, to show tights worn as trousers, to bring the bustier out at night and bead it. In 1982, his dresses made with fine metal mesh first appeared and were a hit. His clothes can be found in the collection of the Victoria and Albert Museum in London and have been the subject of exhibitions at the Fashion Institute of Technology and the Metropolitan Museum of Art, both in New York.

7.3 Luxury brands

The luxury value proposition is about timelessness, heritage, and exclusivity. Luxury brands compete on product categories other than clothing, such as watches, cosmetics, leather goods, art de la table, and writing instruments. Even if such companies do own a clothing business, they usually present a limited number of pieces with a lower fashionability compared to fashion designers, with the aim of building a more contemporary image that can support the core business. Most luxury houses began long ago in the leather goods business, such as Vuitton and Hermès, or in hard luxury (jewels) such as Bulgari or Cartier. Around the original know how, these firms built a complete offering of other product categories, accessories and clothing included. Some companies, such as Chanel, became famous with fashion clothing but then after the departure of the founder moved their core business into other categories, such as cosmetics or timeless accessories. Famous fashion designers such as Lagerfeld for Chanel and Fendi and Jacobs for Vuitton collaborate on fashionable clothing collections. But at the very heart of this model lies not the designer's creativity, but the brand with its heritage and iconic products, which are often reinterpreted so they are always up to date.

In terms of business models, these companies are vertically integrated both in terms of retail and manufacturing. They strictly control every step and activity of their value chain. An example of this is Louis Vuitton, which sells its products only through directly operated boutiques worldwide and wields tight control over all the production phases within its internal facilities. Brands that started as luxury usually do not enter into line extensions, as the brand should remain exclusive. They prefer instead to go for brand extensions, stretching the brand image into different product categories. Hermes, for instance, has no accessible or younger lines, but under the same name and within the same market segment it offers leathers goods, watches, jewels, fragrances, silk accessories, art de la table, and eyewear. Luxury houses use communication to reinforce the brand heritage, iconic products and the dream of the brand rather than mainly portraying the seasonal collection.

Cartier's history begins when Louis François Cartier (1819-1904) followed the steps of his grandfather by becoming a goldsmith apprentice to Adolphe Picard, producing handmade jewellery in a small workshop in Paris. When his mentor died in 1847, Cartier succeeded him and the Cartier company was born. From 1853 on Louis François and, after his death, his son Alfred with his three sons (Louis, Pierre and Jacques) were able to expand the business of designing and selling luxurious jewellery to the most influential clientele in the world, including virtually every crowned head in Europe, most of the maharajas of India, and the Kings of Siam and Nepal. Under Louis Cartier's management (until 1942), the company was tirelessly innovative. He revolutionized the art of jewellery in all its forms, and took *haute joaillerie* (high jewellery design), clock-making and accessories to the apex of art: The Art of Cartier. By 1968, Cartier had evolved from a family business into an enormous multinational organization that continues to keep the magic of Cartier alive today. Cartier has preserved its special status because the company has always been able to balance tradition with innovation. Cartier jewellery for women has forever been among the most beautiful in the world, and remains a collector's pleasure. In the business of watches, Cartier made wristwatches in a variety of forms – round, square, tortue, tonneau, rectangular, and oval – rather than limiting timepieces to one or two shapes. Each watch makes a statement in terms of the art of living; the "Santos" (1904) or the "Tank" (1917) models are still considered classic examples of style and design today. Cartier consistently uses the best quality for watch cases, dials and movements (Cartier wristwatches are produced with movements by Jaeger, Vacheron, Le Coutre, Cartier itself and The European Watch). Distribution is managed through directly operated stores and exclusive multibrand jewellers globally. In terms of communication, Cartier leverages its heritage and connections with the arts. In 1984, the Cartier Foundation of Contemporary Art was founded as evidence of the determination to bring Cartier into the 21st century by forming an association with living artists.

In 1989/1990 the first major exhibition of the Cartier collection, "l'Art de Cartier", was a triumphant success at the Musée du Petit Palais in Paris, while the second great exhibition of "l'Art de Cartier" was held at the Ermitage Museum in St. Petersburg. In 1995, a major exhibition of the Cartier Antique Collection was held in Asia.

7.4 Premium brands

This is a wide and quite heterogeneous group. The common trait is that business is positioned in the medium to high price segment (from upper bridge to diffusion) for a younger customer compared to luxury or fashion designers. A premium strategy is followed in terms of price, distribution and communication. Industrial and distributive realities and the vision of an entrepreneur are what bring these companies to life, not the inspiration of a designer. (Evidence of this are the made up company brand names – Diesel, Miss Sixty, Coach, Gant, The North Face).

Their know how is both industrial and commercial, but these companies are usually not integrated in production and retail. They do, however, manage large networks of external suppliers and distribution channels, rigorously controlling the brand concept. The value proposition for these brands is the brand image, connected with the price/quality ratio, and service (to retailers and consumers). The price/quality ratio is attained through product specialization, building special relationships with key suppliers by offering different quality/prices and outsourcing assembly in low-cost countries. Service, instead, is provided by fast and continuous deliveries and replenishments. Therefore, time to market is a key success factor in this business model.

Most of these companies were, at one time, manufacturers or small enterprises specialized in one product category. Over the years, the original product specialization gave way to an expansion of product range and product categories toward a lifestyle offering (extensions in sportswear, fragrances, accessories). At the same time, these players developed strong brands, created directly operated retail networks in addition to their wholesale clients, and made their communication evolve towards models very close to those of fashion designers (the catwalk, the designer spokesperson, from TV to printed magazines as favorite media). The aim of this evolution was to target a younger audience (i.e. the ZZegna line for Zegna), upgrade the perceived image (Miss Sixty), and reposition as designer brands in new markets (Max Mara). In some cases, premium brands built a portfolio made up of directly owned and licensed brands. Examples are the Aeffe Group[1], the Burani Fashion Group[2], Diesel[3].

The Diesel company was created in 1978 in Molvena, in Northeastern Italy, within an industrial area that had been home to historical Italian clothing groups such as Benetton, Stefanel and Marzotto. The history of Diesel is the history of his entrepreneur Mr. Renzo Rosso. Born in 1955, Rosso attended an industrial textile manufacturing school and in 1978 he joined forces with several other manufacturers in his region to form the Genius Group, which created many successful brands still widely known today in casualwear and jeanswear, such as Katherine Hamnett, Goldie, Martin Guy and, of course, Diesel. In 1985, Renzo took complete control of the Diesel brand by buying out his other partners and becoming the sole force behind the brand: "With Diesel I wanted to be free to produce only clothing that I liked". Diesel is a simple name, well-known all over the world, and easy to remember. In the 1980s, the company was specialized and strongly product-oriented: the Diesel line was based on high quality denim jeans with a medium/high price positioning. The key competitor was considered the American brand Levi's. The real innovation was the approach to communication. The now famous Diesel advertising campaigns started in 1991, and ever since have been characterized by a single creative execution in every market of the world. Diesel appropriated the "consumer products make better living" theme (so beloved by ad-

---

1. Aeffe Group includes own-label brands, such as Alberta Ferretti, Moschino and Pollini, and licensed brands, Jean Paul Gaultier, Blugirl and Authier.
2. Burani Fashion Group's main brands are Mariella Burani, René Lezard, Mila Schön and Stephen Fairchild; the company also produces leather apparel, accessories and footwear under brand names like Braccialini, Baldinini, Francesco Biasia, Coccinelle, Mandarina Duck and in the fashion jewellery Valente.
3. Through the Staff International company Diesel controls or has licensed brands such as DSquared, Maison Martin Margiela, Sophie Kokosalaki, Vivienne Westwood.

vertisers from the 1950s onwards) and translated it into the "Diesel – For successful living" campaigns. But Diesel's images of consumer paradise must be interpreted very ironically. In fact, the standard promise of "success" found in most advertising is exaggerated and made absurd. Serious themes seem to be lurking everywhere in the Diesel ads, but any suggestion of worthiness is undercut by a final admission that it's all just a joke. The "For successful living" concept has not only been understood and appreciated by the public but also by the advertising establishment (which was initially very skeptical about this approach)[4]. In 1982, Diesel became a joint-stock company and since then turnover has skyrocketed, from 3.5 million Euro in 1985 to 110 in 1991, to 800 in 2007 in a completely self-financing system. In terms of products, the "traditional" casualwear of the 1980s evolved into more sophisticated "oriented workwear" in the 1990s, and into premium casualwear in recent years.

The brand started a successful business of leather goods and shoes, and entered into licenses as a natural way to expand the offering to the final customer. Diesel's licensed products accurately represent the ethos, design and spirit of the company. Present license agreements include: eyewear (an extensive collection of glasses by Safilo, Italy), fragrances and cosmetics (licensed to the L'Oréal Group) and watches (produced and distributed by Fossil, USA). All the company's products target a discerning consumer concerned with being on the cutting edge of fashion. Parallel to its wholesale distribution through multibrand stores and corners (in major chains and department stores), since 1996 Diesel has been opening directly operated retail. Flagship stores and single-brand stores are the ideal vehicle to bring the Diesel concept to life in its entirety, providing enough space to showcase all Diesel collections.

7.5 Fast vertical retailers

In the last two decades, the fashion scene in the mass market has changed dramatically due to the entry of a new actor who has imposed new value propositions and business logics. This is the fast vertical retail model. These retailers are specialty chains with wide geographical reach (e.g. Promod, Mango, Terranova,

---

4. Diesel advertising won awards at the Cannes Film Festival in '95, '96 and '97 ("Grand Prix" in the film category, "Golden Prize" in the print category and the "Advertiser of the Year Award" in '98), by Eurobest ("Top Award" in '94, "Grand Prix" for print campaigns in '95, '96 and '97), by Epica ('97 "Golden Prizes" both for print campaigns and TV commercials), to name just a few.

Zara, Top Shop, and H&M). Before them, the mass market was characterized by low price and low fashionability. Their innovation in terms of value proposition was to offer a flow delivery of new fashionable merchandise in large and welcoming stores at very convenient prices. These companies are called vertical because they do not restrict their activity to retail distribution: in order to be fast and fashionable they go as far as conceiving the design of the collection. In doing so, they bring about a process of integration of the research and development functions for collection production. In addition, they take over some of the functions that are typical of the clothing industry. In fact, the very term "retailer" risks becoming inadequate, as these firms sell something different from the source articles they purchase, combining the competences of a number of different suppliers. This change involves a more direct relationship with manufacturers of semi-finished textile products, so vertical retailers see greater integration.

The core features of vertical systems can be characterized as follows:

- complete control over the whole value chain (design, manufacturing, logistics and distribution);
- standardized store concepts and coherence between the retailer and the product brand; collections and models are designed by own design teams and sold under the company's brand (and sub-labels);
- quick responses to market and fashion trends are ensured by the fact that quantitative and qualitative information from the point-of-sales is quickly passed back to the design and procurement teams;
- sales risks associated with fashionable items are minimized by the acceleration of all processes within the value chain;
- higher profitability is achieved by collecting margins normally shared between producer and retailer.

In several European countries, specialty chains adopting a vertical system are increasingly eroding the market shares of traditional players, such as department stores and family-owned independent stores. In addition to verticalization, these retailers are also taking a fast fashion approach. "Fast fashion" is not a retail format, but a strategy adopted by leading specialty chains based on shorter and shorter product lifecycles and a tight and efficient supply chain allowing for fast turnover on the shelves. European specialty chains such as Zara and H&M which have adopted a fast fashion model are growing at about three to four times the rate of the sluggish apparel industry as a whole. These results are possible because leaders in fast fashion experience better inventory turns (5-7), net margins (15-20%), and full price sell-through (>80%). At the heart of any fast fashion retailer is speed, and in order to implement the speed strategy, retailers need a flexible supply chain, possibly forsaking low-cost production in Asia in favor of fast but higher-cost local production.

Inditex is a Spanish group of fast fashion retail chains listed on the Stock Exchange. The Group is present in 64 countries, with more than 3.200 stores across eight different brands/concepts: Zara, Kiddy's Class, Skhuaban, Pull and Bear, Massimo Dutti, Bershka, Stradivarius, Oysho, and Zara Home. The Inditex concept of production in proximity (which represents 50% of total production) means that fashionable products are manufactured in the Group's own factories or by suppliers whose processes are significantly integrated with the Group. The Inditex business model is based on a mix of sourcing patterns: fabric sourcing is 60% external and 40% internal, while manufacturing is 50% in-house. External suppliers, a high percentage of which are European, are often supplied with fabrics and other materials by Inditex. In the case of in-house production, Inditex directly carries out fabric supply, marking and cutting, and the final finishing of the garments, subcontracting the garment-making stage to specialized companies located mainly in the Northwest of the Iberian Peninsula.

Hennes & Maurits is a Swedish fast vertical retail chain, listed on the Stock Exchange with a global presence. H&M does not own any factories, but does have 21 production offices for direct procurement: 10 in Europe, 10 in Asia and one in Africa. These offices handle contacts with the approximately 700 suppliers that manufacture H&M's products (primarily in Bangladesh, China, and Turkey). Production offices are responsible for placing the order with the right supplier in terms of price, quality, and time. Ensuring the safety and quality of the goods is the result of extensive testing, including checking for shrinkage, twisting, colorfastness and dry rubbing. At H&M,

lead times vary from two to three weeks up to six months, depending on the nature of the goods. In recent years, H&M has reduced the average lead time by 15-20% through developments in the buying process.

7.6 Does the conglomerate strategy work?

Since the mid-1990s, many fashion and luxury companies have grown though acquisitions on the pathway to becoming multi-business and multibrand groups. Monsieur Bernard Arnauld paved the way in just a decade by building the first international luxury group: Louis Vuitton Moët Hennessy (LVMH). In Italy, companies such as Gucci, IT Holding, Mariella Burani, and Prada followed the route of building a portfolio of businesses and brands. The fervor surrounding the multibrand group tied into the conviction that this business format would ensure plentiful financial and managerial resources on one hand, and would mean acting as talent scout and incubator for new creative talent on the other (since the group could finance the experimental phase involved in launching or relaunching a brand). For companies that gravitated into the group's orbit, the idea was to guarantee the financial and managerial resources needed to grow. A reasonable assumption, but things didn't always turn out as expected. There are as many reasons why as there are points of view. As far as the management literature is concerned, multibusiness and multibrand groups would be well-suited to foster growth in a fragmented system such as fashion, because such groups have certain organizational resources that single firms don't have:

- ability to access to the capital market and expedite listing;
- quality management;
- worldwide distribution and production structure;
- capitalization of experience and a strong position in relations with suppliers.

In light of what has taken place in the international fashion system since the late 1990s, many grey areas surrounding this business model have been exposed pertaining precisely to the factors listed above.

- *Access to the capital market/listing.* While nearly all the French luxury brands and vertical retailers have gone public, few Italian fashion designers or premium brands have followed suit. The advantages of listing, in fact, are not always clear to all players. Granted the market makes more resources available, but more resources can also send the group "off the rails" strategically speaking. For example, businesses are beginning to realize that listing on the stock market, or even allowing outside investments in company share capital, only provides useful financial resources to large companies run with a managerial focus, firms that already have a strategy and clear objectives in place. But the same strategy has penalized firms that only use the financial lever to seize opportunities. Companies that opt for listing are certainly obliged to follow given regulations, but also to generate substantial – at times bordering on voracious – growth to satisfy the demands of the capital market. For family-run firms, in particular when the family is numerous, the advantage of going public is undoubtedly linked to enhancing the value of the shareholders' wealth and its liquidity. However, some groups have postponed listing several times, or abandoned the idea altogether, claiming that the compulsory growth and margins would be detrimental for a fashion company that has to constantly innovate and explore new directions.
- *Quality management.* Buying brands often goes hand in hand with recuperating licenses and the need to manage the supply chain. In following this strategy, beyond the importance that finance and distribution networks take on, enormous pressure is generated on human resources in multibrand groups, especially at the executive level. In contending with projects that grow in number and complexity, what we note in group structures is actually a lack of managers, and the few who are available are sought after at an international level. Fashion and luxury companies should

"implant" managers with experience in other sectors; instead they tend to scout almost exclusively inside the sector, justifying this with the distinctive specificities of these industries. Certainly, these specificities do exist in the product area, but probably not in retail or human resources. Until a new managerial class gains expertise, we can look to middle sized, second or third generation family firms which have "raised" their human resources "at home". In fact, these are the companies that offer the best guarantees in terms of continuity of top management needed to implement long, complex projects and make them profitable.

• *Capitalization of experience and a strong position in relations with suppliers.* A clever multibrand group can exploit its strength to help suppliers invest and grow, and in exchange attain the most advantageous conditions. Nonetheless, it's not uncommon to see groups that use their strength to gain progressively better conditions, but often the autonomy, quality and innovativeness of suppliers suffers, and their very survival is jeopardized. Sadly, Italian districts have first hand experience of this issue. What's more, in some cases the synergies and economies gained for purchasing fabrics and materials can be seen in the standardization of products which should in theory belong to different lines or brands. In sum, it isn't an entirely foregone conclusion that a group is capable of managing suppliers in a virtuous and differentiated way, in particular in the current cost cutting climate.

• *Worldwide distribution and production structure.* Retail has been one of the key investment areas for all fashion and luxury firms in recent years. In one sense, greater orientation toward the market and direct/indirect coverage of the market is undoubtedly a positive factor that has boosted margins. However, today objections are being raised regarding certain aspects of leading groups' retail strategy. Firstly, the race to open gigantic flagship stores and monobrand boutiques has raised the level of fixed costs (increasing both the distance to breakeven for businesses, and the rigidity of the economic and financial structure), causing financial difficulties for some groups. What's more, protests are heard against the retail policy of the leading groups (and big monobrand companies as well), which proposes standardized product assortments worldwide in "cloned" stores in various international fashion streets. This has diminished the variety and richness of cities' historic centers and provoked increasing boredom among globe-trotting customers, who find the same things everywhere they go. This being the case, it appears that if a group truly wants to win the battle on the creative front, it has to actually "conceal" its strength and global exposition if it aims to convincingly introduce new talent to its trendsetter clientele. Instead, the chance to access an efficient, specialized supply chain is most certainly a crucial factor for individual brands. But this is where the group's ability to act as talent scout comes in, not only to recruit designers, but top-level specialized manufacturers as well. These companies are few and far between, however; they don't graduate from the schools every year like designers, and they are not as easy to integrate and manage.

So what's the use of multibrand groups? No doubt they serve the interests of stakeholders and managers, to allocate profits and losses and to boost bargaining power with distribution and the press. Further, the brand portfolio strategy makes it possible to segment demand, targeting the same customer (luxury or fashion) yet offering different products, occasions for use, styles and price ranges. All this while avoiding excessive stretching, which dilutes the equity of individual brands. Within this framework, then, the Gucci Group targets show-off and fashionista clients with the Gucci brand, while Bottega Veneta is for customers looking for understated luxury, and Balenciaga instead is edgy fashion for the trendsetter customer segment.

Do multibrand groups create value for consumers? At a time when the fashion product is becoming more and more trivial, it seems we can assert that multibrand groups create value if they offer products with a soul and an unbeatable quality/price ratio. More than generating synergies, the paramount ability of such groups might be knowing how to replicate success stories, which entails brand building in the businesses where their competencies lie, as well as talent scouting. Till today, few have succeeded. Many brands bought are still in the red, although the impact on group earnings is immaterial because these conglomerates are protected by their size. In some cases, however, striving to replicate success stories could actually hinder the ability to grasp which business model is best suited to each individual brand. There have been exceptions to the rule, of course, in recent years (see Bottega Veneta). Nonetheless, we still believe it is important to underline that the focus on short term economic results and the lack of vision and long-term orientation force niche, emerging and specialized brands down a path of compulsory growth through brand extensions and retail openings. The risk is to alter the physiological development cycle of the brand, or distort its vocation. For example, launching a fragrance that lacks consolidated brand awareness is running a high risk. What follows then, is that within a multibrand group, it's no simple thing to replicate success stories. Often, in fact, a few cash cow brands bring in the turnover that finances a multitude of other brands being initially developed or to be repositioned.

Now more than ever before, financial capacity is important because groups need to attack several markets, and continually increase their visibility. But the new big conglomerates (financial more than industrial) may not represent a real turning point, much less the only available route. In fact, in some way the risk in this sort of concentration is standardizing the offering, stifling creativity. Behind these massive structures, in fact, there are people who, by nature, are inclined to follow the "tried and true" path to success.

8 Consumer segmentation

8.1 About consumer segmentation

Consumer segmentation is the process of classifying people into relatively homogeneous groups in terms of their needs and reactions to marketing initiatives. To segment customers a company should ask itself a list of strategic questions, such as: Who are my customers? What are their characteristics? Where do they live, work and play? Why do they choose my brand/product?

Demand segmentation allows a company to identify and analyze the needs and desires of the so-called *target*. In fashion in particular, segmentation helps to define, season by season, the specific features of the brand's offer system with respect to general market trends. However, at a time when the importance of individual consumers and one-to-one dialogue is increasingly recognized, segmentation can be regarded as artificial and weak since the definition of segments relies on theoretical assumptions. In real life, different groups move from one segment to another, becoming moving targets. The description of segments is, however, a fair compromise that allows firms to try to match their offer with the needs and desires of a group of people.

There is no single way of segmenting the market. There are numerous segmentation variables, and each firm has to use the best mix to meet its own objectives and market needs. Although there are many different approaches to segmentation, all of them have to meet certain basic requirements. First, they have to offer a precise definition of each segment to avoid overlap (requirement of the minimum variance *within* segments, and the maximum variance *among* segments). Secondly, the segments must be achievable by the firm economically. Finally, each segment must be targeted by a specific brand mix. As the market changes, so segmentation criteria have to change too. The recent development of communication systems (the Internet, for example) means single individuals can be reached through a micro-segmentation approach. The consumer is looking for a pluralism of lifestyles and must be targeted through a combination of segmentation tools.

> There are no longer widespread movements in youth culture, like for instance punk. Nowadays there are many sub-cultures that have niche tastes and lifestyles. A significant example is the hundreds of specialist youth magazines that relate to very small segments. In addition, the proliferation of virtual worlds implies that the consumer is becoming increasingly more elusive in the mass, but increasingly more accessible in the niche through new tools such as Internet and social networks.

There are two segmentation macro-categories, and these depend on how customers are grouped together. These macro-categories are based on *descriptive* and *behavioral* segmentation variables. The objective of descriptive segmentation is to describe the individual without taking into account his or her purchase or consumption behaviour; geographic and demographic criteria of segmentation are used here. Behavioral segmentation, instead, groups customers on the basis of their way of thinking, buying and consuming.

8.2 Descriptive segmentation

This type of segmentation considers the *individual in general*, on the basis of widely available objective data and statistical information. The two main criteria of this segmentation are geography and socio-demographics.

Geographical segmentation divides the market into different units – countries, regions, provinces, cities, and even suburbs. The assumption is that the characteristics and thus the needs of individuals vary as a function of place of residence.

One particularly interesting geographic segmentation method in fashion is based on the anthropomorphic and socio-cultural characteristics of the population. Anthropomorphic characteristics make it possible to segment the market on the basis of height, average size, and drop. The populations of Northern Europe, for example, are on average taller and have different sizes and drops than the populations of Southern Europe. Socio-cultural characteristics, instead, show attitudes towards color and use of certain fabrics (natural rather than synthetic ones), buying habits, and dominant retail formats. Combining the anthropomorphic and socio-cultural characteristics of the population, gives us seven international macro-segments. Europe is usually divided into two geographical areas: the pan-German area (Germany, Scandinavian countries and East Central Europe), the Latin area (Southern and Mediterranean Europe), and Britain. Asia can be divided into three sub-regions: Japan, the countries of South East Asia and Australia, and greater China (China, Taiwan and Hong Kong). The American continent divides into North America (the USA and Canada), and Central and South America.

Socio-demographic segmentation divides the market into groups that share characteristics like income, age, gender, profession, and family life cycle stage. The underlying assumption is that consumer behaviors are influenced by these variables. Higher income is associated with the search for higher quality in many industries, fashion included. Consequently, markets are divided into a high, average or low income range.

Age remains a fundamental criterion for segmenting the fashion market, but the construction and interpretation of segments is very different from the past. The classic age segmentation distinguishes between: children, adolescents, young people, adults, and old people (usually over 60). Additional segmentation methods have now been developed, among which generational marketing[1].

---

1. W. Strauss, N. Howe, *Generations: The History of America's Future, 1584 to 2069*, William Morrow & Co., 1992.

A generation is defined by dates of birth, a cohort by important external events that occur during its formative years. In the US, for instance, people born between 1930 and 1939 are often labelled the Depression Generation, but those born between 1912 and 1921 are the Depression Cohort, since they became adults between 1930 and 1939. In reality, a plethora of names exist for some generations. Shown below is an example of one of the most current methodologies on the international scene.

- *Pre-Teen*. Very young but precocious, highly sensitive to fashion and novelty. They come from families that have higher purchase power than in the past (double income); they have few siblings; they tend to have group identity with their age group; they are ambitious and want to imitate young people who are a few years older than them. This is a very fragmented market.
- *Teens or Net Generation* (1981-2000). They grew up with technology and electronics; they look for everything that is new; they are independent, strongly oriented to consumption but also very mobile in their lifestyle and therefore require products that can follow them. This is a very changeable and trendsetting market.
- *Generation Flex* (1965-1980). Also known as Generation X, this was the first post-modern generation. It has experienced important changes in social life (the disappearance of political ideologies, the increase in divorce, new illnesses, flexible work); it is made up of cynical and mistrustful consumers who are value-oriented and do not pursue any one specific lifestyle.
- *Boomers* (1945-1964). The '60s generation, oriented to well being, health and career. It is made up of strong, refined consumers who redefine the life stage formerly known as "aging".
- *New Seniors* (<1945). Given greater life expectancy, this is the generation that will represent an important market in the next ten years in terms of dimension. It is characterized by consumers with young attitudes, strong purchasing power, who are active and independent, oriented toward products that fit their specific needs (clothing, travel, fitness, etc.).

Some authors put the Pre-Teen Generation, Teen and Flex groups together into a macro-category known as the Visual Generation. This group of young, post-modern consumers grew up in a world dominated by the media. They are very sensitive to visual symbols and communication. As symbols nowadays form lifestyles and collective identities, it is necessary to study the symbols rather than political beliefs, cultural level, or purchasing power, in order to understand this generation. It is a difficult generation to classify by known stereotypes since the purchase and consumption behavior of these individuals carries the marks of the free choices that make styles, symbols, and messages. The anthro-sociologist Ted Polhemus defines the young people in this group as "style-surfers" or "symbol surfers"[2].

At the other extreme of the market are the New Seniors. They belong to a segment that will have the greatest demographic strength in the new century, and they are very different to the senior markets of the past. Nonetheless, in the high-end of the market and in fashion, product strategies have yet to change. For the most part, brands continue to neglect problems of wearability, comfort, and service level expected by customers who have plenty of time, who are very oriented toward quality, and who want to learn about and understand product attributes and brand history. What's more, this group is made up of people who are often freer to experiment, since that are far removed from aesthetic obligations that arise from belonging to a group, as is the case for adolescents, nor do they need a corporate uniform, as with the adult segment. In the future, the brands that become first movers in adapting simple product features, making elegance functional, and selling these adaptations not as a medical compromise but instead as an aesthetic element of design, will win an enormous market. New Seniors are young in spirit, and they will appreciate firms that can lever this characteristic.

The socio-demographic variables need to be combined with one another, and they also need to be integrated with other criteria. Although they are very easy to use, and are fundamental for identifying the characteristics of different segments, these indicators do not reveal the motivations that make consumers behave in a certain way. Instead, psychographic segmentation does throw light on these motivations.

8.3 Behavioral segmentation

This type of segmentation considers the *individual as a consumer*, and attempts to go beyond descriptive factors to find causal factors that can be used to build market segments. The main segmentation criteria are based on purchasing behavior, lifestyles and benefits.

---

2. T. Polhemus, *Street Styles*, Thames and Hudson, 1994.

Segmentation by *purchasing behavior* is centered on the knowledge, attitudes and reactions of the individual in product purchasing. The purchasing process concerns the evaluation and selection of a product-service-brand combination by the buyer. Individual buyers are divided on the basis of three variables – user status, occasion of use, and brand loyalty. With regard to user status, consumers can be grouped into the following categories: non-user, potential user, new user, habitual user and former user. Occasion of use, instead, relates to the purpose or context of use of a specific product, without regard to the consumer's characteristics. (This criterion is widely used in fashion). The third variable defines different segments on the basis of the level of loyalty towards a product or brand: consumers with strong loyalty towards one brand only, towards two or more brands, occasional loyalty, or not loyal.

Psychographic segmentation considers *how the individual lives*. The underlying assumption is that the consumer buys a product reflecting his or her characteristics and behavior, both as an individual and in relationship to the reality he or she lives. The Oxford English Dictionary defines a lifestyle as "a way of life" and lifestyle segmentation aims to examine the way people live. Lifestyles are identified through activities (profession, hobbies, holidays, sports), personal interests, opinions/attitudes on socio-cultural events (politics, culture, education).

Psychographic segmentation differs from demographic segmentation because individuals with the same characteristics in terms of demographics may have different characteristics in terms of psychographics. Psychographics has been very successful in fast-moving and in high-involvement consumer goods industries where the concept of lifestyle is crucial. A market for psychographic research exists in many countries, where lifestyle analyses are regularly produced and diffused through tools such as semiotic maps.

A relevant dimension in fashion is the consumer attitude towards the adoption of a new product. According to the product life cycle stages we can identify different types of consumers who should be reached using different marketing strategies:

- Fashion innovators adopt a new product first. They are interested in innovative and unique features. Marketing and promotion should emphasize the newness and distinctive features of the product.
- Early adopters or Fashion opinion leaders (celebrities, magazines) are the next most likely adopters of a fashion product. They imitate the fashion innovators and bring the product into a more popular and accessible style. The product is produced by more companies and is sold at more retail outlets.
- Late majority adopts a fashion product at the peak of its popularity. Marketing is carried out through mass merchandisers and advertising to broad audiences.
- Laggards or Late adopters are consumers who are late to recognize and adopt a fashionable style, and to so in the moment its popularity fades and the fashion product is often marked for clearance.

A further fundamental criterion in the fashion and luxury industries concerns the perceived importance of the fashion content compared with other values such as price and brand prestige. Combining attitudes towards fashion with socio-demographic variables results in three macrosegments – affluent consumers, value oriented consumers and fashion victim consumers.

- Affluent consumers are those who buy a particular product for reasons of status or exhibitionism. They are generally well-off adults or young adults, they tend to be classic in their way of dressing, and they are very brand oriented and fairly brand loyal.
- Value oriented consumers are mature and savvy; they look for value in the offer as the right mix of price and perceived quality. They generally belong to the average income segment (but not necessarily), and they are transversal with regard to age.
- Fashion victims (also defined as a fashionista – a person who is a fashion enthusiast) are usually young consumers. They are fashion conscious and they buy the brand to show that they belong to a certain social group rather than a social class like affluent consumers. They are not brand loyal and they are transversal with respect to income, although they are willing to spend.

The geographic distribution of the three segments is not homogeneous internationally. Affluent consumers are particularly concentrated in Asia and the Middle East, and value oriented consumers in Europe. Fashion victims seem more evenly distributed internationally, which confirms that young people are increasingly creating a global segment.

Benefit segmentation considers *what the individual wants* with regard to the values and benefits he or she is looking for from the product or brand. The assumption is that someone who buys the same class of products is driven to do so by the search for similar benefits of the same intensity. In the field of cosmetics, for example, a possible set of benefits for a lipstick could be: long-lasting, lip-drying protection, coloring, and so on.

To define a segment, every set of benefits can be traced to demographic variables (young *vs.* adult consumers, of low *vs.* high education) and lifestyles (understatement *vs.* showing off). Benefit segmentation is used above all for communication campaigns. Advertising allows the firm to make the connection that is rarely made by the consumer, between expected benefits and product attributes. (A typical example is the Geox shoes headline "the shoe that breathes" which emphasizes the breathable effect of the innovative shoe's sole).

The new consumer: client-user-partner

Modern individuality is flexible, multidimensional, and it emerges as the aggregation of daily choices rather than as the result of rigid and fixed lifestyles. Thus personal identity depends increasingly on the characteristics and number of lifestyles that are adopted. In the face of this, the traditional segmentation model has to be replaced by a *market construction* approach that can anticipate consumer needs. For this reason, the most advanced firms go from psychographic segmentation based on lifestyle to segmentation based on *mind set*[3]. The unit of analysis is no longer the individual, but the mental category and behavior that occur in different life occasions.

The fashion firm has to move close to many behaviors through a relational and participatory model. The offer system has to create a sort of friendship with the final consumer. The purpose of this is not just to satisfy current needs, but also to suggest new ways of using the product. There are firms, in fact, that co-design their product with their customers, allowing a free choice of sizes, colors, accessories and materials.

---

3. J. Lopiano-Misdom, J. De Luca, *Street Trends*, Harper Business, 1998.

In the context of purchasing and using goods, to talk about protagonism in consumption means to recognize the explosive role of new technologies. In the current scenario, the individual is no longer a consumer or a customer but a user who wants to create content and have a hand in developments. There's been a shift from the use of highly specialized niches which have technical functionalities as their center of gravity, to mass consumption which is technically simplified but aesthetically sophisticated. This transition has coincided with the target of users expanding from the male to the female segment, from techies to young people. For example, the upsurge of a very young, female public into the world of consumer electronics has noticeably uplifted aesthetic contents in goods such as digital cameras, MP3 players and telephony. (Proof is in the plethora of partnerships with designers).

This new way of using technology has caused a radical lifestyle transformation. Thanks to the simplicity and ubiquity of technology, we can listen to music or view content anywhere, anytime. We can be constantly connected, and continually mix work and pleasure throughout our day. As the boundaries separating home, work, and leisure have disappeared, so has the rigid division of space and time in the "continual fluidity of roles and expectations of individuals" (as hypothesized by the English philosopher Zygmunt Bauman, considered the theoretician of post-modernism[4]). In the liquid-modern society, speed is what counts, not duration. And to be fast, you always have to be connected.

The iPod is the cult creation of the 2000s. Credit goes to its neutral, emotional design, and its simple, revolutionary interface; it forgoes an excess of useless functions, and focuses on doing one thing and doing it well (reproducing music). But the enticing aesthetic and the functionality of the interface aren't enough to explain its planet-wide success as compared to other MP3 players. The iPod is popular above all because it offers freedom: the freedom to listen to the music you want, the way you want it and wherever you want it. The key feature is the integrated system that Apple

---

4. "Liquid modern" is how we can define a society in which the conditions under which its members act change faster than it takes the ways of acting to consolidate into habits or procedures. Liquid life cannot stay on course, as liquid-modern society cannot keep its shape for long". Z. Bauman, *Liquid Life*, "Introduction", Polity Press, 2005.

created by linking the iPod with iTunes. ("The best digital jukebox with the number one music download store inside"). The iPod+iTunes solution should be seen as a total experience that can be had with the technologies, and the ability to work on contexts of use through an interactive design approach. Users can organize their personal playlists, share music, access compression formats without sacrificing sound quality, integrate a single tool from their PCs to their home stereos to their cars: all this means freedom of movement and action that this system offers users.

8.4 Main drivers for luxury consumption

Now we'll focus on the evolution of the motivations underlying luxury goods consumption specifically. If consumption is a language expressed through the goods we consume, individuals say something about themselves, claiming membership in this or that group, defining their identity in relation to others. Social distinction has always been the basis for fashion and luxury consumption with an ostentatious or *hetero-referential* logic. Added to these motivations, more recently we've seen luxury consumption for the purpose of fulfilling the personal need for self-realization, pleasure, experience, and fun, in other words, *self-referential*. In this research stream, the *recreational shopping* and *hedonistic consumption* theories explain that the gratification engendered by the act of buying something, whatever that good or service may be, is an essential purchase motivation. The hedonistic consumption theory[5] contributes to placing the emotional dimension at the center of the purchasing process, in other words, the capacity of goods (in particular luxury goods) to elicit sensations and emotions.

Below is a sampling from some of the most recent literature[6] on luxury goods consumption which provides a picture of an ex-

---

5. According to Groeppel and Bloch (1990), the recreational shopper is not less rational than the economical shopper, but is stimulated by accessory aspects of the point of sale that make his or her provisioning process more enjoyable and entertaining. In actual fact, a single purchasing experience is often motivated by a mix of pleasure and necessity, which prompts consumers to enter the store to satisfy a functional need and at the same time to experience fun and pleasure.

6. Some of these trends were taken from research conducted by the English consulting firm Ledbury Research, which has worked for years in the field of luxury brands, http://www.ledburyresearch.com.

tremely interesting situation: the gradual integration and co-existence of hetero-referential and self-referential consumption logic, even in the same consumer.

- *Conspicuous consumption.* Conspicuous consumers[7] spend to impress others and to make certain that others are aware of their socio-economic status. These were (and still are) the traditional consumers of ostentatious or "show-off" luxury. Given the growing number of wealthy people, however, it's becoming more difficult to show off. So, these consumers are migrating toward new consumer territory: sending their children to posh schools or members-only clubs. Within this consumption model we find the traditional components[8], known as the *snob effect* (I buy because the item is rare and expensive; the more expensive it is, the more I buy) and the *bandwagon effect* (I buy because other people whom I admire buy and I find this reassuring). This approach is most often found among customers in emerging countries.
- *Selective extravagance.* This defines an individual consumer who displays consumer behavior that sometimes moves up (trading up) and sometimes down (trading down). Such behavior is more and more common in the middle-to-high market range. The phenomenon is also known as rocketing: i.e. spending large sums of money, beyond one's income level, on a few important and expensive (luxury) items, and penny pinching on everything else, compensating with private label brands and discount products. Selective extravagance is especially common in Western markets for the segments labeled "luxury rich, asset poor", in other words, members of the middle classes with a luxury culture, but who have little by the way of wealth, who occasionally buy these products. These are normally consumers who are more price-sensitive, more informed and deman-

7. T. Veblen, *The Theory of the Leisure Class: An Economic Study of Institutions*, Macmillan, 1899.
8. H. Leibenstein, "Bandwagon, Snob and Veblen Effects in the Theory of Consumers' Demand", *The Quarterly Journal of Economics*, 64 (2), May, 1950.

ding both in terms of product and service, less loyal and less brand sensitive. Rocketing is often a choice dictated by one's pocketbook. (But not always – this buying behavior can also express a lack of interest in certain product categories and/or an ethical impulse to compensate for waste). By comparison, *mix and match* brings together luxury and mass market consumption with an overriding aesthetic perspective. An individual's search for trendy clothes runs the gamut of high and low brands and products.

- *Fractional ownership.* Sharing is seen as a major future trend among more careful and disenchanted consumers. Fractional ownership is a way to lower the entry cost of goods that were once for a select few by renting or sharing; chartering yachts and private jets, co-purchasing even bags and clothing. This way, the status symbol is no longer associated with real buying power. In the most exclusive port, the truly rich rub elbows with people who rent big boats just for the weekend. In luxury accessories, the concept of rent has gradually morphed into the idea of a loan. In other words, service offered by specialized shops and sites is becoming more intimate and personalized, as if the customer is given the chance to borrow clothes from "a trendier friend's closet"[9].

- *Self-treating.* This refers to the personal pleasure associated with the consumption experience, an idea that's also linked to the concept of connoisseurship. Connoisseurs are people who are respected by their friends for their expertise in refined and complex products, such as wines or watch mechanisms. This type of consumption appears conspicuous only to a restricted circle, and personal pleasure is always the primary driver of consumption choices.

- *Early adopter.* These consumers are the first to buy innovative products and serve as models for reassurance/emulation for everyone else. They're the first to recognize a style

---

9. J. Michault, "New Year's Coming and No Outfit? Rent It", *International Herald Tribune*, January 10, 2006.

or a new technology, and are continually scouting for trends (products, brands, or technologies). Early adopters aren't loyal; they choose luxury only when it's associated with the concept of innovation.

- *Conspicuous austerity.* This refers to spending large quantities of money on goods and services that convey an image of simplicity or austerity. It can also indicate a lifestyle in which a person openly and deliberately uses goods and services that convey a lower socioe-conomic status. In this case, non-consumption, or consumption of goods that offer an image of austerity, can be differentiated. In fact, either these consumers don't want to impress anyone, or they have money and they know how to spend it, or this behavior may also convey a transition from "I'd like to but I can't" to "I could but I don't want to". Ethical considerations are often the drivers of this approach.

- *The snob-slob paradox/omnivore-univore.* The basic premise of consumer sociology is that cultural choices are shaped by social standing. Nevertheless, how people's position in society differentiates their aesthetic choices is still a matter of debate among sociologists. Today, experts seem to have come to a consensus on the "omnivore/univore theory". The American sociologist Richard Peterson[10] observed that the stratification of tastes in modern society does resemble a pyramid, but one turned upside down. In other words, the higher classes differ from the lower classes in terms of range of tastes (in fashion, music, art, food, and so on), the latter having much more limited tastes. The sociologist referred to omnivores (higher classes), who can be distinguished by their eclecticism, transversal consumption, and a greater cultural tolerance as compared to univores (lower classes), who show less tolerance and far more limited tastes. The main example given is music, where high classes enjoy various kinds of music (from traditional, such as opera, symphonic music, and jazz to more

---

10. R.A. Peterson, R.M. Kern. "Changing Highbrow Taste: From Snob to Omnivore", *American Sociological Review*, 61 (5), 1996, pp. 900-907.

popular, like rock and rap) while lower classes tend to prefer just one type of music (rap for Afro-Americans, or heavy metal for suburban youth in Europe). This interpretation seems lend particular support to trading down and excursionism of traditional luxury customers who enjoy mixing product types and price ranges, as we've seen. According to Peterson and other sociologists, therefore, a change has taken place, and will be consolidated, in marking status which once set "highbrows" against "lowbrows", and now contrasts "omnivores" with "univores."

8.5 A customer-oriented culture

As the above analysis shows, as experience becomes increasingly subjective, the use of luxury and fashion follows a less and less homogeneous approach: the customer is ever more transversal in terms of age, lifestyle, and income bracket. Segmentation has to be implemented on small numbers in an attempt to pinpoint which customers create value for the brand, then targeting them with specific marketing strategies.

To read the market, therefore, we have to shift our lines of site: not *the* market but *our* market, that is, made up of our customers, ours because they buy in our stores. (In emerging countries, for example, where the company doesn't have its own retail presence, one of the key factors in supporting the decision to open on-site is the number of purchases made abroad by customers from the country in question). Customer Relationship Management (CRM) is a corporate philosophy that starts with profiling the clientele, and ends up designing services and marketing initiatives aimed at various segments identified through profiling.

Firms need to take a snapshot of their customers and the trends that impact them through a series of key parameters. However, companies must be aware that no variable taken on its own can adequately depict the consumption process. The critical point becomes not so much whether to opt for lifestyle segmentation rather than one based on age groups. Instead, firms have to integrate a profile of objective data (receipt analysis: amount purchased, frequency of purchases per season, number of items purchased, etc.) with observations of subjective behavior (impulse buys *vs.* planned purchases, satisfaction or dissatisfaction with a given level of service, etc.), crossing this segmentation with the positioning and attributes of the product/service offered.

Conducting analysis in this way is at once more on-target and in-depth. Deeper knowledge of customers makes it possible to anticipate their needs and preferences, and to align the organization accordingly while avoiding a gap between the target objective and actual consumption. A focused marketing strategy (in keeping with the principle of "different actions for different customers") enables companies to optimize investment levels and returns while enhancing the satisfaction of top customers. The stronger customer loyalty achieved in this manner increases the frequency of purchases, the average sales receipt, and the opportunities for cross- and up-selling (selling more than one item at the same time and selling more expensive items).

PART FOUR

Brand management

9   Branding as positioning

9.1 What is a brand?

A brand can be defined as a name, term, sign or symbol or a combination of all of these things, intended to identify the goods or services of one seller and to differentiate them from those of competitors. Branding is all about creating a difference. Branded goods are distinguished from unbranded goods by their intrinsic and symbolic value and therefore command a premium price. The intrinsic value is tangible and associated with product attributes such as performance, durability, workmanship, precious materials. The product and its attributes are the starting point in building any brand identity. The symbolic value is intangible and associated with the social distinction or the emotional value the brand is able to communicate. Armani's clothes are made from the best materials and have a very refined look. But they would just be nice clothes if the brand Armani didn't create a story along with layers of memories and emotions behind these products. A brand name creates a common identity for the product and highlights the ways in which it's different from other products.

Creating a brand that people want means increasing profit for the company. Some decades ago the world of industry and that of marketing were separate and spoke very different languages. Few believed that marketing and communication expenses could ever be considered an asset. Nowadays the brand has become the most important corporate asset in many industries, and industry and marketing are strongly interconnected. Fashion and luxury companies spend millions of euro on creating brands.

Some brands have been around for years and have kept their image, such as Hermès, Ermenegildo Zegna, Chanel; others have been around for years and changed their image, like Burberry or Gucci; some brands are new creations, such as Zara or Seven Jeans. Whatever stage the brand is in, its owner wants to ensure that it has a clear positioning. Brand identity and brand image are the strategic objectives, above all in businesses where the role of intangibles is greater, such as in fashion, design, and entertainment. A strong brand image helps the business add value for the customer and for shareholders; over time it creates an asset for the company called "brand equity". Determining the brand equity, meaning the value of a brand, is an extremely important aspect of strategy and marketing both for the producer and the customer. The purpose of this section is to provide an in-depth review of three dominant theories in the field of brand equity management.

Advertising practitioners began using the term "brand equity" as common nomenclature for this concept in the early 1980s. Since that time, interest in the brand equity concept has steadily risen. Each effort has produced a slightly different way of defining brand equity and to date, there is no one widely accepted, conclusive definition of brand equity. In addition this concept is probably more relevant in mature industries (such as fashion) and in large rather than small companies; it also varies geographically. Still the most common approach is to define the brand as an asset. Currently there are three dominant theories of what constitutes brand equity. The three categories of brand equity measures are: those that assign it a strictly financial value, those that express it as the means for brand extensions, and those that attempt to measure it from the consumer's perspective.

a. *Brand equity as financial value.* Those who support the financial theory feel that without placing a monetary value on each brand, corporate executives have no way of knowing the total worth of their companies. The importance behind the need for this knowledge comes into play when a company is posturing itself for acquisition or attempting to ward off a take over.

b. *Brand equity as potential for brand extensions.* A second view of the financial implications of brand equity is the school of thought that correlates brand equity with *brand extensions*. Here, brand equity is a measure of a mature brand's ability to assist in the development of similar brand types (extensions). The thought is that the more equity a brand has, the better able it is to lead to new avenues of expansion. The emphasis shifts from the near-term to measuring future growth potential. For the first time, we begin to see references to consumer perception, brand loyalty, and the attitudinal dimensions of consumer behaviour. Researchers in this field study the associative affects of brand equity and brand extensions and how they can be applied in meeting the long range planning goals of a company. It is a loyal customer who is willing to try and adopt brand extensions when they become available. Financial considerations become important when contemplating an acquisition or introducing a new brand. By assessing current brand value and past performance, a prediction can be made about potential future growth. The same holds true for brand expansions. Attention is given to brand attributes such as: brand name, attitude towards the original brand, and the fit between the existing brand and the new one, to name just a few.

c. *Brand equity as customer perspective.* The third area of study deals with a consumer-based perspective of equity. Researchers who study this stream feel that with the knowledge of what goes into purchase decisions, they or corporate marketing managers can then determine what value (equity) the consumers place on a particular brand. The question becomes how to build *meaning* for the consumer. Researchers of the consumer based segment examine the attitudinal and behaviour patterns of consumers to determine brand equity. Keller (1993) and Krishnan (1996) offer one popular model of *brand image*. Both feel the backbone to building brand loyalty is to first establish a strong *brand knowledge base*. Brand managers can the use the knowledge base as a springboard for long-term brand loyalty marketing strategies. According to Krishnan (1996), a consumer's knowledge of a brand is the result of the *memory* of various *associations* he or she has with a particular brand. By linking the various brand associations the consumer has, a complex memory structure for that brand results. The more associations, the richer the memory becomes. The goal of the brand manager is to "carefully cultivate a unique image that cannot be readily copied or imitated by other brands"[1]. Understanding this memory association theory enables brand managers to put into action strategies that could make a brand more unique. When necessary, they increase the quantity of associations to bolster weakening brands. Finally, as associations become fatigued, they bring them up to date or put a more positive spin on them, thereby reinvigorating them. Keller (1993) uses a multi-step approach in developing his brand knowledge model (see *Figure 9.1*). The two major elements of the model are *brand awareness* and *image*. Within the awareness segment are brand *recall* and *recognition*. The make up of brand image is dependent upon *type*, *favorability*, *strength*, and *uniqueness* of *brand associations*. Keller believes that by building favorable brand associations, the consumer will develop a positive attitude toward the brand. The more needs the brand satisfies, the more positive the attitude, the more positive the brand knowledge imprint. As the strength of the memory imprint increases, so does the likelihood that the information (knowledge) will become ac-

---

1. Krishnan H.S., "Characteristics of Memory Associations: A Consumer-based Brand Equity Perspective", *International Journal of Research in Marketing*, 13, 1996.

FIGURE 9.1   **A MULTI-STEP APPROACH IN DEVELOPING BRAND EQUITY**

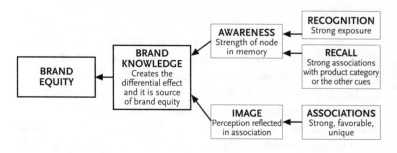

Source: Adapted from Keller, 1993.

cessible to the consumer when he or she actively thinks
about a product.

Branding involves creating mental structures and helping consumers organising the knowledge. After establishing the consumer knowledge structure of the brand, brand managers need
to determine what actions to take to capitalize on this knowledge
structure in order to have loyal customers, the best thing a company can have.

In the following chapters we will always make reference to
brand equity from a consumer perspective. In other words, the
brand is defined by the values of the people who use it, and the
value profile of the people who buy a brand is effectively the profile of the brand. Successful brands understand this; consequently
they place the customers at the center of their corporate culture
and never cheat them. Even if the current fashion is to increase
the so-called "shareholder value", brand managers should always
remember that their success and survival depends soley upon
happy and loyal customers over the long term. If it's true that
the aim of each brand is to build awareness and a lasting positive image in the consumer's mind, brand image is the simply
the consumer's perception of what the company is willing to
stand for with its brand. This is where the concept of brand identity comes in. Identity is the promise the company makes.

The brand can be seen as a product, a set of values, a lifestyle.

Identity tells about the brand history, and sources of uniqueness; it communicates the organisation's core beliefs and values. Identity inspires employees who become the first ambassadors for the brand. Brand image is the sum of consumer perceptions about the brand which may not coincide with the brand's identity unless the brand promise is clearly stated. The identity of any brand has to have strong rational and functional support that serves the deeper needs of the customer. Having that as a framework, the brand can elevate its proposition to the subconscious mind of the customer. The rational and functional base, with emotional content, connects with people beyond their expectation, where the competition cannot go.

> The first time people see an identity they must be provoked by it so that an interest develops. The most quoted example is that of Apple. Towards the end of the 1970s when IBM was internationally established and reputed as a gigantic IT company, Apple Computers suddenly came in with a provocative product with a relevant identity – an apple. At that time people might have said that it's irrelevant to connect a computer and an apple. But the apple was already associated with the genius of Newton's theory of gravitation. In Biblical expression, the apple comprised the symbol of Eve being tempted to indulge in pleasure. Somehow this kind of semiotic brand appeal intrigues and creates curiosity and relevance in the customer's subconscious mind. IBM at that time used to talk literally, as a sum of all the technical greatness of its computer system. But Apple took the route of invention through the emotional path of history. When the understanding of an identity is very prosaic, its charm is lost.

In order to create a strong brand image, a company should be able to build a strong and shared brand identity first, and then be able to communicate this identity in a consistent and relevant way through all the contact points for the customer. Branding is about integrating; the brand is in different places at the same time but it needs to speak only one language. This is particularly relevant in the case of fashion and luxury where under one brand there are several product categories, several distribution channels and communication media. What's more, the product, being seasonal, cannot represent the identity of the company over the long term.

9.2 The brand identity model

Managing successful brands is widely considered as much an art as a science. This certainly applies to fashion and luxury brands, as creating a demand for something very expensive which is not really needed is an art, while managing multiple products, markets, and channels under one brand is a science. Managing these kinds of brands is even something more than that. Luxury and fashion brand management is a balancing act: keeping with the traditions, breaking from them, balancing old and new, staid and stylish, nurturing the roots of tradition and know how, at the same time staying fresh, relevant and contemporary.

Keeping the dream alive is the key success factor. The difference between brands that are successful for generations and all the others lies in their approach to the future. Brands that won't last are happy with the existing product, while great brands are never happy with the here and now and constantly seek new improvements in order to satisfy a changing and increasingly sophisticated consumer base. These brands are dreamers and creators of the future with a solid grounding in their past.

Mr. Bernard Arnault of LVMH gives his formula for creating a star brand that can be presented as follows: define the brand's DNA starting with and leveraging on the brand's history, appoint the right designer to express that DNA, create a great storytelling and marketing buzz, and tightly control quality and distribution. Star brands are born only when a company manages to make products that "speak to the ages" but feel intensely modern[2]. We might humbly add that star brands are those which build a memorable experience for their customers.

The Industrial Revolution in Europe made travelling a leisure activity because of new means of transportation. Wealthy people wanted quality and custom made equipment for their travels. Mr. Louis Vuitton met this need when he opened his first store in Paris in 1854. His products were innovative, expensive, and very high quality. In order to make them distinctive, Mr. Vuitton used the monogram LV together with a pattern of very

---

2. B. Arnault, S. Wetlaufer, "The Perfect Paradox of Star Brands: An Interview with Bernard Arnault of LVMH", *Harvard Business Review*, 2001.

simple graphic symbols and the mark of universality that could be easily recognized by anyone. In few decades, the name became a legend in the art of travel by creating luggage, bags and accessories as innovative as they were elegant and practical. A century and a half later, the legend lives on and LV has become a powerful brand that is an enduring status symbol around the world. The LV experience is lived in the stores, only lavish, usually huge monobrand boutiques where people feel as if they were living in another world and travelling through different senses, collections and expressions of contemporary arts. The timeless message of LV as the art of travel has also been effectively represented recently through communication. Moving from traditional print ads, in 2008 Louis Vuitton decided to show a 90-second television and movie theater advertisement with a travel theme. This captivating corporate advertisement, Vuitton's first, presents travel as a personal journey, without recognizable stars or products, or references to the brand or even recognizable places. Images and music combine to create an experience of escape as the camera encounters landscapes and faces as if in a dream. The LV ad follows the Louis Vuitton's "Core Values" corporate campaign featuring Mikhail Gorbachev, Catherine Deneuve, André Agassi and Steffi Graf on the theme of travel as a personal journey.

Bottega Veneta was established in 1966 in Vicenza, Italy by the Moltedo family. By the 1970s, Bottega Veneta had become the accessories label of choice for customers who appreciated understated luxury. The brand has earned its reputation through its signature "intrecciato", a unique leather weaving technique created by Bottega craftsmen. Bottega's popularity continued through the 1980s as it opened shops in Europe, North America and Japan. The style was discreet and tendentially high-end, and the brand adopted the motto: "When your own initials are enough". By the end of the 1990s, the brand moved towards a flashier, logo-driven aesthetic with a departure from the original stylistic identity. In 2001, the Gucci Group acquired a controlling stake in the label and appointed German designer Tomas Maier, nine years at Hermès, as creative director. In 2002, Maier presented his first accessories men's and women's complete ready-to-wear collections. He brought the brand back to a more understated and classical look. Lines were simple and clean, with ladylike silhouettes and Greco-Roman inspired draping and folding predominating. The color palette used largely light-toned neutrals and faded colors to build the understated elegance look. Eyewear was launched in 2003 followed by fine jewellery and home furnishings in 2006. Further positioning itself as a lifestyle brand, Bottega Veneta has designed namesake suites at St. Regis Hotels in New York and Rome. Today the brand fully interprets the dimensions of a luxury brand: unsurpassed quality, stylish design and opulent materials, exclusive distribution and refined communication.

In order to analyze the complexity of positioning in fashion and luxury we came up with a model which identifies four main elements in building a brand identity in these industries: heritage, style, retail, and communication (*Figure 9.2*). These four drivers define the long-term positioning of the brand in terms of aesthetic and visual codes, and represent the framework and the point of reference for the seasonal strategies in terms of product, store and communication. An effective positioning allows brands to build strong, favorable and unique associations in the consumer mind, which leads to a positive brand image. In fashion and luxury industries, the stylistic identity is the core of brand positioning as each company first makes an aesthetic statement through the product. The designer or the entrepreneur decides what type of product to make – classic, trendy or avant-garde – also based on its history and profile of competencies. Giorgio Armani started from the women's jacket, Valentino from the red evening dress, Diesel from the 5-pocket denim. Then, the stylistic message should be conveyed in the right way through the store concept and the communication message. Again, branding is about integrating.

FIGURE 9.2   **THE BRAND IDENTITY MODEL**

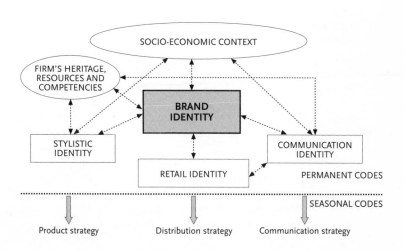

To succeed in an ever-changing environment, it is vital to have both internal consistency and external relevance. Internal consistency is important for positioning the brand: stylistic identity, communication identity and retail identity should all refer to the same brand DNA so the customers know what to expect from the brand. External relevance means to be able to catch up with market evolution and the socio-economic context and update the brand identity in order to be fresh and contemporary for the customer always. Brand identity management is not simply a matter of keeping everything from the logo to the packaging consistent. Companies must also strive to reinterpret their brand equity as channels, competitors and customers change around them.

Mary Quant was set to launch the mini-skirt and by 1969 it was estimated that more than 7 million people owned at least one item bearing the designer's daisy logo. Despite its global appeal, Mary Quant was indelibly linked with London, a brand associated with the cultural attraction of the swinging 60s. Because Mary Quant had been so successful during the 60s, the brand became associated with the decade, and when the fashion scene moved on to the 70s and 80s, Mary Quant was left behind. The iconic designs that made it first cutting edge, and then contemporary, finally made it seem stale.

In the following chapter we will further develop each element of the brand identity model.

10.1 What is heritage?

Any company builds a lasting, successful brand first by developing and creating an effective story. Storytelling is an integral part of modern branding – a strategic tool for communicating brand values. Storytelling is deeply rooted in human nature: as human beings, we make sense of our experiences through stories. This explains why stories are also becoming a tool for businesses to build an emotional bond with their customers. If a brand is willing to be more than just a list of adjectives and is willing to achieve depth and realism, then a brand needs to have come from somewhere and be going somewhere. It must have lived, and be living, in real time. Moreover, companies build their brands through stories that explain to the customer the buying and using experience. Storytelling is also about educating about the product and quality; it serves to propagate cultural standards. All brands can create a story even if they don't own one. For instance, in the absence of any stirring corporate history, Dove created its own narrative with the realization of the Campaign for Real Beauty and the Dove Self-Esteem Fund. Criticizing the harmful and unrealistic expectations the beauty and fashion industry inculcates in women's minds, the Campaign for Real Beauty pitted Dove against the bulk of prevailing Western culture.

But great brand stories stem from the reason a brand exists. Apple wanted to free creative spirits while slaying the Microsoft dragon. Coco Chanel set out to re-invent fashion and liberate women from tradition. When the story is authentic, it talks in mythological way about the brand competence and legitimacy and becomes heritage. A company's heritage has a major impact on building brand positioning and image since consumers trust and value the rich and long tradition and history of a brand. The more positive and extensive past a company has, the more likely a customer will continue to believe in the company's image. Companies with a strong heritage shed a positive light on their present standing and usually continue to win success in their future ventures. History counts as a promise of potential sales. For instance, LVMH Group's acquisitions of niche brands, such as the Italian fashion brand Emilio Pucci or the fragrance brand Acqua di Parma, served to leverage their history and project its magic into the future. Heritage is also a way of understanding the key resources and competencies the brand has developed as something unique. Many companies have a long history, as *Table 10.1* indicates.

But history becomes heritage only when the company is able to create a charming story around it. Heritage is made of four building blocks (*Figure 10.1*): *place* (i.e. Paris for Hermès, Biella for Zegna or Milan for Armani), *people* (the founder, the family, the designer inspiring the brand such as Coco Chanel or the Ferragamo family), the *brand legend* (the story told as a legend: the art of travel for Vuitton, serving queens and Maharaja for Cartier, Ferragamo as shoemaker of the stars), the *products*, in terms of iconic products (the Kelly for Hermès, the trench for Burberry, the Polo shirt for Ralph Lauren) and proprietary know how and manufacturing techniques (the "intrecciato" for Bottega Veneta).

Competitors can imitate a brand or its products – but not its history. Therefore a firm should creatively interpret the value in its brands by developing an authentic and evocative vocabulary, imagery and emotional memory. Leveraging heritage means connecting brands to compelling stories and experiences. A brand's

TABLE 10.1   THE AGE OF STAR LUXURY AND FASHION BRANDS

Fashion and luxury companies	Country of origin	Date of birth
Moët & Chandon	France	1743
Harrods	UK	1834
Tiffany	USA	1837
Hermès	France	1837
Cartier	France	1847
Levi's Strauss	USA	1853
Louis Vuitton	France	1854
Burberry	UK	1856
Bulgari	Italy	1884
Gucci	Italy	1906
Neiman Marcus	USA	1907
L'Oréal	France	1907
Rolex	Switzerland	1908
Ermenegildo Zegna	Italy	1910
Chanel	France	1910
Prada	Italy	1913
Salvatore Ferragamo	Italy	1927
Lancôme	France	1935
Christian Dior	France	1946
Emilio Pucci	Italy	1948
Valentino Garavani	Italy	1961
Luxottica	Italy	1961
Ralph Lauren	USA	1967
Giorgio Armani	Italy	1975
Calvin Klein	USA	1978
Versace	Italy	1978
Dolce & Gabbana	Italy	1985

iconography is defined by scouting for people, imagery, quotes and stories that made the brand. Questions to be asked are: what has the brand's role been in history? What has been the cultural impact of the company or products? How are the brand and products associated with iconic events and experiences? The execution must be about more than a timeline. Authenticity cannot simply be asserted but it must be brought to life in the minds of target audiences. In this respect, a corporate museum is the ultimate show-

FIGURE 10.1   **THE CONCEPT OF HERITAGE**

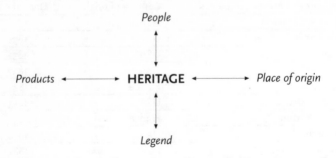

case of firm's history and a strong brand-building tool. Heritage is transformed into a unique brand statement that conveys the themes and messages the brand want its audiences to receive. They can take the form of large-scale museums open to the public, such as the Ferragamo, or they can be small, highly-focused exhibits in corporate offices. The corporate archive is also a tool to use to leverage the heritage. The creation, ongoing development, storage, management and Intra/Internet delivery of historical collections is of key importance in fashion. And companies are increasingly investing in creating digital archives of products, advertising campaigns, documents, images that can be accessible to all brand stakeholders: designers, employees, clients, students, press.

10.2 Leveraging heritage. Best cases

Originally a shoemaker in Bonito, Italy, just outside of Naples, Salvatore Ferragamo moved to the United States in his 20s and worked in a shoe factory in Boston. He immediately disliked the mass production of shoes, preferring instead a specific shoe made for each specific customer's unique wants and needs. It was after this experience that he moved to Hollywood and began making original shoes for celebrities, fast becoming "Shoemaker for the Stars". California was a dreamland in those years and so was its film industry. Salvatore began to design and make cowboy boots for westerns and Roman and Egyptian sandals for epics by major directors and producers. Eventually he moved back to Italy, but continued to customize his shoes, using only the best Italian leather and focusing on women's preferences for style and comfort. Today, his main operations continue to be family run. It is this strong heritage for fine Italian shoes and family strength in the business built a loyal, unwavering customer base. The importance of heritage in supporting the Ferragamo brand identity can be seen in the following aspects:

- *People.* Behind the Ferragamo company there is the founder and his family. Salvatore was both an artist and an innovator. In his constant search for "shoes which fit perfectly", he studied human anatomy, chemical engineering and mathematics at a university in Los Angeles. In the post-war period, all over the world the shoes of Salvatore Ferragamo became a symbol of Italy's reconstruction, through design and production. These were years of memorable inventions: the metal-reinforced stiletto heels made famous by Marilyn Monroe, gold sandals, and the "invisible" sandals with uppers made from nylon thread (which in 1947 were to win Ferragamo the prestigious "Neiman Marcus Award", the Oscar of the fashion world, awarded for the first time to a footwear designer). In 1940 he married Wanda Miletti, the young daughter of the local doctor in Bonito, who had followed him to Florence and who was to bear him six children, three sons and three daughters. When Salvatore died in 1960, Wanda suddenly found herself at the head of the company. At first alone, and later with the help of their six children, she successfully managed to overcome the enormous problems posed by the demanding legacy left by her husband.
- *Product.* The Ferragamo shoe is built as a masterpiece of beauty and comfort. Ferragamo introduced colors and unusual materials. Each model was unique for a specific client. He used to say that in his shoes a woman could become a princess and a princess a queen. A museum was created in Palazzo Feroni, Florence, with a unique archive displaying 100.000 models created by Salvatore and a documentary archive as a living testimony of art in shoemaking with famous iconic products such as the Vara shoe. A line of collector's items was introduced re-proposing iconic products from the past, such as Marilyn's Shoe covered with Swarovski crystals or the classic and timeless wedge.
- *Place.* Ferragamo has always given evidence of his Italian heritage in terms of taste, functionality and manufacturing, meaning that production partners are based only in Italy, every article is controlled in the headquarters, and materials are always high quality (perfect leathers, the softest wools, cashmere and pure cotton).
- *Legend.* Ferragamo is now defined as, "a classic yet modern brand, rooted in artisan and long cultural tradition connecting selective-

ness and self-esteem". Behind this statement lies the story of Salvatore Ferragamo, which he himself recounted in his autobiography, *Shoemaker of Dreams*, published in English in 1957 and later in Italian in 1971. It reads like the story-line of a film: a film where the protagonist incarnates a world of values and qualities through which, in the end, the dream of a lifetime comes true. This legend is told through the organization of intense cultural activities aimed at celebrating the art of shoe making such as the exhibition in Shanghai and in Milan, "Salvatore Ferragamo–Evolving Legend 1928-2008" for the 80 year anniversary of the brand.

Chanel is another brand with a rich history that continues to strengthen the brand today. Chanel brand is about Mademoiselle Coco, the double C logo, Paris – Rue Cambon, some iconic stylistic codes and numbers and products. The legend starts with the story of Gabrielle Chanel who lost her family at a young age and was raised by nuns who taught her to become a seamstress. She was very much influenced by the current events of her time, specifically World War I, and her designs reflected the discontinuities in the way women dressed, as they wore more masculine looks and cuts. Because the cost of materials was high during the war, Chanel used a cheap, knit material called jersey which exemplified both simplicity and masculinity. She also endorsed the fashionable validity of black by creating the "little black dress" in 1926, a dress nicknamed the "The Chanel Ford" by *Vogue*. The iconic dress, a black *crepe-de-Chine* with a pin-tucked front, is still worn in various designs today and Chanel is accredited with its invention and design.

Burberry's style is about London, outdoor garments and the legendary check. Inspired by the tradition of the British military and sports, the brand utilizes the most high-tech, innovative and durable fabrics as a result of its roots in uniforming soldiers, explorers and sportsmen. This heritage has remained consistent in Burberry's repositioning strategy. Burberry's focus – men's apparel and the British lifestyle – would have constrained and potentially hindered continued success in a globalized fashion industry. Accordingly, these stylistic codes have been modified in keeping with the new "One World" image representative of Britain's multiculturalism and Burberry's new global identity. After the Italian designer Roberto Menichetti, a new creative director was appointed, Mr. Christopher Bailey, whose solid English roots have produced colorful and youthful collections. The style has been revitalized through different forms, colors, fabrics and varied usage of the signature check pattern.

Stylistic identity and the product development process

11.1 Defining the brand offering

As we have already mentioned in earlier chapters, the offer system in the fashion industry, and particularly within the clothing industry, is very complex. This is partly due to the *physical and technical features* of the products (fabrics, models, finishing and accessories), partly to *destination of use* (functions, end uses and occasions of use) and partly to *style of dress* (classic, modern, avant-garde). Complexity is also the result of the degree of innovation of the distribution service in the whole offer system. Therefore, rationalizing the process of collection development is a must.

We should, however, be aware of the need to safeguard creativity and inspiration. These are the two essential elements; without them fashion would not even exist. Therefore the process of product development in fashion companies is the result of the integration of two sub-processes. The first is aimed at defining the seasonal offering in terms of aesthetic and stylistic elements, and is driven by the creative people, mainly designers. The second is focused on defining economic and competitive targets of the collection and is driven by managers from different departments (sales, merchandising, and marketing).

Designers should scout and interpret the latest aesthetic-technical trends (shapes, colors and materials) in order to renew the firm's offering from season to season, without of course distorting the brand's permanent stylistic identity. Interpreting long-term socio-cultural trends, and analyzing the market (consumer and trade) and the previous season's sales, however, are all activities that have to be carried out by commercial or product management. The objective here is to define the entire brand offering in terms of variety and variability (number of collections, number of end uses, models/variants, and price ranges).

The two sub-processes should be performed in parallel, even though they have to converge in the definition of the seasonal collection, which aims to integrate aesthetic creativity with commercial strategy. This is not always easy. Designers would like to renew most of the collection year after year following latest trends in order to give free reign to their creativity and to generate new reasons for the consumer to buy. The commercial view, on the other hand, tends to keep certain items and designs that have been successful in past seasons, as these are perceived as less risky for the company.

The truth is half-way between these two positions. The fashion brand cannot be completely dependent upon the commercial vision because in fashion industries the consumer wants to be surprised and excited by the brand's new proposals. On the other hand, unbridled creativity without any marketing constraints is hardly sustainable or profitable in markets where respect of price points and timely deliveries represent key success factors in order to compete. Managing the product development process in fashion means being able to create a system that is consistent at different levels: short term *vs.* long-term and aesthetic *vs.* commercial variables as indicated in *Figure 11.1*.

Having a strong brand positioning and being market-oriented allows companies to filter and interpret trends in a consistent way, avoiding the domination of pure aesthetic logic. We already discussed positioning and the brand identity in the previous chapter, while in the following one we will examine the importance of the stylistic identity and the collection architecture to ensure company growth.

FIGURE 11.1   MANAGEMENT AND CREATIVITY IN PRODUCT
DEVELOPMENT

	SHORT TERM	LONG TERM
Aesthetic variables	Seasonal stylistic concepts and themes	Stylistic identity
Competitive variables	Seasonal collection architecture	Brand identity and positioning

At this point, it is useful to offer a definition of some key terms in the fashion product area, particularly the difference between fashion, style and design. Where fashion is trendy, and fosters change and progress and faces the future, style isn't trendy; rather, as observed by Polhemus (1994), it is inherently conservative and traditional, making use of permanent stylistic codes and adornment.[1]

By style we mean a distinctive form or quality, a manner of expression that can apply to clothing (crew neck *vs.* turtle neck or denim *vs.* gabardine), cars (convertibles *vs.* station wagons), and art (pop art *vs.* art déco). Within a specific style, decorations, patterns and textures may change. Individual interpretations of the same style are called *designs*. When a style becomes popular, many different designs of that style can be produced. As illustrated in the first chapter, a style does not become a fashion until it gains consumer acceptance at a given time.

11.2 The concept of stylistic identity

The reason we all read fashion magazines is to find out what the latest trends in fashion are. One season it's wide-legged pants, another season it's skinny pants. One season it's bright colors and patterns, another season it's natural colors and stripes and

---

1. The example of primitive societies makes the use of stylistic codes to preserve traditions clear; for instance the tattoo patterns of the Maori or of some African populations all serve to resist change and to mark membership in a specific social group.

plaids. Fashion brands propose new collections every season according to what these trends will be. However, at the same time, they also preserve their own individual stylistic codes in order to maintain their brand identity and positioning.

> Stylistic identity for the Gianni Versace label has always been linked to a concept of "Mediterranean baroque". The permanent codes that have been used to represent his style and identity are Greek geometrical decorations, the mythical Medusa logo, and the color gold. The style has its roots in Versace's own background, the Italian region of Calabria. Also Dolce and Gabbana use permanent stylistic codes that originate from their motherland, Sicily: black, lace, seductive blouses and hot atmospheres from lazy and sunny villages where beautiful young women relax in the shade of the prickly pear trees. On the other end of the spectrum, the success of the Milanese house Prada is due to the invention of a minimalism that lacks the intellectualism typical of the most avantgarde designers, and thus is very easy to access for the wider public. Both for accessories, the core business, and for clothing, Prada has adopted stylistic codes that are linked to simplicity of lines, technical items and research on materials.

Without their own stylistic identity, all brands would be the same every season and as a result there would be no such thing as competition. Although fashion companies exist to offer their seasonal collection styles, these seasonal styles must be consistent with the company's overall identity. Because in fashion the very essence of each brand is rooted, for the most part, in a distinct brand style, it is absolutely crucial that the brand still exemplifies its permanent stylistic codes in its seasonal collection. Customers need to feel consistency and similarity for the brand to be successful; thus, stylistic identity is essential throughout all collections. Stylistic identity should not be a standard or a cage (where uniformity is the very antithesis of creativity), but on the contrary a direction along which to make the brand's style evolve.

Stylistic identity is made up of some aesthetic elements including the brand logo, colors, fabrics, patterns, details, lines and the shape of a piece. Designers must be extremely specific with each factor: looking at the hue, intensity, and selection of the palette for the color; the texture, performance, weight, and feel of the fabric; the direction, seams, openings, stability and crispness of the lines; along with the system of lines, and outline of the shape of the piece. A company such as Armani, for example, always uses neutral, calm colors; very seldom do we see very bright colors in the seasonal line. However, Versace uses very warm and cool colors on a permanent basis.

"I am known as the stylist without color, the inventor of "greige" – a cross between grey and beige. I love these neutral tones, they are calm, serene; they provide a background upon which anyone can express himself. It is a way to connect and combine the other colors. It is a base to work on, and it is never definitive, never dissonant, never a passing trend. It is always something that remains, a versatile base on which, from time to time, to imagine other things" (Giorgio Armani, Armani Press).

Prints are a very important element to a brand's stylistic code. Burberry has its check, Dolce & Gabbana the leopard print and Missoni the waves. These elements are permanent and appear in every seasonal collection. However, if animal prints are the particular trend for a season, they will appear in a company's seasonal collection, but not on a permanent basis. For example, Prada had a coat and lots of accessories in the Fall 2006 collection with a leopard print, but we rarely see Prada displaying this sort of print in other seasonal collections.

The Italian fashion house Missoni became famous in the 1960s thanks to an unmistakable style – brightly colored knitwear with lines, squares and designs that could be freely combined. These patchworks of unco-ordinated pieces could be "put together" into patterns to make a jumper with geometric patterns match a jacket with different colored lines. It was a distinctive style, with a very recognizable product. It was necessary to renew the product in the 1980s, and in the 1990s the firm went into crisis. Total black and minimalism were very far from the Missoni style. Retail minimalism wrong-footed the small firm that was forced to invest heavily in the opening of flagship stores. A process of "cleansing" was started, and the style of the mono-brand boutiques followed the general trend (clean, white, few clothes on display). The colors remained, but the ranges were changed, as were designs, matches, modelling, and materials (leather took on a more important role). Although the jumper still had geometric patterns, it was now combined with a solid-colored jacket, and the "put together" look was challenged. The attempt was to encourage modernization of the style without giving it up completely. Missoni was not credible when it ventured beyond its own style, because it entered territories where it did not belong in the mind of consumers. This is how the difficult subject of stylistic development arises, the possibility of gaining new ground without losing the historic roots that underlie brand identity.

A very important element of style is the presence of iconic products. These are usually historical products which won fame for the brand name, and which become codes themselves. Examples are Armani's women's jacket, the Vuitton monogram line bag, the Hermès Kelly bag, Burberry's trench, and Chanel's suit. This last piece is composed of a knee-length skirt and trim, boxy jacket, traditionally made of woven wool with black sewing trim and gold buttons, worn with large costume-pearl necklaces. These pieces can be reinterpreted over the collections in terms of materials and details but always need to be present in the brands' more basic offering. In addition, these products usually contribute the largest part of turnover and margins.

> The Keepall is the quintessence of the Louis Vuitton leather goods collection. It first appeared in the 1930s, in a canvas version designed as an additional item of luggage that stylish travellers folded at the bottom of their trunks. As air transport rapidly expanded over the 20th century, the Keepall became established as the original cabin bag, the prototype of today's weekend bag. Its multiple uses symbolize a totally new way of travelling, characterized by increased individualism and a tremendous thirst for freedom.

For a fashion brand it is critical to achieve a balance between the new seasonal trends and the brand's permanent stylistic codes. Some brands which opt to be more fashionable will push more in the direction of the season's trends while more classic and luxury brands will decide to innovate just a very small part of their collection and stay close to their founding products and stylistic codes.

> The American Ralph Lauren is an example of a designer brand which possesses a strong stylistic identity rooted in some timeless symbols. The iconic product on which the company built its fortune is the classic polo

shirt with the representative horse and polo player as the logo. Ralph Lauren's style can be described as being classic and timeless with aesthetic elements coming both from the lifestyle of the American upper class of the East Cost and the native American Indians. Mr. Lauren himself defines his identity as "A tweedy English-American look with a French cut". He has always been against obsessive fashionability. "I'm not a fashion person. I'm anti-fashion. I don't like to be part of that world. It's too transient. I have never been influenced by it. I'm interested in longevity, timelessness, style – not fashion".

Valentino opened his first atelier in 1959 on Via Condotti in Rome. The following year, he met Giancarlo Giammetti, who started to work for the maison and soon became its CEO. The first years were identified by the "haute couture" dresses, which were entirely produced inside the maison. At that time, Valentino had 80 seamstresses in his atelier who worked based on the weight of each fabric (low, medium and heavy) with only three sewing machines. This explains why one *haute couture* dress took from two to three months to be produced. In those years, the strategy was to develop and maintain an exclusive image, extending the griffe recognition by limiting its access through high prices, beautiful and precious dresses and an extremely selective distribution, focusing on high margins and low volumes. The griffe gained international recognition, especially with its VIP customers (Elizabeth Taylor, Audrey Hepburn and Luciana Pignatelli, to name a few) and in particular with Mrs. Diana Vreeland, who promoted Valentino's work worldwide. Over the years, the brand values that became Valentino's symbols have been associated to this territory of exclusivity, celebrities, precious and rare materials, rich and glamorous, lightness and joie de vivre, allure/*couture*. From the heritage in *haute couture* and exclusivity comes Valentino's stylistic identity, which is based on four elements:

- *Lace.* Whether white, layered and innocent, or black, transparent and sensual, lace is a Valentino mainstay. A classic way of whispering sex, rather than shouting it.
- *Red.* One of Valentino's most famous motifs, it fuels Valentino's passion for design and joie de vivre.
- *Fur trim.* A touch of fur – real or faux – will add instant glamour to a look.
- *Ruffles.* Ruffles and bows interpreted by Valentino exude a sophisticated charm. "Ruffles make you look as if you are dancing when you are still, and what is sexier than a beautiful woman dancing?" (Valentino Garavani).

11.3 The seasonal collection architecture

Again with reference to *Figure 11.1* let's now move from the long-term dimension of brand positioning and stylistic identity to the short term aspect of the seasonal offering. To compete in fashion, brands are offering a new product collection each season. What is a collection? Within any industry, a company's offering is made up of one or more product lines. The concept of line identifies sets of products that are homogeneous in terms of functions, occasions for use and/or product category. The key word in fashion companies is not "lines" so much as "collections". The collection is based on the season. Just like the line, the collection is a set of products grouped according to different criteria.

Historically, the collection comes from French *haute couture* where the *couturier* usually presented a limited series of completely new models every six months. Renewal in *haute couture* involved all the models, while modern collections are the result of a mix of models with different purposes. Some are totally renewed from one season to the next, and others are just carried over with small changes. This mix between seasonal and continuative items in each collection changes as a function of the positioning of the brand. The seasonal part of the collection is larger in ready-to-wear women's clothing and minimal in men's formal wear. It is also clear that the roles of managers and creative people differ according to the collection structure. Creative people's involvement is greatest in the fashionable part and least in the more basic portion of a collection.

Figure 11.2 presents the flow of activities that takes place during the seasonal cycle of product development and shows the departments involved. It starts with the Brand or Merchandising Department defining the collection guidelines, followed by activities connected to making the sample collection that will be presented during the fashion show (in case of designer or premium apparel brands) or in the brand show rooms. This is the collection that will be sold during the sales campaign. Orders collected from buyers will be produced and then finally delivered to the point of sale (directly operated by the brand or owned by wholesale or retail clients).

FIGURE 11.2   **SEASONAL ACTIVITIES IN PRODUCT DEVELOPMENT**

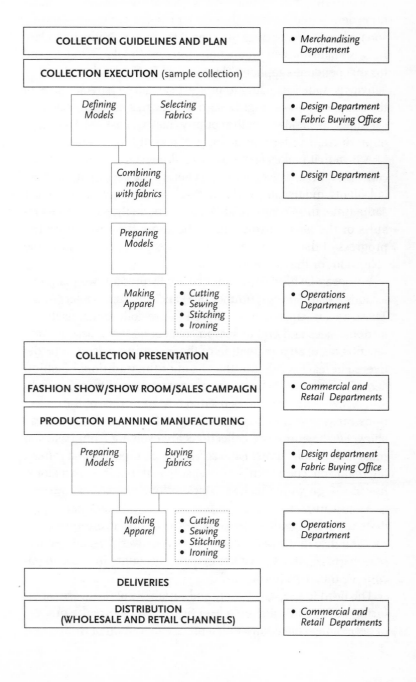

Some specific issues regarding the fashion production cycle are worth mentioning here. All fabrics cannot be purchased after orders are in; instead there is a need for pre-orders for reasons related to respecting the overall lead time. Production planning is made for own production structure ("make strategy") and for independent suppliers ("buy strategy"). Production planning activity is done according to product category, characteristics of the supplier, and timing. Design of activities in manufacturing is strongly dependant on the country (Italy *vs.* East Asia) and type of production system (*façon vs.* purchase of finished product).

A firm that makes fashionable clothing starts working on the collection three to twelve months before the presentation to retail clients and usually works on three seasonal collections at the same time: the Commercial Department analyzes the sales results of the *past* season and at the same time monitors the progress of the *current* season while designers are creating the collection for the *upcoming* season.

European fashion companies generally present two main collections a year: Spring/Summer (S/S) and Autumn/Winter (A/W). These are anticipated and followed by pre-collections, flash collections, sales and end of season collections. *Pre-collections* represent a taste, an anticipation of the incoming season to be delivered at least three months ahead of the traditional fashion show. This preview is becoming more and more diffused in fashion. A few years ago, stores used to buy 20 to 30% of the collections early; now they buy 50 to 60% before the official runway show. Furthermore pre-collections are evolving from basics to most fashionable items. *Flash collections* are capsules that refresh the main collection with the latest seasonal trends, which stores buy in-season with a make-to-stock rationale.

American and fast fashion retailers, on the other hand, produce up to 24 small collections a year in order to renew their merchandise in the sales point on a flow delivery basis. They also have permanent sales with store-wide discounts in order to encourage the turnover of goods.

The need to keep the variety and variability of the seasonal offering under control should lead firms to structure the process of developing collections with a precise definition of timing and

needs in terms of resources. In what follows, the deve\
of seasonal collections will be described and analyzed. Th\
or significant activities are:

1. defining the collection guidelines and plan (merchandising plan);
2. executing the collection and making the sample collection;
3. presenting the collection.

We will now go more in detail on the specific process of creating the collection architecture that is the heart of any fashion company.

The collection guidelines

The process starts with setting down guidelines that should lead to the collection's general features. This activity is carried out by the Product/Style Department together with the commercial staff. The starting point is the final analysis of the sales of previous collections for the same season. This is obtained by gathering information on *sell-in* (sales to trade customers) and possibly *sell-out* as well (sales to the end consumer). The quantitative information (customer statistics, markets, ABC analysis) then has to be enriched by qualitative elements collected from the sales network (distributors, agents, retailers) and/or directly from customers. Other information such as complaints, returns, and defects, is also very important for providing the full background of past sales results.

Sales analysis along with marketing and retail reports should all result in decisions about the collection positioning against different customer segments, different channels, geographic markets and competitors. Additional decisions pertain to the internal resources that are already available and those that should be developed. The Design Department contributes to defining the collection objectives from the standpoint of setting down seasonal stylistic codes. Seasonal codes concern fashionable patterns, materials, colors, details and also product types. They have to evolve seasonally as a function of the development of fashion, while remaining consistent with the long-term stylistic identity of the firm (see *Chapter 10*). The relation between seasonal codes and stylistic identity is particularly important in market segments where product creativity is fundamental, therefore in the high-end of the market.

Once the general input for the collections have been outlined both from a stylistic and marketing perspective, the next move is building the Collection/Deliveries Plan. Also called the Merchandising Plan, it represents the kick-off of the process of design and product development for the season; it must be scheduled according to the specific seasonal cycle of the company. The Collection Plan is drawn up by the merchandiser or by the Product Development Department with the contribution of the Marketing, Sales and Production Departments. The plan outlines desired level of complexity defined in terms of number of stock keeping units (SKU[2]), product range, price positioning, target gross margin, product cost structure, choice of carryovers (fabrics, style, color/washes that will be presented again from the past collections).

Starting from one specific brand/line (i.e. Giorgio Armani or Emporio Armani), the decision of how to allocate SKUs within the collection should follow a certain hierarchy. In other words, how many SKUs should be allotted for:

- gender (male, female);
- end uses (special occasion/free time/active) and color stories;
- product classification (suit, jacket, sport pants, 5-pockets pants, knit, jacket);
- fabric (cotton, linen, wool, technical);
- fit (slim, regular) and style (double breasted *vs.* single/button *vs.* zip);
- color (wash for jeans);
- drop/length.

---

2. One SKU defines the number of combinations of different fabrics, fits, styles, colors/washes and drops/lengths. It does not include the size. For instance one fabric (denim) per 2 fits (regular and slim), per 4 styles, per 3 colors, per one drop makes a total of 24 SKUs.

After deciding on SKU allocation, the price positioning of the collection should be evaluated. Pricing is a strategic issue that is influenced by many factors, such as the market positioning of the line, competitors, and gross margin target. Other considerations are: first, the retail mark-up is very different from one country to another, therefore usually companies focus only on strategic countries or clients; second, pricing is impacted by currencies and customs duties. As a general consideration, price ranges should not be too high but at the same time there should be a balance in terms of entry, core and top prices. After defining the product and price ranges, the feasibility of target gross margin can be evaluated through simulations.

Lastly, seasonal carryover and full-year carryover should be checked, considering that SKUs, fabrics, fits, washes can be all carried over from season to season. Carryover is usually much higher in basic, almost out in fashion. It is important to find a balance between the advantages of continuity and the need to renew products. A high degree of innovation involves greater workloads in the following stages of the manufacturing process: product industrialization, testing, production launches. An increase in workloads must be checked in advance in order to ensure production capacity and respect of timings.

When laying out the structure of the offering, it's very important to establish the timing of the delivery to the stores. The aim of carefully planning deliveries is to favor a better sell-out for each season. In particular:

- to reduce to a minimum the time that the product is in the shop, so that what arrives systematically is what can best be sold at the time of delivery;
- to encourage continual product renewal of the product in the sales point, and ensure that the customer returns, through the systematic arrival of new product packages (approximately every 15-20 days);
- to maximize sell-outs thanks to the greater matchability of the items and the greater degree of assortment, which is the result of the product spending less time on the shelves in the sales point.

For instances the design and sale of the seasonal collection in terms of "color stories" allows companies to achieve the following objectives:

- to guarantee a greater product characterization and identity in the store;
- to reduce the possibility that agents or retailers will put the offer together "to please themselves" (so-called "buying as a single product" from collections that were instead designed as coordinates or matchables);
- to satisfy the needs of differentiated delivery times for different markets, and offer the possibility of differentiated delivery dates for a certain number of color stories (market A: foreign, opinion leader, tourist area; market B: other customers);
- to encouraging better timing of the purchase of textiles and productive activities.

Executing the collection

After the Collection Plan is defined, the execution phase starts. It provides for the organization of many activities pertaining to the operational stage of collection development, the production of prototypes and the sample collection and the definition of timing. Sample collections are created according to following criteria:

- they should represent the collection identity;
- they present customers with options in terms of styles and fabrics and help to make their orders easy and properly structured.

Timing is very important: delineating a real program of activities instead of a simple calendar entails determining the standard workloads of the resources, and estimating the needs of the resources generated by the Collection Plan on this basis. The advantage of using tools like a properly developed collection plan and an activity-based plan is that this leads to easier control of the progress of the collection. As a result there is a higher probability of reducing delays and costs, both as regards the collection and production, and a higher probability of making a suitably full complete collection.

Sometimes it is not easy for product management to convince the creative staff of the need for planning, as it is considered a limit on their capacity for expression and on the time needed for developing stylistic ideas. However, the current needs of the market impose increasingly stringent working times. As a result, planning improvement is now a necessity that cannot be ignored.

Presenting the collection

Once the sample collection has been set up, it's presented to the retail and sales network (for the wholesale cannel) for the purpose of refining the collection's match with market demand. A growing number of firms also involve particularly influential clients (key clients) in this phase in order to receive feedback. As the decision to further increase or reduce the collection size is made here, the way these decisions are taken often means that they have great weight in the outcome of the whole development process.

The importance of input from retail and the market varies according to whether the firm stresses a high level of creativity or greater focus on quality and service instead. In the former case, the process is characterized by the greater autonomy of creative people over marketing. In the latter case, working with clients is an important competitive tool. Customized and exclusive offers are also frequently made in this case, as is the use of personalization on the basis of client demand. Exclusive offers and personalization both require close collaboration from the early stages of design onwards between the client and the manufacturer. The contribution of clients to highly innovative offers is usually only sought at a later stage, for the screening of the definitive collection.

11.4 Who makes trends?

Trends and fads originate continuously from fashion firms as a result of designers' interpretations of input originating from many heterogeneous sources. For instance Bollywood movies, fusion cuisine, design hotels, day spas, the iPod, celebrities' looks

FIGURE 11.3   **TRENDS' MAKERS**

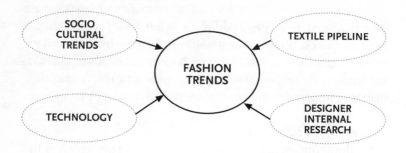

and lifestyles, blogs and social networks are all examples of phenomena that have become trends in recent years at different levels. Some have immediate impact on the catwalks, others act on a deeper level on expectations associated with using a fashion item. (For instance, younger consumers, used to Internet communities, expect more direct involvement in communication and a more active role in designing fashion goods). In *Figure 11.3*, we identify four major sources of trends for fashion and luxury firms: major socio-cultural trends, technology, the textile pipeline, internal research.

Socio-cultural trends

Starting from major socio-cultural trends, these are long-term trends, as was minimalism or fusion, or green environmental concerns influencing not only fashion but many areas of contemporary societies (architecture, music, the arts). These trends may become MindStyles[3] that shape the landscape of the collective imagination upon which companies can position themselves conceptually when it comes to defining their brands and products.

The textile pipeline

Traditionally, the process of fashion trend forecasting (colors, materials, looks) has been formalized by well-defined actors and

---

3. This definition comes from the Italian research institute Future Concept Lab.

institutions. This process emerges from the interaction of three actors in the textile pipeline:

- Bureaux de Style are the first to start in forecasting. Mainly based in France, they identify emerging general trends likely to have an effect on the textile industry in the following years. They work as groups of sociologists, designers, producers and materials experts and collaborate with national and international opinion leaders to produce and sell information about general trends. This information becomes available in *Cahiers de Style* which cover different areas (colors, yarns, cloths, print designs, and so on).
- Fiber producers and/or the international secretariats for natural and synthetic fibers. They carry out their own research and/or interpret the suggestions from the Bureaux de Style. They manage information about trends as a service to their own customers. They are the first producers to give information about fashion trends as they have to design their product 24 months before it comes out on the market.
- Product Fairs for semi-finished goods (yarns and textiles) such as Pitti, Première Vision, Interstoff and Unica. Fairs are the final stage in the process of seasonal trend development, as well as occasions for gathering, comparing and discussing trends from the Bureaux de Style and fiber producers. Trends displayed at textile fairs become input for the lower stages of the pipeline (clothing producers). Textile firms contribute to emerging trends with their own interpretation of general trends, as a way of presenting their own sample collections of yarns and textiles to their clients.

Seasonal trends are strengthened in the commercial relationship between the different actors in the pipeline. The producers of yarns and textiles interact with their own opinion-leader manufacturer customers to finalize the features of the seasonal offer. It is at this stage that general trends are finally incorporated into a finished product. *Table 11.1* shows seasonal timing. Nearly two years go by from the conception of color and fiber trends to the presentation of collections in store windows, excluding pre-collections.

TABLE 11.1   **DIRECTIONS OF THE FASHION SYSTEM:**
LEAD UP TO SPRING-SUMMER '09

June '07 – Color meetings
Intercolor
International textiles

June '07 – Fiber suggestions
Innovations
Technology
Trend information
Yarn trends and fabric trends consultation meetings (Première Vision, Milano Unica, Interstoff Asia)

October '07 – January '08
Work in progress for yarns and fabrics
Yarn exhibitions for weavers (Filo)

January/February '08
Designer collections
Menswear and Women's wear Autumn/Winter '07

February '08
Fabric Exhibitions in Europe:
Munichfabricstart (weavers' pre-collections) – Munich
Milano Unica (textiles) – Milan
Première Vision (fabrics) – Paris
Indigo (textile designers) – Paris
ModAmont (accessories) – Paris
Texworld (garment textiles) – Paris
Pitti Filati (yarn exhibition for knitters) – Florence

March '08
Fabric Exhibitions Asia:
Interstoff Asia H.K. (fabrics)
Intertextile Beijing (apparel fabrics)

April '08
Salone del Mobile – Milan (design and lifestyle)

May/August '08
The fairs in the world:
Bread & Butter (young fashion) – Berlin
ISPO (sportswear) – Munich
CPD (women's wear) – Düsseldorf
Magic (menswear and sportswear) – Las Vegas
Pitti Uomo (menswear Spring/Summer '08) – Florence
Menswear – Designers Collections Spring/Summer '08

September '08
Women's wear – Designer collections Spring/Summer '08

October '08 – February '09
Sales campaigns
Industrialization, production and deliveries

March '09
The collections are finally in the point of sales

Source: Elementi Moda, Milan.

Technology

The fashion and luxury sectors have never been characterized by frequent technological innovation. However, advances in the fiber and fabric sectors have recently led to innovations in finished products as well. In the fabric field, for example, Goretex has revolutionized sportswear. In the same sector, a trendsetter is Tactel by DuPont, which is extremely soft, fast-drying, and 20% lighter than other fabrics. The widespread use of Lycra has allowed many product categories to maintain their original shape after extensions with a new look and fit. Meryl by Nylstar is a collection of high performing fabrics (soft, resistant, antibacterial, antistatic) with innovative applications in apparel.

Designers and internal research

Fashion firms can receive many suggestions from the outside, but it is only an ongoing process of internal research that transforms external input into original and innovative products. Usually fashion firms can count on two sources of internal research:

1. exploratory market research;
2. exploratory technical research in the product-style area.

Exploratory market research draws on many sources, which can be divided into two groups:

- *Trend analysis.* This allows medium and long-term market forecasts of a socio-cultural nature to be made, relating to both to society as a whole and to the specific business target. Few firms develop the relative research as an internal activity; they usually purchase consumer trend studies that are carried out by external professionals (psychographic research). To be effective, such research should be anchored in the socio-cultural features that are more salient for supporting an individual firm's positioning.
- *Relationships with actors in the competitive system.* Industry fairs, visits to customers and suppliers, and the systemic study of competitors are important sources for analyzing market trends and testing the market positioning of the firm.

Research in the product area is not limited to receiving input from marketing. Such research usually goes forward with its own exploratory activities. As in the case of marketing, exploratory product research is fed from aesthetic-technical areas:

- technology: machinery, finishing processes, specialized fairs, industry representatives, and technical journals;
- market: specialized fairs, style consultants, magazines;
- product: developments in yarns and textiles, coloring agents, products for finishing.

A designer with a strong personality will generally not adhere fully to market trends, but will develop them in an original way. Designer research follows routes that are not classifiable. Sources of inspiration come from history, art, architecture, travelling and nature, and over time they are collected within personal archives that represent a valuable asset for the firm.

Each brand has to select what is good for the target customer from the general trend scenario. It's like being on a highway: you have your direction, but then it's up to you to decide when to exit and go. In addition, trends do not always last the length of time we expect; contrary to what we might think, many fashion cycles last for years and not just seasons. Surveys have shown that color trends have a five to seven year cycle (from one season to the next there is a variation, e.g. we see a family of pink which develops), although the "classic" colors always sell – in general better than any of the trend colors: blue and beige are always sold in S/S; grey is always found in winter.

Furthermore, fashion design is a practical craft. What it can achieve is constrained by current lifestyles and mind sets, technical methods and, above all, by the limits of the human body and its range of movement. Because of these limitations, fashion often spends more time looking backwards than forwards: designers often imitate the style of another generation. The roots of much modern fashion lie in rediscovering, recreating and recycling the past (McDowell 2000). Innovation in fashion is rare; a radical change in direction is even more so and that's the reason why anything too avant-guarde is seldom commercially successful. Retro trends are not an invention of the last century: for example, Dior's "New Look", with its narrow waists and ample skirts, was reminiscent of the Belle Époque. The big difference is that today it does not take a hundred years for a trend to return, because all resources needed to develop and propagate it have been greatly simplified and accelerated.

In fact, due to growing globalization in the media and in consumer phenomena, trends shift from the micro to the macro (from the extreme to the mainstream) faster than ever before. Along with long-term cycles, short-term crazes appear ever more frequently. Fashion as an industry has developed into a very fast-moving sector with numerous collections every year and new trends every month. With the rise of "fast-fashion" retailers, consumers have an overload of trends to choose from. They ingest so much information from magazines, blogs and word-of-mouth that they're able to quickly digest the trends, buy what they want, and style things in a unique way.

In the face of the supermarket of trends that are constantly proliferating, which ignite more quickly but fizzle out just as fast, today the company that wins the challenge of overcrowding is the one that can interpret and reinvent trends within the context of its own stylistic identity. An objective dimension, a diktat that applies to all, is juxtaposed with a subjective aspect, where the role of the art director is to serve as filter in relation to the company's personality. (This role is supported by management, from an executive level – owner, President, CEO – to more specific functions such as brand manager and merchandiser).

All brands don't occupy the same territory. The same trend might take on a different interpretation in a radical brand as opposed to a modern or classic one. What's more, today brands have to know how to adapt to local contexts, proposing a global style yet at the same time one that is customized in terms of wearability, cultural sensitivity, diverse aesthetic tastes, etc. Differentiation is also a function of the distribution format and store location.

If it's true that trends are information available to everyone, companies with a strong identity have to build their competitive advantage by leveraging their codes. This is also because today a product that burns out after a single season is mass, while in the high end of the market goods are expected to leave a mark, to last over time. Proof lies in luxury brands: as the fashion/seasonal component in their collection augments, they feel the need to reassert their heritage by revisiting classical themes. (An example is Vuitton, who rediscovered the Keepall, a classic of the travel bag collection).

Leading companies manage their stylistic identity with expertise, leveraging permanent concepts that may relate to various levels of their offering: product concepts (the white shirt for Ferré, the driving shoe for Tod's, the button down for Brooks Brothers, the Polo for Lacoste and Ralph Lauren, the fireman's coat for Fay); shapes (silhouettes, more flowing or structured garments, Fendi's baguette); fabrics (design, look, performance, weight, touch, nylon for Prada, cashmere and tasmanian for Loro Piana); patterns/workmanship (animal prints for Cavalli, the check for Burberry, paisley for Etro, pinstripes for D&G, finishing for Diesel); details (tailoring, use of logos... H for Hermès, H for Hogan, F for Fendi, Ferragamo's gancino); colors (warm, cold, neutral, intense or melange, Valentino's red, Benetton's green, Armani's greige, D&G's black); lines (stitching, cuts, pleats, trimmings).

From the standpoint of continuity in an offering, products can follow a seasonal logic (innovative) or they may be carry-overs (continuative). In a context which is becoming more crowded, noisy and complex, where companies have to sell as much to sophisticated Western connoisseurs as to status-driven consumers in emerging countries, leveraging icon products is essential to make a company's proposal recognizable, to promote customer loyalty, and to minimize the fashion risk. Furthermore, such items offer the company a much higher return in terms of profitability as compared to the more innovative portion of the offering (where high margins have to compensate for scanty volumes and investments in research). With image products companies communicate, with continuative items they do business.

The communication strategy should evolve in this direction as well. The rationale behind the offering has changed drastically because industrial brands have become retailers. Consequently, the two traditional collections have been substituted by mini-collections segmented according to delivery times, occasions for use and channels. Despite this, communication rarely varies during the season. In November advertising, the same shoot is used as in September, without considering that a different product is in the stores. As with style, image identity should also have a permanent component, linked to the deep-seated identity of the brand, and a more dynamic dimension as well. Up till now, the evolution in communication has been a seasonal phenomenon associated with renewing the offering. In the future, instead, hypothetically fast fashion could be coupled with "fast communication". This could modify the message and in doing so recapture the attention of readers in the same way that fresh collections in stores renew the interest of their customers, spotlighting image products at the outset of the season and carryovers later on.

Today the challenge for fashion companies is to be progressively more dynamic in the approach to the market (different collections, different launches, different media) and at the same time increasingly clear in building their proposals. To go from falling in love to having a relationship, one has to reveal one's character and distinctive personality, with respect to general fashion trends.

12.1 Fashion "make-to-order" and fashion "make-to-stock"

There are two business logics that fashion companies may follow, in particular within the clothing segment:

- The "make-to-order" logic, where firms produce only the portion of the seasonal offer that has already been sold to retail clients. According to this logic, firms follow these stages: building the seasonal sample collection, presenting the collection, acquiring orders, launching production and delivering products. This process allows the firm to minimize unsold stocks that would be out of fashion the following season. Make-to-order is the traditional logic of high-end fashion designers.
- The "make-to-stock" logic, where firms produce the offer that is planned for the season on the basis of sales forecasts. This logic is followed for basic items that are sold year after year with minimal modifications. These are the stages: sales forecasts, production planning, production launch, sales and delivery. This process guarantees a much more

rapid delivery time compared with the make-to-order logic. For this reason, make-to-stock applies both to companies working on basics (styles and volumes can be forecast in advance) and to quick fashion companies that produce mini-packages in order to shrink time to market and lead time. The make-to-stock logic does not differentiate substantially from the business logic in other consumer goods sectors and is quite common in the mass market.

While up until the 1990s make-to-order and make-to-stock existed in a pure state, the two business logics have moved closer together in recent times, resulting in mutual contamination. For everyone, the key words are now speed and market proximity.

Historically, make-to-order was characterized by long lead times (meaning the time from when orders are taken to when products are delivered, on average 3-4 months), and an even longer time to market (from design to delivery of a collection, usually around 9 months). This system gave garment workshops the advantage of minimizing risks (because it guaranteed low levels of leftover stock for the producer) and long lead times – which meant the chance to plan and compensate for inefficiency in timing and resource allocation. Plus, cash flow was predictable. However, there was also a disadvantage: the company was far from the market. It wasn't possible to fine-tune merchandise on offer (which remained unchanged with respect to the season and upcoming trends) and customer service was lacking. As a consequence, in recent times traditional make-to-order began to evolve: the main collection was enhanced by pre-collections with staggered delivery times; seasonal lines were integrated with mini-packets or "flashes"[1].

The ability to deliver (to the right place at the right time) and to replenish stores became critical success factors. To ensure service (prompt delivery), make-to-order companies began to work a part of their collection with a quick fashion logic. In doing so, a portion of seasonal sales were satisfied through make-to-stock. (Before getting any feedback on sell-out, companies gambled on certain articles, producing them in excess of orders, lead times being equal).

---

1. See also page 179.

The pure quick fashion logic, opposed to make-to-order, was a model developed by companies that worked on time to market with an eye to service. This model was common in other industries, but in fashion there existed an additional critical dimension: variety. The point of departure was make-to-stock, but in order for this model to work, a continual supply of new/valid products (in terms of fashion content and stylistic distinction) had to be fed into it. Speed in terms of time to market (product development) was a vital prerequisite. Quick fashion companies had a pull-based strategic orientation. As opposed to make-to-order garment manufacturers, these firms sold in season, working not on the basis of orders received but through continually monitoring sell-in. Quick fashion was very close to the market: lead time did not exceed two weeks, and time to market ran from 20 days to 2 months, depending on product complexity. This was possible because the several months it took to arrange the sample collection, typical of garment producers, were eliminated (along with related research investments).

The advantage of quick fashion companies was their ability to make a garment with high fashion content very fast. Traditionally, quick fashion was a follower – it didn't create new trends, like the big fashion houses did, but spotted the major ones and copied them. This was done with an extremely compressed time to market, and sample collections which were reduced in size and repeated over time. Critical success factors were the production network (flexible and decentralized) and distribution based on wholesale diffusion centers located in easy-to-reach places for retailers. It was a quick response of the pipeline. Suppliers and outsourcers had to upgrade their internal setup: they too had to adopt a more flexible structure to guarantee fast, frequent delivery, and smaller reorders.

The major disadvantage of this model arose from the challenge of brand building, since permanent stylistic codes which characterize the product were lacking, and no investments were made in image (neither in advertising nor in stores, since this was an exquisitely wholesale model).

In order to achieve a differentiated market positioning, quick fashion companies have started to introduce make-to-order main collections, in which some recognizable stylistic codes are identifiable, combined with weekly mini-collections aimed at refreshing the merchandise in the store. Today the two logics exist side by side in fashion firms, as the offer systems contain both fashion and continuative items.

12.2 The sales process*

Given this premise, the objective of the sales process in fashion is to obtain customer orders as quickly as possible. Within the make-to-order logic, the order represents the starting point of the productive and logistic process (purchasing raw materials, manufacturing and delivery). In the make-to-stock logic, however, the order is only the information which marks the beginning of the distribution process.

The make-to-order logic is, as we've said, more diffused in the fashion system. Here the sales process starts with the presentation of collections to the sales network. The sales network is made up of show room managers or commercial managers (area managers, key client managers and agents). The sales network is presented with the whole seasonal offer (themes, technical features, price ranges and level of service). The objective is to illustrate the concept of the collection in terms of target, positioning, and selling proposition to all the people involved in sales. This is very important since the tangible and intangible contents of the collection risk being left by the wayside, or ignored completely, in the many steps before the product actually reaches the end consumer.

There are usually two shows for the sales force. The first of these is more spectacular, and the objective is to transmit the image of the collection. The second show is more technical: the product and collection managers explain, item by item, the reasons for the choices of specific textiles and colors, and the assortment options of the various items. Once the collection has been presented to the sales force, there then follows a series of stages – budgeting, presenting the collection to customers, acquiring orders and managing after-sales service.

---

* This paragraph was adapted from Saviolo S., Testa S., *Strategic Management in the Fashion Companies*, Etas, 2002, chapter 9, par. 9.1.

The budgeting process

Before the collection is presented to customers, the sales budget is generally drawn up, usually by product line/brand and geographical area. This is an important chance to give the sales network responsibility for their specific results. In fact, if the sales network is to be motivated, it must be involved in defining objectives. The firm's commercial management and the sales network discuss the "potential" for each geographical area as part of the budgeting process. This is an evaluation of existing and new clients interested in the line/brand. The aim is to determine the medium-term actions (from one to three years) that have to be implemented for every combination of line/brand/geographic area. This is how market-oriented firms build up a detailed customer database for each area; customers are rated on the basis of their past orders/sales potential as priority 1, 2, or 3. Usually for fashion companies the number of customers is very high, even though only a few of them contribute greatly to turnover. For this reason, it's fundamental to create a customer database in order to select the most suitable line/brand mix for each particular area. The budgeting process is much easier if existing customers and new customers are already identified in terms of their sales potential. Where this is not the case, budgeting becomes pure imagination, or risks being left wholly to the agent/representative, who may not be fully aware of the commercial strategy of the firm.

Presenting the collections to the trade

The trade customer sees collections in the firm's showrooms and through the sales network. This network, based on representatives and agents, is the most traditional sales structure. These people are not employees of the firm, and may in fact work for one or more firms with a commission on sales. Agents work through direct contact with customers (these may be retailers or also intermediate manufacturers in the case of the higher stages of the pipeline), and take their orders. The agent visits the smallest and most traditional customers directly, while sales to large, structured customers generally take place in the show room and are managed by the agent. However, the problem of this sales formula is linked to several factors:

- the increasing width and variety of fashion collections means that it is increasingly necessary for the agent to make a selection of the offer to be presented. If the agent receives no guidance from the firm, there is a risk that this selection will be made on the basis of agent's personal decision;
- agents usually consider the customer as their own asset, and are only rarely willing to supply all customer information to the firm, which would allow the firm to connect the product to the channels that are most suitable to the brand;
- the concentration and sophistication of distribution means that the role of a commercial intermediary is less and less important. By the same token, sales people are needed who are well-integrated in the business culture, and who understand relational marketing, the product, and how to handle service. Agents cannot, and should not, be creative people, yet they still have to understand the creative culture and language of the firm if they are to transmit these features to the lower stages of the pipeline.

For all these reasons, the leading firms moved long ago towards sales though the firm's showrooms or through representatives who specialize in product types (knitwear, accessories or coats), customer types (boutiques, department stores or specialist chains), or geographic areas.

Selling through the firm's showrooms allows all the products in the collection to be shown under the direct control of the firm. Customers visit the showroom during the sales campaign, which usually coincides with the period of the fashion shows and trade fairs. The showroom is a simulation of a shop/setting where customers can make an immediate evaluation of the suitability of product assortments. This suitability seems an imperative, given the complexity of collections and the importance of global coordination within distribution (the product and visual merchandising).

The order acquisition process

The timing of the sales campaign varies from firm to firm, generally covering a period from two to six weeks, for which the sales network is given a weekly budget. It is worthwhile to check whether significant qualitative and quantitative objectives have been attained, even after the first few weeks. This kind of control is increasingly necessary for the rapid identification of market trends and for planning purchases accordingly. The sales process is very closely related to the sourcing of materials (fabrics, accessories). To guarantee delivery times that meet the current needs of the market, given the long working times that are a feature of the textile pipeline, some of the purchases and production have to be made "blind" – without any certainty of total orders. Leading firms manage this structural uncertainty through accurate customer segmentation, which allows them to project orders from the first few weeks and estimate total needs up to the end of the campaign. This requires *fine-tuning* progressing sales and production planning, and entails not only the use of very sophisticated information systems, but also a sales structure that is integrated with the firm.

Managing service to the retail client

Evolving distribution and retailing formats require collaboration and support from the agents and the firm's sales network towards the retail client. This assistance generally consists of checking the quality of assortments and deliveries, providing support for sales point activities (visual merchandising), replenishing during the season (of both running products and infra-seasonal ones), and replacing defective items. It means creating the conditions for moving from a maximization of the sell-in (sales to trade customers) towards a maximization of the sell-out (sales to the end consumer). Service management implies a closer customer/seller relationship that can be used as the basis for developing knowledge and building deeper trust.

12.3 Retail structures in fashion and luxury

Retail trade provides an interface between producers and consumers, representing the final segment of the fashion and luxury goods chain. While distributors act as intermediaries between manufacturers and retailers as importers and/or wholesalers, retailers engage in commercializing goods directly from manufacturers or from wholesalers, selling products directly to consumers, usually without developing or changing products further. Most retailers undertake sales and administrative activities such as customer service, product merchandising, advertising, inventory control, and cash handling. Retailers in luxury and fashion can be classified according to two criteria and five categories[2]:

- *non specialized*: department stores, hyper- and supermarkets, mail-order retailers;
- *specialized*: specialty chains, independent stores (mono or multibrand).

What follows is a brief description of the five categories.

Department stores

A department store is a retail establishment which specializes in selling a wide range of products organized into departments. Main product categories usually are: clothing, accessories, fragrances, cosmetics and home collections, with no predominating merchandise line. Additionally such stores may select other lines of products such as toiletries, electronics & photographic equipment, jewellery, toys, and sporting goods. Department stores mostly offer brands and they give those brands a dedicated space in terms of visuals and merchandise (wall units, shop-in-shops, corners). Private labels represent a limited part of the offer. Examples of department stores include in House of Fraser, Selfridges, and Debenham in the UK; in Italy, la Rinascente and Coin; in France, Printemps and Galeries Lafayette, and El Corte Inglés in Spain.

---

2. Our classification follows K. Aspinall, *Long Term Scenarios for the EU Textile and Clothing Industry*, OETH, 1997. Aspinall identifies six main types of retail channels: independent stores, specialty multiples, department and variety stores, hyper- and supermarkets, and mail order. In some European countries, itinerant retailing still accounts for a significant share of the market. In addition, retailers' outlets are on the rise.

Hypermarkets

Hypermarkets are superstores combining a supermarket and a department store. The result is a gigantic retail facility which carries an enormous range of products under one roof, including full lines of groceries and general merchandise. Hypermarkets, like other big-box stores, typically have business models focusing on high-volume, low-margin sales. Due to their large footprints and the need for many shoppers to carry large quantities of goods, many hypermarkets choose suburban or out-of-town locations that are easily accessible by automobile. Aggressive pricing is not only financed by high sales volumes, but also by the low cost of sales space, greater autonomy in terms of logistics when compared with smaller retail outlets, a faster turnover of goods and longer opening hours. Examples include Auchan, Carrefour, and Tesco.

Mail order retailers

Mail order retailers, such as La Redoute in France and Otto Versand in Germany, sell products by mail. The buyer places an order for the desired products with the merchant through some remote method (by phone or via Internet). Then, the products are typically delivered directly to an address supplied by the customer, such as a home address; occasionally the orders are delivered to a nearby retail location for the customer to pick up. Some merchants also allow the goods to be shipped directly to a third-party consumer, which is an effective way to send a gift to an out-of-town recipient.

Specialty chains

Specialty chains (or multiples) have a wider geographical reach, with some very large players, such as H&M, C&A and Zara (Grupo Inditex). Some are directly owned and operated (e.g. C&A) while others have a franchise structure (e.g. Benetton). The economics of sourcing and marketing differ from what independent retailers deal with. Specialty chains are also called verticals as their main characteristic is the control these companies have over the products they sell. In fact, specialty chains sell their own branded production, manufactured by favored suppliers. For larger chains, network economies are achieved through the use of advanced information and management systems (electronic point of sale, electronic data interchange and just-in-time) and national media advertising. Speciality chains can be further classified as *single-industry specialists* (e.g. Promod, Mango, Pimkie, Benetton, Terranova, Gap, Zara, Kiabi, Top Shop, C&A), *single-product specialists* (e.g. Yamamay and Tezenis for lingerie or Tie Rack for accessories), *single-client specialists* (e.g. Prenatal for mothers-to-be), and *single-occasion of use specialists* (e.g. Decathlon and Sportscheck in sportswear and activewear).

Independent stores

Independent stores are self standing points of sales specialized in one or more product categories. They carry different brands and sometimes their own private brand. The difference between specialty chains and these stores is that they are not multiples; instead there is usually just one independent store. The selling surface is limited and the merchandising is directly managed by the store owner. Independent stores are still the dominant retail format in many European countries such as Italy, Spain, Portugal and Poland. However, these retailers saw their presence dramatically reduced in the last decade due to the emergence of aggressive specialty chains.

A recent evolution in the format of independent multibrand stores is towards the development of concept stores. Also called destination boutiques, these are large multi-brand spaces where products are sold in an environment proposing a unique and sophisticated retail concept. Concept stores have strong identities and autonomous capacities to attract customers. They are big (> 10.000 sq ft); they are located in trendy and high traffic areas; and they usually combine art space, cool portable electronic gadgets, a bookstore, an antique homewear section, a groovy restaurant as well as the "must-have" fashion items of the season. The objective of the concept store is not to make immediate or occasional sales, but to attract and maintain groups of customers who are searching for a shopping experience beyond the purchase itself. The chance to enter a sales point without being obliged to buy something guides the final consumer towards a more open and less "frightened" relationship with the brand. As a result, the concept of *store loyalty* is being added to the traditional *brand loyalty*.

This makes for a completely different relationship between the retail brand and the industrial brand. In fact, it is extremely important to ensure consistency between the identity and positioning of both the brands, which have to share a common vision and a common target. The best global examples of stores that have fully developed this format are Colette in Paris, Corso Como 10 in Milan, Joice in Hong Kong and Maxfield in Los Angeles, Jeffrey in New York, Restir in Midtown Tokyo, Villa Moda in Kuwait and Podium in Moscow.

With reference to the 1990s and early 2000s, the European fashion retail market has been characterized by growing levels of concentration (although the industry remains fairly dispersed with the persistence of small family-controlled ownership structures) and the rise of specialty clothing chains adopting innovative marketing strategies *vs.* traditional independent stores or department stores. While people routinely shop at hypermarkets, they simultaneously look for variety and fashionability at specialty retailers. Over the last ten years, specialty chains have captured a chunk of department stores' market by targeting and tailoring offerings to well-defined customer segments and then improving operations to increase efficiency.

The growing market share of speciality chains at the expenses of departments is not just a European phenomenon. A similar process started long before in the US. A possible explanation of the loss of appeal of department stores lies in the fact that department stores are product emporiums filled with too much merchandise. Consumers often see them as having high prices, not being very innovative, and offering mediocre service and product knowledge. Furthermore, the availability of an increasing number of product categories at affordable prices in hypermarkets (such as underwear and hoisery) is having substantial implications for the space allocation and the merchandise carried by premium clothing retailers, such as department stores. On the one hand, department stores are skewing the mix of their merchandise in these categories away from basics to fast-growth micro-categories (e.g., high-end designer jeans) and exclusive brands.

In order to achieve assortment distinctiveness at competitive prices and to defend and increase shares in the "battleground" categories, some retailers, such as la Rinascente in Italy and Marks & Spencer in the United Kingdom, are partnering with their suppliers to carry even more proprietary brands and merchandise. What's more they are radically enhancing the fashion sensibility and quality of their private label, and re-assorting their stores to enrich the in-store experience for their customers and to drive conversion. It is likely that, in the future, a place will remain for "destination stores", which appeal to customers also through the theatricality of the shopping experience. These premium department stores (such as Harrods and Harvey Nichols in London, and Galeries Lafayette and Printemps in Paris) still offer consumers a "dream world" reminiscent of the golden age of department stores. For instance, since 2004 in the Printemps Store in Paris, concession shopfits have been upgraded and mass-market labels such as Zara and Mango have been replaced by higher-end brands. The focus will stay on high fashion brands, and a concierge service has been introduced, along with 10 personal shoppers and a Maybach luxury car to transport customers and their shopping bags to their hotels, a bid to cash in on tourist sales.

After this overview on the structure of the retail business, we will move to the firm level, analyzing the different options available to companies in terms of distribution and retailing.

12.4 The distribution and retailing process

Choices in terms of distribution channels and store formats are fundamental elements in building the brand identity and the brand experience in fashion and luxury. This is because the consumer does not perceive the product as standing alone, but as part of a wider system in which the retail experience proves fundamental. Market-oriented firms should conceive the commercial and retail process not just in terms of final sales, but also as part of the wider system of information and marketing intelligence that involves the whole company. The creative people and the product area, who can't know the needs of the wholesalers, retailers and end consumers, have to be guided by brand and commercial managers. In fact, these are the people who are responsible for analyzing the market in terms of the mix, assortments and range. The commercial area, in turn, has to guide product managers on the basis of the needs and feedback that come from the market. The end customer will never see the whole collection in the firm's showroom like managers do. He or she sees and forms opinions only on what is available in the sales point. If what the sales point shows is the result of a progressive selection made by everyone in the chain (agents, wholesalers, retailers, store directors), the brand is not able to communicate its own potential. Thus its value and identity are compromised. Therefore the distribution and retail strategy is becoming more and more important in these companies. Activities which relates to distribution and retailing are structured along three levels:

- *the distribution strategy*. This is a medium to long term plan of action defining the brand's tactics for entry into new markets in terms of positioning, channels, partners and retail formats;
- within the above, *distribution policies* will define the retail identity and retailing activities market by market in terms of buying, merchandising, field marketing and sales and service techniques;
- at a more operational level, there is a set of activities for executing the above strategies at a *store level* (administration, people management, promotion).

12.4.1 The distribution strategy: selecting channels and formats

The distribution strategy starts with the selection of the channel(s) in which the brand will be sold in each market. With reference to the structure of distribution channels in fashion and luxury, we can distinguish between (*Figure 12.1*):

- *Direct/Retail channels*. The company itself manages the retail network, which is directly operated (Directly Operated Stores) or franchised (the image delivered is the same);

FIGURE 12.1   **CHANNEL STRUCTURE**

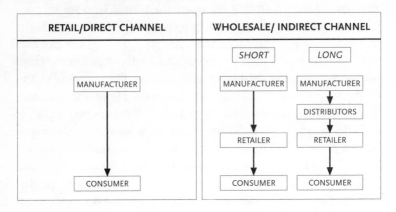

- *Indirect/Wholesale.* The company does not control the retail activity but it interacts with distributors and retailers (department stores, multibrand boutiques, concept stores).

Selecting channels

The trade channel selection is a fundamental phase in defining the firm's distribution strategy. The retail and wholesale channels have different timings and require different strategies in terms of products and service (from deliveries to replenishment to CRM). In the short wholesale channel, the brand directly handles relations with retailers, mainly multibrand boutiques and department stores. In the long wholesale channel, the brand has to work with distributors to agree on issues such as the distribution criteria for the specific market (number and profile of retail doors), the pricing and margin structure of the local offer and payment conditions.

In an industry where time is crucial, the choice of a direct or indirect channel has a particular effect on the quantity and quality of market information that the producer can obtain in a reasonable time. Sell-out information in the indirect channel gets back to the top of the supply chain with a sizeable lag. This information has to be relayed by different subjects (the retailer, the agent or distributors, and the commercial department), and often becomes available only when new collections have already been developed. Conversely, the indirect channel may be the only option available on emerging foreign markets, or when seeking wider market coverage.

The direct channel allows companies to obtain better quality information more rapidly. The sell-out of directly managed stores can be read every day, so that analysis can be done to determine best sellers and slow sellers. On the basis of these data, seasonal re-assortments can be made guaranteeing an assortment that is complete in terms of sizes and models in the sales point. Further, these data can be cross-referenced with information about consumer characteristics, and this sets off a very useful learning process for the development of both the offer and the brand.

Usually luxury and fashion brands decide to be present on the international markets with a mix of channels. This despite the fact that the trend, above all in luxury, is moving more and more in the direction of a larger contribution of retail sales to company turnover.

In the last two decades, a third channel that we might call *transnational* has shown an impressive rate of growth in fashion and luxury. This term actually refers to two major channels that share a common feature – neither are connected to single domestic markets: the Internet and the travel retail.

Despite the enormous potential of the *Internet* as a retail channel, luxury and fashion firms are latecomers to the Web, and with few exceptions, have only recently initiated e-commerce. This is especially true for the high-end (designers and luxury brands), while the situation is different for retailers or premium brands selling basic items with a global market reach, such as sportswear brands. The reasons why Internet sales have been slow to take off, in particular for clothing, relate to the difficulty of accurately characterizing the product online in terms of fit, touch, colors, and details. Compounding this challenge is the personal, often emotional nature of an apparel purchase that is hard to re-create online. By the same token, however, the Internet offers companies the chance to reach new targets (young, emerging countries) and to establish relationships with their customers through customized design and CRM tools like profiling, clustering promotions, loyalty programs and customer satisfaction surveys.

Luxury and fashion brands which have already developed an e-commerce section have mainly focused on limited editions of accessories and gifts developed for the Web only. This serves to limit investments and complexity from a managerial standpoint. Indeed, online sales may lead to some technical problems related to the transfer of warehousing from distribution to the firm (necessitating a huge ad hoc investment in logistics); consequently, these problems affect the width and assortment of the offer, sizes and drops. There is also the possibility of channel conflict with the traditional distributive structures. Finally, most compelling is the high return rate in apparel products purchased online. Taking all these reasons together, we can easily see why for many years most sites purely displayed merchandise or referred consumers to retail stores where the company's products were sold[2].

Nevertheless, companies are learning to think of the Web not as an alternative channel or medium, but as a tool to integrate in the more comprehensive corporate strategy. For example, a website can be used as a way to drive in-store traffic and enhance how the company engages with customers, letting them know about fashion sales, special offers and giving general clothing advice. The better customers feel about the e-commerce website, the more they will buy from the physical stores too. What's more, the Web has given rise to new luxury and fashion players such as online retailers, one example being net-a-porter.com, and on line discounters such as Bluefly.com.

---

2. We would also like to add the difficulty of regulating a territory whose legal confines are not yet very clear (consider the worldwide reach of Internet as compared to physical distribution which is often limited to certain countries) and the anonymity of selling on the Internet, which gives counterfeiters a huge advantage. The online sale of counterfeit luxury and fashion brands is becoming a major problem for brand owners. So, brands are taking a stand. Some are deciding to fight, taking legal action against these sites, while others are beginning to consider the possibility of selling directly, giving their clients a safer choice. Since more and more mainstream consumers are already shopping online, brands and retailers are investing in improved online shopping experiences by using state-of-the-art technologies, such as sophisticated analytics and personalization tools.

Eluxury.com is a leading beauty and fashion retailer of more than 100 of designers and luxury brands. The LVMH-owned site is the only authorized e-tailer for Louis Vuitton products (aside from the brand's own website); they also sell clothing and accessories from hitters like Dior, Fendi, Marc Jacobs, Dolce & Gabbana and Versace.

Yoox.com is an Italian Internet mail order retailer of men's and women's multibrand designer clothing and accessories: from vintage collectibles to capsule collections by cutting-edge designers and unique assortments of books, design and art objects. Founded by Federico Marchetti, a former investment banker, near Bologna in 2000, Yoox.com has become a highly profitable e-commerce company that serves 53 countries worldwide and has over 4 million visitors a month. The company's concept is to buy up overstock or unsold items from previous seasons in a direct relationship from renowned fashion houses (including Dolce & Gabbana, Diesel, Gucci, Armani and Cavalli), manufacturers or retailers and sell these goods online at discounted outlet prices. This enables luxury brands to off-load last year's merchandise without undermining their brands or cannibalizing sales at their existing stores. In addition to its eponymous website, through Yoox Services (established in 2006), the company operates the online stores of Italian fashion houses Emporio Armani, Marni, Diesel, Stone Island and C.P. Company.

Travel retail has to do with sales in airports and airline catalogues. It is a fast-growing market due to the increase of tourist flows, particularly towards Europe. A major force behind this growth is the transformation of airports into destination retailers. Inside airports, retail spaces are designed to have a shopping mall feel, transforming the airport into a veritable living space. The top product categories sold are perfumes and cosmetics, followed by fashion and accessories and gourmet goods.

Sales of luxury items are on the increase as passengers are a "captive audience" and are more likely to treat themselves to expensive brands while waiting for a flight. In order to get passengers into a buying mood, stores more frequently program an events schedule comparable to downtown stores and propose new products with exclusive offers. Retailing inside airports is based on a concession model. The Airport Authority provides space to brands, and in return asks for royalties calculated as a certain percentage on sales depending on product category. The Airport Authority also requires a guaranteed minimum, generally expressed as an amount per passenger. Expirations of concessions are staggered over time; the average duration of contracts is five years for shops and ten years for bars and restaurants.

Selecting formats

After determining the mix of direct and indirect channels, a second level of decision within the distribution strategy is the format(s) the brand will have within each channel. A retail format is one typology of the point of sale characterized by a specific location, dimension, and assortment. In the direct channel the different retail formats are the flagship store, the self-standing store and the shop-in-shop. Among formats within a wholesale distribution we have corners, wall units and the open sale. In the following we will describe the different retail formats within each channel. Formats in the retail channel:

1. *Flagship store.* The leading store within a group, usually the biggest in size and stock holding, used as a benchmark against which other stores are measured. Independent, directly owned and operated, offering the brand global image and lifestyle concept. Location: top global capital cities worldwide, street level only, huge dimensions, from 200 to 5.000 sqm selling surface. Offer: all brand product categories + coffee shops and leisure areas. Sales people are hired and managed by the brand.
2. *Self standing store.* Independent store, directly owned and operated. Location: high street, malls, airports, hotel arcades, with independent entrance. 70-200 sqm. Offer: a large selection of the brand product categories. Sales people are hired and managed by the brand.
3. *Shop-in-shop.* Medium-sized, branded store not street level but still directly operated (department store, malls). Location: inside an independent retail entity, 50-120 sqm selling surface with walls but with no independent entrance. Offer: main brand product categories. Sales people are dedicated.

Formats in the wholesale channel:

1. *Corner.* Retail space personalized with the brand image within an independent retail entity (department store). Location: no independent entrance, no walls. Offer: a selection of the brand product categories. Sales people can be dedicated.
2. *Wall unit.* Retail space within department stores organized as a wall dedicated to the brand and with the brand name on top but no personalization. Frequently used for leather goods (shoes, bags). No dedicated sales people.
3. *Open sale.* Retail space at the lower level of department stores with a multibrand offer focused on one product category (accessories such as wallets, small leather goods, and jewels). No dedicated sales people.

A diffused method of entering multibrand distribution for fashion and luxury firms (mainly department stores and large speciality stores) is through the corner. This is a small area (10 to 30 sqm) that is devoted to a specific brand. It has a personalized layout and a co-ordinated offer mix. The corner makes it easier to show the single brand identity and image to consumer within a multibrand distribution format. The corner assortment and merchandising mix is directly managed by the industrial firm, and the end consumer perceives the world of the brand clearly. The corner also creates the conditions for the better service management to the trade (replenishments, flash collections, handling returns), because sell-out can be monitored on a daily basis, and a good level of assortment and image can be maintained. The corner is based on different contractual formulas which vary according to the degree of control from the industrial brand. The brand may manage the space completely in terms of assortments, sales staff, sell-out surveys and visual merchandising, or it may delegate all these activities to the retailers. The greater the brand's control, the easier it is to transfer the firm's own commercial policies to the sales point. This also increases the chances for consumers to get all the information they require.

One of the most interesting forms is the partnership corner. Here the producer and the retailer have an almost equal share in the investment and costs of managing the space, and they co-operate to give each other the information needed to optimize sell-outs. In addition, the soft corner formula is quite common where the retailer has a strong brand identity and an established clientele. This formula allows for the personalization of the space needed by producers without weakening the retailer identity. As a result, the sales point maintains its own identity even in the presence of strong industrial brands. The corner is almost mandatory for firms that seek to affirm their brand identity, but that are not able to create a network of directly operated stores. This is above all true in those geographical areas where there is a widespread distribution structure and numerous medium to large multibrand retailers.

From the flagship to the open sale there is a decrease in terms of firm's control over the overall image (windows, dedicated spaces, packaging, sales people, personalized shopping bags, etc.) and the distributor's commercial policies (pricing, markdowns, etc.). There is a trend towards harmonizing policies among all channels (the so-called integrated multichannel management). The purpose of this integration is to avoid possible distortions in the perception of the brand, and competition over the same brand among different channels.

12.4.2 The store management

At a store level, managers work towards meeting personal and location sales metrics and customer satisfaction standards by maximizing the customer's experience. They manage all phases of store operations to ensure maximum sales and profitability. Activities are roughly the following:

1. getting customers into the point of sale;
2. converting them into customers buying merchandise once inside the point of sale;
3. doing this in the most efficient manner possible.

In order to lure the customer into the store and increase the traffic, first the firm should resonate with each store's local target audience. Stores located in resort destination differ from those in downtown areas or in airports in terms of needs and shopping habits. The firm should integrate its media program with the right mix of advertising inserts, direct mail marketing, door hangers, out-of-home advertising, and in-store signage to drive traffic to its doors.

Once the customer is into the store, planning activities should help to increase the so-called "conversion rate", that is the number of sales receipts divided by the number of visitors. There are some general guidelines to design the store layout. For instance, the high margin items should be placed in high traffic areas while the in-demand articles should be put in low traffic areas. Complementary items should be near each other, and items needing frequent restocking should be near storerooms or cash registers. In terms of store design and communication, signs and graphics provide information and can add personality, beauty, and romance to a store's image. Also, good lighting should do more than illuminate space – it can highlight merchandise, sculpt space, and capture a mood that enhances a store's image. Contemporary lighting design requires an in-depth knowledge of electrical engineering and the effect of light on color and texture. In terms of merchandise display, there are many options depending on the brand's and product's positioning. In fact, when an item such as a fragrance or a scarf is displayed in a glass case, it implies luxury; an item in a glass case with a lot of space around it implies extra-luxury. But luxury and high fashion stores are also more frequently adopting a "bazaar display", displaying candels, leather goods, scarves, and other small goods the same way bargain stores do to increase the fun in the shopping experience. Once the customer has already purchased one item, it's easier to sell an additional one. Thus apparel retailers strategically place impulse buys like hair bows and costume jewellery by the cashier the same way supermarket checkouts display candy and magazines.

Retail activities should be performed in a productive way. Accordingly, space productivity represents how effectively the retailer utilizes its space and is usually measured by sales per square foot of selling space. This indicator is also most commonly used for planning inventory purchases. It can also roughly calculate return on investment, and is used to determine rent on a retail location. When measuring sales per square foot, selling space does not include the stock room or any area where products are not displayed. A retail store with wall units and other shelf space may want to use sales per linear foot of shelf space to determine a product or product category's allotment of space. A further indication of retail performance is the so-called sell-through analysis. Sell-through is a calculation, commonly represented as a percentage, comparing the amount of inventory a retailer receives from a manufacturer or supplier against what is actually sold to the consumer. A good retail business will try to maximize the sell-through in each season.

12.5 The retail identity

Within the retail and wholesale channels, firms can better express the brand image through a consistent and inspiring retail identity. Developing an unique retail identity is fundamental in order to give to the brand's entire retail network a consistent image. The reason we talk about retail identity and not store identity is related to the need to define an identity not only for retail formats but also for wholesale formats (corners, wall units) and even the websites. The same brand is in different places at the same time and should speak the same language.

We define the retail identity as the integrated system of policies related to the space planning, merchandising, design and visual communication (*Figure 12.2*).

The retail image can be defined as the overall perception the consumer has of the brand's retail identity. The point of sale becomes a strategic marketing tool contributing to the creation of the total brand experience thanks to innovative solutions in terms of visual merchandising and space planning. The result of a strong retail identity is a positive store image – i.e. the positive overall perception the consumer has of the store environment. The retail identity and image should be consistent with the brand's stylistic and communication identity to deliver a strong message to the customer. The continuous search of fashion designers for new ways to communicate brand values has determined a new trend in fashion retailing called *retail architecture*. Retail architecture provides a means for fashion to manage space and trans-

FIGURE 12.2   **THE RETAIL IDENTITY**

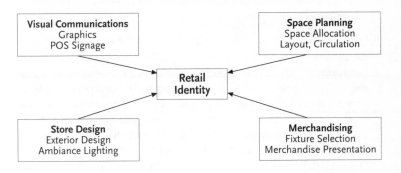

form it in a memorable experience. Brand building practices that existed mainly through advertisements are now extending to the architectural ambience of the store.

> Prada is all about non-conformity, therefore the company has decided to break away from the traditional model of "flagship stores" and create a new retail format: Prada Epicenters. At the end of the 1990s, Prada commissioned the architect Rem Koolhaas to create an innovative but consistent retail experience for Prada customers. The Epicenters are the reflection of the brand's cutting-edge products and are destined to provide a research for new spatial relationships, materials, technology applications and service strategies. At the moment Prada has three epicenter stores, located in New York, Los Angeles and Tokyo. Prada selected the top modern architects to design these stores, making them the subject of serious intellectual inquiry: in addition to Rem Koolhaas, who designed the US Prada stores, Herzog & de Meuron (Basel, Switzerland), who also designed the London's Tate Modern, were the architects of the Tokyo Epicenter.

> The Chanel store in Ginza district in Tokyo was designed by Peter Marino, an American architect who has created flagship stores for the world's most chic luxury brands, from Chanel to Louis Vuitton. The Chanel building projects a very strong and direct image of the brand: striking forms, clear black-and-white contrasts and powerful lettering. The exterior of the building is made out of black glass and steel, symbolizing the iconic quilting. It actually has a huge TV screen projecting the runway and various scenes

depending on the season. The Chanel building also contains a concert hall and a restaurant by the name "Beige Tokyo" – the favorite color of Coco Chanel.

The Japanese "zelkovas" trees inspired Toyo Ito, the world-famous Japanese architect, in his design of the Tokio flagship store for Tod's. Concrete bands which look like tree branches criss-cross the exterior of the building. In fact, the picture of the Tod's building really shows the relationship between the tree and the building. Furthermore, thanks to these concrete bands, the store actually has no columns inside; just sales area with product displays, which helps Tod's to concentrate all attention on the products. The architect managed to make the building very different from other fashion buildings in the district and at the same time he created a distinguishing identity for Tod's flagship store.

Within the framework of retail identity, service identity and design of the service policy have become the new frontier of luxury and high fashion. Service is where the human touch, the luxury/mass market differentiator, has to be given expression, observing and anticipating – not following – the needs and desires of the clientele.

We are convinced that the luxury business involves exactly this: anticipating desires, seeking to exceed standards so that there is no limit – nor will there ever be – on what can be luxury. The human touch also has an ethical dimension: the customer gives us the honor of coming to us, and must be respected, listened to, and thanked. Lastly, the human touch means passion. We can find passion in every line of work, even the most humble, but in luxury it's a requirement because we're working with beauty, with excellence in craftsmanship, with history and with culture. Passion must be authentic, and be transmitted to the customer, along with pride in the brand that we represent, the brand we have the honor of working for. In historical luxury brands, the search for excellence, ethics and passion are ever-present. They constitute the value dimension that shapes the service policy. These values must then be filtered by the brand identity, its specific language, and its classic or fashion character, for the expert customer or for a wider market. Simply having a service policy would be a point of arrival for some luxury brands.

What is important to realize is that in luxury different levels of service already exist which differentiate an authentic luxury proposal, that is, unique and memorable, from everything else that's sold as luxury. From this perspective, since hotels are built on service, they perhaps represent the sector in which this search for differentiation and excellence has reached its epitome. The new orientation is based on the conception of a hotel that welcomes guests and makes them feel at home. Also, image is redefined through design. The big international chains traditionally considered luxury (the Hilton, the Four Seasons, Sheraton, etc.) offer standard experiences and service in all their locations. Instead, for the new concept of hospitality, it is the etymological value of the word that counts (from the Latin word meaning "friendliness to a guest"). This concept is based on service proposals created for individual locations. In fact, such proposals often incorporate the *genius loci*, or spirit of the place, to welcome guests in the local service culture. In hospitality, the Asians are experts. For example, the celebrated Oriental in Bangkok sends all its personnel to a Buddhist monastery for a week to absorb, not to study, what the spirit of service should be: a particular grace, never saying no, taking care of others. Likewise, the five-star experience in Indian or Indonesian resorts begins with the local tradition of hospitality and etiquette, making the guests' experience unique, blending it with that of the journey. If the value dimension and the human touch are essential in building a service identity, *service design* proves just as critical. This term refers to the careful design of all the phases and moments of customer interaction in the sales point and with the firm.

There are several examples of firms in the sector that are working on planning a brand experience through service. Some begin with very structured training on products and sales techniques, such as Louis Vuitton, Zegna, and Hugo Boss. In fact, these companies organize lessons for their personnel in a corporate retail academy to explain the technical specificities and wearability of their products. Books are also compiled with guidelines for sales staff on how to carry out their duties. Other brands set down very precise rules regarding how to "manage" the consumer in the sales point. For example, the corporate policy of the cosmetic brand

Khiel's includes the principle that consumers must be served by their own sales person for at least 20 minutes, and they must be made to feel welcome. This motto can be seen in the polished visuals, in the appearance of personnel, who communicate human touch and courtesy, in the simple little table laid with coffee or tea evoking a sense of hospitality, and in the sofas that make customers feel at home. Another example is Cartier. In addition to having built a true service identity in Cartier boutiques the world over, the company has come up with a control system to verify how consistently and precisely directives are implemented. Monitoring is done by a number of mystery shoppers who make visits several times a month, and a questionnaire filled in by internal personnel giving a qualitative evaluation of store performance.

12.6 The Customer Relationship Management

Service is always increasingly representing a source of differentiation and competitive advantage. It has therefore become fundamental for companies to develop an integrated process of client orientation (*Figure 12.3*).

Customer Relationship Management (CRM) suggests those marketing instruments veered at managing the relationship of ones own customers in an increasingly personalized logic. Such tools have traditionally been applied in the consumer goods market. In fashion and luxury the number of limited customers, the difficulty of information gathering and the centrality of the designer have often tried to justify the skepticism that has for a long time dominated the face of CRM.

However, always a greater number of companies in the industry have begun to implement CRM strategies with the aim of consolidating profitability and the loyalty of their customers. By profiling their clients it is possible to develop targeted actions to improve the frequency of visits at the points of sale, cross and up-selling, and brand loyalty. Evolved companies also use the gathered information to take strategic decisions; for example observing the geographic origins of tourists or of business men that buy in other cities may possibly help evaluate new potential points of sale.

FIGURE 12.3   **THE INTEGRATED PROCESS OF CLIENT ORIENTATION**

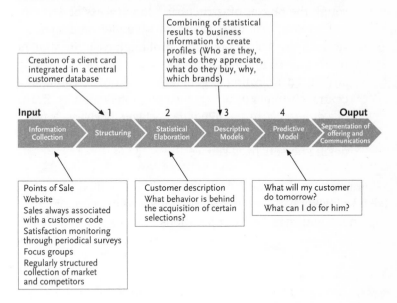

The challenges to face are considerable, starting from the profound cultural change which involves the adoption of these tools. The primary point of contact between a company and the customer is the sales personnel, where in fashion and luxury there is a higher turnover and where often the value of collecting information is misunderstood. Moreover many stores are located in geographic areas where service culture and client orientation are limited. Criticism also lies in the integration between profiling customers at the points of sale and on the website, a topic which puts off most general requirements in coordination of marketing actions on traditional and online media.

The fulfillment of a CRM system that truly places the customer at the center of business strategies is based on two pillars:

i. an inner customer oriented culture, or better the alignment of the entire organization in respect to a business culture which promotes knowledge and customer service through various organizational approaches (product, business, service units);

2. the integrated management of customer information through the phases of: structuring the process of data collection from customers (client cards); understanding of customers that hold more value (profiling); customization of marketing/communications operations and of the offering structured according to generated profiling; creation of a central customer database; customer interaction by means of a differentiated and integrated network of channels (website, brick and mortar) offering one single image and proposing personalized services.

Companies in the industry which have implemented CRM with determination have begun to succeed in customer portfolio management, with significant implications on market performance.

13.1 The image identity

If the product incorporates the tangible dimension of fashion goods, it is communication that provides sustenance for symbolic contents. In fact, how a product is represented is what transforms it into a brand in the mind of consumers, what superimposes a lifestyle, a world of values on product attributes.

In fashion and luxury, communication almost always focuses the so-called "dream factor," alluding to an exclusive world, a happy few celebrities. At the same time, though, communication must also share the dream, making the brand an object of desire in the eyes of the general public. This is done by leveraging the aspirational factor in luxury, and building a powerful, desirable imaginary[1] in the mass market.

Visibility, consequently, becomes an essential ingredient in the success of the major brands. Visibility is achieved through campaigns by the best photographers with the most sought-af-

---

1. In sociology an imaginary is the set of values, institutions, laws and symbols common to a particular group, and the corresponding society.

ter top models, by systematically buying ad space in the first pages of glossy magazines, by occupying high-impact outdoor spaces and choosing the biggest locations in the most prestigious shopping streets. Visibility is the result of both the vast investments in communication (on average from 5% to 12% of turnover) and the power of the codes a brand employs. The language of fashion, based on the aesthetic of images without text, with the product as protagonist, represents a means of communication that is: *high impact*, because it builds dreams by using models and celebrities; *consistent*, because centralized decision-making by the designer/art director promotes congruity between image and style; and *universal*, because the form of expression is the image, which can be understood with no need for translation.

Fashion has always used visual tools for communicating – photographs, shows, showrooms, models, displays, videos and sample collections. This is because symbolic elements are more important in the purchase of a fashion item than functional attributes. These symbolic features are more easily delivered through communication based on images and aesthetic representations: the more refined the communication, and therefore the more "useless", the more this kind of visual support is needed.

Fashion is, in and of itself, a form of communication. By producing messages, it communicates on its own, and does not easily tolerate the imposition of another language, such as the one used by advertising agencies[2]. However, the predominance of

---

2. Fashion designers do not make a great use of advertising agencies. On one hand it is argued that the presence of designers would be too overbearing as they want to steer the creativity. On the other, that the agencies do not have Art and Copy Departments accustomed to the fashion language. In reality, fashion firms and communication and advertising firms are both playing on the same turf – creativity. This would make meetings between designers and art directors turn into personality clashes that would be too hard to overcome for the sake of finding a common approach. The separation of the two worlds has resulted in a difference of language. Fashion has traditionally regarded itself as "above" the agencies, and has denied itself the communication potential that the agencies could offer. The agencies, for their part, have not developed the necessary sensitivity to operate in an industry with different rules to those of consumer goods. There is also the problem of size. Modern advertising agencies are more like factories than creative workshops. Their excessive rigidity and bureaucracy puts off designers, who are looking for a personalized relationship.

image (as opposed to text) and focus on the product often translate into the so-called "logo picture" – i.e. essentially similar images of different brands, which is also due to crowding on the same media channels.

To communicate in a different way, fashion companies have to match the world of communication with the world of the brand, representing a lifestyle which must be consistent in every single element (from the shoot to the pack, from the fashion show to the store window). One of the best examples ever of integrated and highly differentiated communication in the luxury industry is Hermès.

Hermès has a history. It came into existence in a Parisian workshop in 1843, and therefore is now in its sixth generation. One of its business assets is thus the time factor. Time is written into its mission: to make a product of outstanding quality with no concessions to marketing. (Making a good product takes time). Hermès tries to innovate without ever turning away from the values of tradition, values which are also the subjects of its communication. For example, the mercantile spirit that has always characterized the history of Hermès has led to the development of an ethnic theme related to travel in its communication (under the headline "Hermès, the only elegant luggage"). Hermès uses institutional communication that is intended to arouse emotion. Its objective is to communicate the world rather than the product. (The house magazine is called "Le Monde d'Hermès"). The world of Hermès is for a select few; it is almost aristocratic. The obvious use of the logo as a communication tool is avoided; in fact, the logo is used only as a signature (like an artist's initials on a painting). The result is that the products do not have a label on the outside and the visuals of the brand campaign leave out the trademark. Communication codes are the color orange (a random choice due to the wartime shortage of the traditional brown wrapping paper), the "bolduc" (the ribbon that is wrapped around packages), the gift box and the theme that the Group offers each year. The whole communication system and some of the production system revolve around the year's theme, always inspired by the concepts of travel, dreams, nature: the Tree, the Hand, Fantasy, the Mediterranean, L'air de Paris, Orange Hermès and Rose Indien, etc.

Just as Hermès was the messenger of the gods whose duty was to liaise with the world of human beings, Hermès is a "messenger of dreams" in the luxury world.

FIGURE 13.1   COMMUNICATING FASHION/LUXURY VERSUS CONSUMER GOODS

	HIGH-END BRANDS	MASS BRANDS
OBJECTIVE	Brand Image	Brand Awareness
MAJOR TARGET	Trade and Opinion Leaders	Final Consumers
PLANNING	Seasonal	Yearly
FOCUS	Product Intangibles Visual	Story Attributes + Benefits Copy
TOOLS	PR (editorials and word of mouth)	Promotions (trade discounts)
ADV MEDIA	Printed magazines	Traditional Media + Interactive Media
EVENTS	Catwalk	Sponsorships
CELEBRITIES	Endorsement	Testimonials and Product Placement
STORE	Prestigious location The Flagship /the temple of the brand)	High traffic location Open Door and Accessibility
BUDGETS	High as a Relative Percentage on Sales	High as Share of Voice
INTERNAL PLAYERS	Designer; Art Director; Press Office	Marketing or Brand Manager
EXTERNAL PLAYERS	Free-lancers (e.g. photographers, stylists)	Advertising Agencies, Media and Research Centers
MEASUREMENTS	Press Return	GRP and Sales

Strict internal supervision of the communication process, the predominance of image over words, the importance of Public Relations as a mouthpiece for speaking to a competent audience (the press, buyers, and opinion leaders): these are the key differentials for communication in the high-end brands of luxury and fashion with respect to mass markets goods *(Figure 13.1)*.

Mass market fashion brands tend to mimic the language of high fashion in an attempt to create an aspirational effect (see the use of top models by H&M or Victoria's Secret). But then they give priority to an array of high diffusion media (billboards, TV, Internet, unconventional tools) to reach a younger, wider audience.

For mass market goods, communication belongs in the more general sphere of marketing; for prestigious items, instead, communication is a lever of creativity. As such it comes under the direct control of the CEO/art director. Both with reference to mass market brands and luxury, communication must be considered an integrated process with clear cut objectives.

13.2 Communicating the product, the brand, the corporate identity

Integrated communication refers to a strategic design that provides for the synergetic and scientific use of all the means available to achieve a particular objective. Integrated communication is above all necessary for a brand that has to communicate the intangible values of a lifestyle. If all the messages coming out of the firm (external communication) and all those circulating within it (internal communication) are consistent, the perception will be reinforced. If the messages are dissonant, however, one kind takes something away from the other. For this reason, all the communication specialists (public relations, press offices, image and communication agencies) have to share the same vision: that of the firm. Vision includes internal communication as much as external communication. In fact, fashion companies have three different objectives in their communication:

1. *Brand awareness.* The brand should be known and well-recognized among competitors.
2. *Brand image.* Image is more than simple awareness: it is about building relevance. It's not enough to be known; consumers have to associate the brand to specific values. Fashion companies do not speak to everyone. In fact, their target is limited to those customers who can actually partake in the lifestyle they propose, or to the wider but nonetheless select pool of aspirational consumers.
3. *Reputation.* Reputation is a very important asset and an increasingly critical aspect of a company's communication. Reputation has to do with the attempt to align key audiences (shareholders, banks, local authorities, employees) with the strategy of the company. How is a given company perceived? It's reputation will determine whether or not banks, private equity funds and shareholders are willing to invest their money and whether or not talented people are willing to invest their lives. Nowadays internal communication, investor relations, issue management (prevention and crisis) and social responsibility programs are as important as advertising and event creation, if not more so.

FIGURE 13.2   **LEVELS AND TOOLS IN FASHION COMMUNICATION**

- **Product:**
  - Objective: support sell-in (wholesale) and sell-out (retail)
  - Tools: advertising, editorials, fashion shows & events, catalogues, windows and pop material, website

- **Brand:**
  - Objective: build awareness and/or image
  - Tools: logo, heritage, designer/entrepreneur spokesperson, celebrity marketing, flagship, website

- **Corporate:**
  - Objective: reputation
  - Tools: internal communication, investor relations, foundations and sponsorship, charity, exhibitions, website

---

Figure 13.2 sums up the most common tools used to achieve the different communication objectives.

Therefore, messages and tools should be designed and planned with an eye to specific objectives, with increasing complexity for people who handle communication and coordination of different activities, different media, and different countries. What becomes critical is tight internal control and investments, not only in economic resources but in human resources as well.

13.3 The integrated communication plan

The starting point of any communication strategy is the communication plan, which defines target audiences, key messages, media planning, budget, calendar, and responsibilities in accordance with the more general corporate strategy for the year. *Figure 13.3* sums up the planning process from the definition of strategic objectives down to the implementation of a communication plan.

An integrated communication plan must set a target budget and assign resources to each component of the plan. Depending on the size of the budget, trade-offs will probably have to be made between methods to achieve defined goals. In addition, the company needs to align internal and external resources to

FIGURE 13.3   **COMMUNICATION PLANNING**

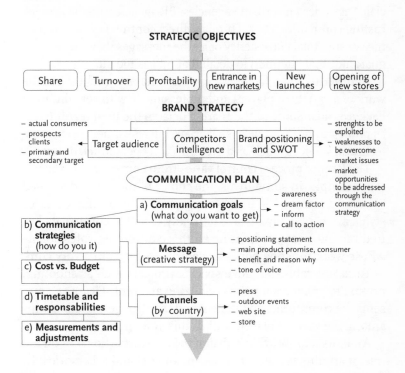

carry out the plan. After identifying the appropriate mix of communication vehicles, the Communication Department has to determine the costs of the plan, compare them to the budget, and adjust accordingly. The final step is to create a tactical implementation calendar that outlines when each vehicle is released and who is responsible for getting it done.

13.4 The communication system

One peculiarity of fashion companies is their direct control over a number of activities, from developing the concept of the ad campaign to post-production, from planning media to the press office and organizing events. This is not the case with mass market companies, where such activities are usually delegated to external specialist agencies (advertising agencies, PR agencies, media centers, casting companies, etc.). Through direct control, fashion companies ensure total consistency of all the messages they convey, and guarantee that attention to detail that makes the difference.

In order to do so fashion companies have to orchestrate the work of a variety of players and professionals with very different backgrounds. Some of them are crucial to the final result (such as photographers, models, stylists, architects); others offer more technical services (such as drivers, security personnel, dressers).

The level of process control varies from company to company. (For example, in some firms, the choice of models is delegated to casting companies; in other companies the designer and/or stylist are personally involved). In any case, the complexity lies in directing and coordinating all those different professionals whose work must be perfectly coordinated within a very compressed timetable to realize specific projects such as shooting, putting together a show, or organizing an event. *Figure 13.4* presents the communication system and the strongest relationships among the various players within this system.

An indispensable role is that of the designer who takes on the role of art director, as is the case in apparel and accessories. In fact, in addition to control over style, the art director is also in charge of every aspect of image, from the ad campaign's message to store design.

Centralizing image-related decisions by assigning them to the designer ensures the tightest possible control over consistency between product and image. By the same token, for fashion companies designers are the key spokespeople. The applause on the catwalk at the end of the show exalts their personality, transforming them into a lifestyle, in other words, into the tangible representation of the essence of the aspirational values of the brand. Identity is the key word, and having a brand with a name that corresponds to a person is important because creating a myth surrounding a person is much simpler than doing the same for a company.

Even when the decision is made to call in external professionals, the firm should control the consistency and synergy of

FIGURE 13.4   **THE FASHION COMMUNICATION SYSTEM**

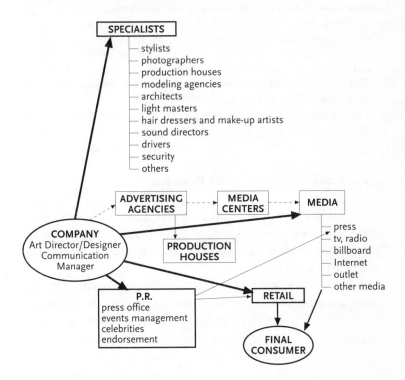

all the messages it transmits by means of a single vision that directs the internal and external actors involved in the communication process. To this end, the integration role played by the stylist appears especially vital.

A stylist is an expert who uses art and science to make people and objects look good in order to make a statement. There are different kinds of stylists: fashion stylists, editorial stylists (also called fashion editors), wardrobe stylists, catalogue stylists, set stylists, food stylists, etc.

The fashion stylist defines the right style to interpret the mood of an editorial, a photo shoot, or a runway. The type and extent of activities carried out by these professionals vary depending on the brand they are working with and the relationship with the designer/art director. When producing a photo shoot, the stylist (who is also called a fashion editor if this person works on the editorial staff of a magazine) might participate in the following phases (with a varying degree of decision-making autonomy): location research, stage design, choosing and arranging clothes and accessories (outfit), casting, coordinating the photographer, hair dresser and make-up artists, lighting and music mood, post-production.

Fashion editors are responsible for the magazine section on new trends; they identify stories and select outfits from the various collections for the editorials on these pages[3]. Fashion editors are not involved in preparing text. Journalists usually handle mainly gossip and lifestyles. This has undoubtedly influenced designers, who have in turn transformed collection presentations into shows in order to be talked about.

Lastly, often stylists do "look advising" for celebrities, and if they work for a brand name, they help search for and select celebrities to work with.

13.5 The evolving role of Public Relations

As shown in *Figure 13.2*, advertising serves to create visibility by promoting sales. However, qualification, hence the chance to attain a price premium, depends first and foremost on Public Relations (PR) activities.

PR refers to the series of activities undertaken to create strong relationships with stake holders (clients, media, local community, employees, investors, opinion leaders) to make the company known and build its reputation, diffusing a positive image and influencing the public opinion.

Managing PR means tracking all the public actions of a brand, the shows, the presentation of the sample collection, the launch of a new line, the opening of a new boutique, special events (usually society gatherings, or those related to fund-raising or the arts, sports and music sponsorship), celebrity dressing (providing garments to people in the world of show business, art, and culture, either on loan or as gifts), managing relationships with key clients. The objective is to promote the brand image to final consumers, even if the initiatives themselves generally target those who work in the industry and opinion leaders. Opinion

---

3. The fashion pages in magazines are above all concerned with trends and image; they do not offer information about the quality, composition, comfort or other functional values of the items. The competence of fashion stylists and journalists is thus often restricted to the aesthetics. The format of the magazines would not encourage a technical approach since the pages devoted to fashion match the editorials, which are promotion rather than information.

leaders talk about the events, and they get talked about, and this should bring the event to public notice.

As the press is the key target for fashion companies, major PR activities involve the Corporate and Product Press Office (indeed most of the work is related to getting products photographed and published).

The work of the Press Office includes:

- managing images and video archives;
- issuing and distributing news releases and other prepared publicity to the news media and public for the benefit of its members or clients[4];
- building and keeping contacts with international, national, local and industry press (the mailing database is the most precious treasure for a communication office and has to be constantly updated);
- monitoring and measuring media coverage results (quantity and quality) and generating corrective actions for the future.

The Press Office therefore has to know "who does what" in the press and has to be able to talk the same language. More important still, clearly, is the Press Office's ability to send a message that is consistent with the philosophy of the firm. This means that this office has to absorb the firm's culture and the concept of the brand. Consistency with brand identity should not only pertain to the message, but also the medium and the context.

The Press Office uses press reviews to measure the result of its own work, both quantitatively (in terms of the number of times the message has been sent out) and qualitatively (i.e. the positive and negative mentions in the media). These evaluations are necessary for future actions and for personalizing them to suit specific interlocutors. *Figure 13.5* shows the main measurements for evaluation.

---

4. Materials may include press kits and press releases, catalogues, look books, newsletters, files for the Web.

FIGURE 13.5 **AN EVALUATION MODEL**

MEASURING OUTPUT	• Media Coverage (media impression, readership)
	   – Number/quality of articles
	   – Number of media/consumers attendance
	   – AVE (Advertising Value Equivalency)

MEASURING IMPACT	• Consumer research: awareness, recall/retention, understanding, favor, education, endorsement
MEASURING RESULTS	• Short term: phone calls/emails, website contacts, word of mouth, tests • Long term: consumer loyalty, reputation, brand equity, leadership, increase in turnover

In order to be validated inside the company, communication offices have to deliver concrete results. These offices should extend their influence to the Internet, to brochures, and to the house organ. (From the point of view of integrated communication it is important to take charge of internal communication as well). What should always be kept in mind is that the final aim is not to reach the media but consumers. One of the strongest PR tool in fashion and luxury is VIP management.

Dream building and VIP management

Today's society is no longer dominated by a social élite as it once was in the days of the aristocracy. Yet a "powerless élite" still exists – the world of show business, culture, and sports – which can set trends, being very ostentatious and highly visible. Mass media plays a key role in this phenomenon by spotlighting more or less famous personages, their lifestyles, and their circles. As a result, the public, potential consumer of fashion products, is attracted by this world, aspires to this lifestyle, and tends to identify with the stars who represent it. Based on this mechanism, which reinterprets the famous trickle-down theory in a modern key, several fashion companies have perfected hugely successful marketing strategies.

Such strategies include: utilizing testimonials for advertising campaigns, dressing celebrities for high-society events for free, using famous people to excite interest in a brand for happenings such as grand openings of new stores, organizing benefits, product placement in films and music videos. These activities guarantee the company a high number of articles, photographs, and mentions in the press, integrating the traditional advertising investment and qualifying the brand as "glamorous" in the eyes of the end consumer.

As a result, the red carpet has been rolled out even further and the night of the Oscars has morphed into the greatest fashion competition in the world. People are almost more interested in discovering who's wearing what, designed by whom, than finding out who will take home an Academy Award. The famous looks – such as the Gwyneth Paltrow's romantic pink Ralph Lauren, Julia Robert's vintage Valentino, Elie Saab's launch by Halle Berry and the Gap t-shirt worn by Sharon Stone – are seen around the world and can enhance the "news effect", in other words the chance for a brand to be talked about for years to come. Dream gowns are still for the privileged few, but the brands in the spotlight cash in with sales in bags, shoes, fragrances, lipsticks, and eyewear.

Associating a brand with a famous face can be done through strategic use of testimonials in advertising, as well as with celebrity dressing for formal or informal occasions more or less orchestrated by the company. When there is an actual contractual relationship, the celebrity providing the testimonial must embody the values of the brand in a credible way.

> This is the case of Versace, a designer name associated in the minds of consumers with the ability to make the most beautiful women in the world sexy. Madonna, Demi Moore, Halle Berry (providing the brand's testimonials in the last few years) all have strong personas; they are splendid women who belong to the world of Medusa, apart from advertising. News of the institutional campaign is fostered by interviews with Donatella Versace talking about her friendships within the Hollywood star system. Public Relations amplifies the effect of advertising; a partnership becomes an official recognition of the brand's reputation.

More recently, however, something is giving way. Prompted by the power of this association, numerous brands, that would not have been able to aspire to spontaneous recognition otherwise, have come onto the scene with aggressive merchandising strategies. The open relationships of the past, the small benefits have been supplanted by million-dollar attendance fees and engagements.

For endorsements to work, instead, a symbiotic choice has to be made. Celebrities have to identify with the image of the brand they're wearing and love it, irrespective of economic advantages. But brands also have to identify with the celebrities who represent them. In fact, companies must learn to choose their brand ambassadors while keeping in mind that in fashion, commercial success and an exclusive image are intrinsically related.

13.6 A new communication scenario

Fashion is contending with the need to evolve its language while preventing this means of expression from becoming trivial. The so-called "photo logo" is no longer enough; investing in advertising is increasingly expensive and not always useful. (Advertising is a sign of the power of a brand which reinforces awareness, but that does not qualify the brand in any way; this qualification, instead, is built via word of mouth). The press, which has played such a crucial role in the rise of fashion, is struggling to find a new language that goes beyond the trade-off between advertising and editorials.

> Fashion shows are certainly the major press coverage garnering event in fashion. The ten minutes that a typical show lasts is when the designer gets the chance to have his entire public (press, buyers and opinion leaders) fully focused on his vision of the future evolution of fashion. The event is more and more a mere communication tool needed to make a statement in terms of creativity and to renew the reason to buy carry over products. (In actual fact, buyers make most of their choices in advance during the sale of pre-collections, and clothes on the catwalk are often different from what will later be sold in the showrooms).
>
> In a competitive arena that is growing more crowded, with hundreds of brands on the catwalks and dozens of cities fighting to take over fashion week leadership, shows are the finish line for designers, the pathway to becoming brand ambassadors. But for brands without substantial advertising budgets, the return on investment in terms of media visibility is not always guaranteed.

New scenarios are emerging on the horizon: the point of sale is no longer a channel but a product in and of itself; event management has sharper focus on emotional and personalized involvement of the end consumer. (This explains the need for strong integration between communication actions and CRM analysis).

The impact of the Web has only just begun. We are in the midst of a major shift in the media landscape from traditional fashion publishing to user-generated content. By 2011, Internet advertising is expected to become the largest ad segment. At the same time, the power of traditional media is waning. On one hand the intense influence of advertising on editorial choices undermines credibility, and on the other consumer interest is becoming more focused on new media (so-called social media) generated by consumers themselves (user-generated content[5]): blogging, podcasting, online video, social networking, wikis[6].

Fashion websites and communities, e-zines, fashion magazine publishers, fashion portals, and social networks are profoundly changing the language of communication, which now has to be more and more interactive, made-to-measure, informative and inclusive. Furthermore, in order to reinforce the overall brand identity, traditional and digital media have to be combined; instead, the

---

5. Citing Wikipedia: User-generated content (UGC) refers to various kinds of media content that are produced or somehow shaped by end users, in contrast to traditional content produced primarily by television and print media. The term entered mainstream usage during 2005, having arisen in Web publishing and new media content production circles. UGC reflects the expansion of media production through new technologies that are accessible to the general public. Prominent websites based on UGC include: Flickr, YouTube, MySpace, Friends Reunited, Facebook, and Wikipedia.

6. A blog is a site where a user posts comments or news regarding a given topic. News is normally organized in chronological order beginning with the most recent information. Podcasting is a neologism that comes from the combination of two words: pod (a popular MP3) and broadcasting. Podcasting is a system that lets users automatically download documents (usually audio or video), called podcasts, using a podcatching client or feed aggregator, which is normally free. A social network is made up of nodes which generally correspond to individual organizations linked by a specific relationship based on shared values, visions, ideas, financial exchanges, commercial or personal relations, etc. A wiki is a collaborative site in which contents can be edited directly by anyone who has access. Ward Cunningham, creator of the first site Wiki Wiki, describes it as "the simplest online database that really works". Wikipedia is one of the most famous wikis.

two are still separate divisions in most of companies (and agencies).

A particularly interesting aspect of all this for fashion and luxury brands is that consumers can exchange information and form alliances within social networks, and this can impact a brand's reputation. A visit to any blog will show how young people discuss their recent purchases, propose their personal hot lists, or tell how they've been treated badly in a luxury shop (and encourage others to boycott it). Consumers have more choice at a product level and less time to choose. Word of mouth carries ever greater influence than any other form of advertising because it's fast, personalized, and seemingly reliable. (In actual fact, however, some forums are indirectly run by brands or by service providers).

For companies, this creates the need for an Internet presence, not only through so-called showcase websites, but by taking the lead in the creation and exchange of information by offering space, content, and services to the community that identifies with the brand. (An excellent example of this is Diesel). Just like in the real world, what happens on the outside has to be monitored constantly.

Many fashion and luxury companies have recently broken the online sales taboo. One reason is because they are aware of the new buying habits of their younger consumers. In addition, these companies recognize that products with their brand, be they original or counterfeit, the season's best sellers or leftovers from years past, are available on hundreds of sites in contexts that would never be tolerated in the "real" world.

To measure oneself up against the language of new media, to capture the opportunities and contain the threats of the Internet: these are priorities of all companies. For those positioned in the high-end of the market, however, the risk is that the impact may be much more intense. In fact, a sophisticated means of communication must be found, one that is selective from a cultural standpoint, in a medium that is accessible by definition and therefore non exclusive.

In a similar context, communication can't be thought of as something seasonal. Communication instead must become a long-term guiding principle of brand identity, the tool used for building intangible values in the minds of consumers, more and more articulated in terms of messages and media.

14.1 Why extending the brand?

A major part of a brand's value originates from its contribution to the launch of new products and services. Introducing a new product under an established brand name has become a popular strategy during the past few decades in many industries. The reasons for brand extension are obvious. Having saturated a market with one product, a brand has two choices for growth: expand into a new market or launch a new product. After the entry of many companies in the stock market, brand extension was needed in order continue to demonstrate quarterly growth for those executives who managed established brands in saturated categories with flat sales. The huge costs of advertising are an additional reason to opt for one brand only in many categories. Last but not least, the "go retail" strategy of the last few decades has pushed in the direction of brand extension: in order to fill the directly operated boutiques and flagships with merchandise, companies had to create assortment in terms of categories within the same brands.

Given the increased popularity of the strategy, academics have produced a wealth of literature on the topic over the years. Brand extension, according to some experts, can be defined as a marketing strategy in which a firm that markets a product with a well-developed image uses the same brand name but in a different product category. This tactic is utilized to increase and leverage brand equity. As stated by Aaker (1996), brand equity is a set of assets (and liabilities) linked to a brand's name and symbol that adds to (or subtracts from) the value provided by a product or service to a firm and/or that firm's customers. This popular definition hypothesizes two perspectives on brand equity: the first sees it as a value for the firm, and the second as a value for the end customers. Much attention has been paid particularly to the effectiveness of the strategy and on how consumers perceive brand extensions. Consumer evaluations of brand extensions seem to depend on the perceived quality of the parent brand, the fit between the brand and the extension category, the characteristics of the product category in which the brand is extended and lastly the sequence of extensions.

Despite all that has been written, there is one major flaw in the literature: it focuses mainly on fast-moving and low-involvement consumer goods and neglects other sectors such as the fashion and luxury industries (Dall'Olmo, 2004). As illustrated in the previous chapters, in fashion and luxury the "functional" *vs.* the "experiential" and "symbolic" attributes of a brand don't simply affect its positioning. In fact, these features also shape the process of consumer evaluation of brand extensions and the managerial decision process leading to the extension strategy. A second peculiarity of luxury brands is the "rarity principle": the prestige of the brand erodes if too many people own it. This creates a trade-off for luxury brand management: the company needs to grow and increase its margins but at the same time it can never sell too much. All this means understanding very well the specific constraints each brand has while implementing an extension strategy. The peculiar characteristics of luxury brands are also considered important enough to make a difference in the relative managerial decision process and extension strategy.

So what are the key success factors in undertaking and managing brand extensions in the fashion and luxury industry that will achieve the initial mission: profitable growth and full expression of the brand's identity? Is success in one category a guarantee for success in another?

14.2 Brand extensions in fashion and luxury

Founded in 1906, the traditional Hamburg company Montblanc is a provider of luxury goods such as writing instruments, watches, jewellery and leather goods. The international brand sells its products in authorized boutiques and Montblanc flagship stores in over 70 countries. The brand became famous as a leader in the niche of luxury writing instruments, made unique thanks to the logo (a white on black star with rounded points), the quality of craftsmanship and the beauty of design. In particular, the core product in the writing instruments segment is the Meisterstück line and the FP 149 fountain pen launched in 1924. Over time, the brand also became associated with symbolic attributes such as prestige, power, success and masculinity. In 1995, the brand started extending into other categories such as watches, leather goods and eyewear and even a male fragrance launched in 2001. Also items for women were recently introduced with the aim of becoming a luxury lifestyle brand.

A fundamental premise to understanding extension strategies in these industries is to distinguish between line and brand extension. By line extension, we mean launching a new line of products with the same brand and in the same product category but changing target (from menswear to womenswear o kidswear), channels (from upscale department stores to specialty stores) or price range (from ready-to-wear to bridge). Examples of line extensions are Emporio Armani for Giorgio Armani, Marc by Marc Jacobs, Boss Donna for Hugo Boss or the Lauren line for Ralph Lauren. We will not consider this brand strategy; in this chapter we will only concentrate on brand extension, that is leveraging on an existing brand to enter a totally new product category (from apparel to footwear or eyewear).

Within the sphere of brand extension, a further distinction must be made between a) strategic brand extension and b) complementary brand extension. The first includes brands that take a side-step into a new market as a means of truly diversifying their portfolio and as the start of a long-term program of strategic change in the direction of becoming a lifestyle brand. In such cases, brands are seeking to become real players within the new business. Examples may be Montblanc in watches, or Armani and Chanel in eyewear or fragrances. With complementary brand extensions, a brand looks to capitalize on a new market segment, typically as part of a wider desire to create a "lifestyle choice" amongst its target audience. These ventures are not core to the brand's long-term strategy. Instead they offer the chance to bolster existing brand values and emotional associations and they create a stronger affiliation with customers. This is the case of most of Louis Vuitton extensions, which are distributed exclusively in Vuitton stores to enrich the brand's contemporary appeal. Another example is Bulgari, which teamed up with Ritz Carlton to create two luxury hotels in Milan and Bali with the objective of creating potential synergies, such as cutlery and photo frames, but mainly nourishing the core brand image.

Both strategies are present in fashion and luxury with mixed results. In the case of strategic brand extensions, companies invest heavily and the risks are usually much higher than in complementary brand extensions. In fact, potential risks include diluting parent brand equity, damaging parent brand loyalty, alienating core consumers and causing fragmentation of the overall marketing effort. Many wonder about how much equity is truly being added to the original brand each time management decides to enter a new lifestyle category. What's more, how many lifestyle companies does the world really need? In this sense, a close look at the global brand scoreboard published every year by *BusinessWeek* suggests that most of all the 100 top brands are very focused on a particular product category and have become the leading experts of their category in terms of credibility and innovation. That leads us to the key question: What is the unique feature that the brand is bringing to the new category that will inspire a repeat purchase? What is Armani bringing back – to the Armani brand first and then to cosmetics – that will tempt people away from the specialist luxury brand Crème de la Mer?

14.3 Successful extension strategies

Of course there is no formula for guaranteeing success, but those businesses that get it right are the ones that followed some common paths in extension:

1. embracing a consumer perspective;
2. innovating the extended category;
3. continuing to nurture the core business;
4. defining the right business model.

Think from the consumers' perspective and avoid confusing them: this is where to start when extending a brand. The first means keeping customers' needs in mind in terms of relevance (Are the brand heritage, vision and the core brand qualities relevant or important to the brand extension category?) and credibility (Does the core brand have qualities that are credible and acceptable to sell the brand extension?). Literature about brand extensions proposes two rules for successful extensions from a consumer perspective:

1. *The more intangible the brand associations, the more distant the product categories open to brand extension.* Brands that are already perceived as "lifestyle" and associated with specific values are more likely to succeed in introducing new and distant categories with respect to brands associated with technical attributes of product features. The Armani brand, for example, is associated with the values of refined elegance, universality and artistic mastery. These values have been successfully leveraged to extend the brand into categories far removed from the original apparel business such as cosmetics and eyewear.
2. *The closer the associations at a product level, the more distant the product categories open to brand extension.* A brand may not have intangible associations but still be able to succeed when there is a strong link between the brand's core product and the extended product. A classic example here is Caterpillar moving into a successful line of tough and masculine

workwear and accessories, leveraging on product-level associations between earth-moving machines and workwear. We would add another very important factor: the core category from which the brand starts its extension process. For instance, there are closer associations between clothing and fragrances than shoes and fragrances; consequently it may be more difficult for a brand starting from shoes to extend into distant categories such as fragrances and cosmetics.

A second aspect of successful extensions is the capability of bringing a new and unique vision and innovate the category with respect to what already exists. Undertaking a "me-too" strategy is simply not enough to make a brand extension investment profitable. Although the most important asset of a fashion or luxury brand is the intangible equity, it is surely not sufficient to simply transpose the brand's codes to new product categories. Brands should propose a definite vision in terms of clients, channels, product features, and technologies, a vision that's new, relevant and different from the existing alternatives and that refers to the unique capabilities of the company. If it's a clear vision, it's easily recognizable regardless of the product to which it's attached. This is perhaps why some of the most successful fashion and luxury brands are associated with people who have strong competencies and personalities and are not trying to please everyone on the market. Innovation gives the brand the credibility it needs to extend within a reasonable scope and reinforce the overall brand image. This is not just a special feature of luxury or fashion, but applies to any industry.

Virgin is the brand of an airline, a record label and a music store chain. Virgin has been cited by many marketing specialists as one of the few successful brands in strategic brand extension; the reason is connected to a reputation for innovation. Virgin's core association is the rebel, recalling Virgin founder Richard Branson. He sets out to do something rebellious in whatever industry he chooses to enter. Therefore Virgin brand identity is based not on what it does, but *how it does it*. As a result, the only way Virgin can be successful with new ventures is to make each one rebellious and new innovative for its respective industry. In the same way, the Apple brand can expand from computers to music players and perhaps phones because it's known for the vision "thinking different", which then creates an expectation of originality. We don't buy an Apple product, we buy the *idea* of what Apple stands for in different product categories.

When in 2007 Prada decided to launch its first phone, it did not just go for a phone with the Prada name and design on it. Instead, with its licensing partner Korean LC, Prada decided to study a totally new concept in phones. As a result, Prada was able to launch an innovative touch screen phone before Apple launched its iPhone. In addition, the phone displays unique features that recall the sophisticated brand in terms of icons, music and functionalities.

Neglecting the core business is one of the most obvious dangers related to brand extension, but actually hard to avoid. While extending the brand, the company has to spend time to keep developing and nurturing its original core business. This is a fundamental step in order to secure the firm's strength to then penetrate in a new product category. Calvin Klein may be cited as an example here. The designer brand started off in ready-to-wear apparel, but few remember this origin in a moment when Calvin Klein is mainly associated with underwear and mass fragrance.

Last but certainly not least is the way the extension is managed. Is the entrepreneur/designer "feeling" the new category and therefore able to transfer to it the stylistic codes of the iconic products? Does the company have the ability to transfer its skills and experience to the brand extension in terms of business models for managing the new category?

The entrepreneur/designer's feeling and passion for the new category is fundamental to innovate and implement a long-term strategy for it. But the business model is also very important and here there are different options:

1. creating *internal* capabilities by setting up a new organization for the new category or entering into an equity agreement with a specialized company;
2. entering into a *licensing agreement*. In fashion and luxury this has been the most popular business model for distant categories such as eyewear and fragrances in order to le-

verage the competencies and market coverage of big licensee partners.

In conclusion, brand extension gives the brand-owner the opportunity to complete the product range by supporting cross-
selling and making both the core and non-core business increase. This strategy is also a way to reach a target that cannot
afford the core product, a tool to strengthen the brand image
and define a lifestyle positioning, a way to get additional communication spending thereby increasing brand awareness.
How can strategic brand extension succeed in a crowded and
difficult marketplace such as fashion and luxury? The answer
is unique for each brand as it lies in a mix of different elements: the existence of a market opportunity; the brand heritage and the original core business; the values and stylistic
codes associated with the brand; the quality and innovativeness of the new product; and the right business model for the
specific category.

In 1910 Ermenegildo Zegna founded the wool mill and launched the brand
name. A century later the Group, a fourth generation family business, has
become the worldwide leader in luxury lifestyle for men.
The company's history has been characterized by two main drivers. On
the one hand, through the approach of high quality continuity: Zegna focuses on great natural fabrics, researches and innovates to attain exquisite manufacturing for high-end men's clothing. This is granted by the control of the whole pipeline: Zegna is the only totally verticalized high quality textile and menswear company in the world, from buying the finest
raw materials to managing its own fully owned stores. On the other hand
the company's key feature is the constant capability to innovate its business model and market approach. Following this second driver, the Group
first created a brand in textile, then launched a ready-to-wear collection,
developed a capillary distribution system and retail network which now
spreads across five continents (Zegna's strong internationalization approach helped the Group enter as a pioneer in emerging markets such as
China, Russia, Brazil, Argentina, and India).
At the end of 1990s, the Company launched a comprehensive strategy of
verticalization, diversification and brand extension. The objective was to
develop the accessories business and enrich the "Zegna Style" world by
combining excellence, quality and tradition with the sophisticated and
cosmopolitan tastes of Zegna customers today. The product offer has thus

expanded into different labels – Zegna Sport, focused on innovation, and ZZegna which meets the needs of the younger, more fashionista clients – so far the product categories comprise of ties, cufflinks, shoes, leather accessories, fragrances, eyewear, underwear[1].

New product categories have to be consistent with Zegna's core values, first of all product excellence is key (product development highly focues on quality – i.e. the use of Pima cotton for underwear, the richness in materials and in details, the high innovation with optimum wearability and comfort, as well as elegance and style).

The aim of brand extension is twofold. The first is to fulfill the brand image and defines a lifestyle positioning consolidating the relevance of the Zegna brand with existing clients. The next aim is to enlargen the potential customer base also to those that cannot buy the core-collection and create an "entry door" for the many aspirational customers, especially in the emerging markets. The expansion of the products' range creates more cross-selling and up-selling opportunities: for example, when a customer buys a Zegna suit he will probably also buy a Zegna fragrance; the brand extension also produces reverse cross-selling, trading up, increasing the core business.

Finally diversification is a way for the Group to have more visibility: extension increases the consumer's brand exposure thanks to the higher exposure to advertisements and the wider number of doors in which new products are distributed. All in all, this helps to create a successful business with the best brand image exposure.

---

1. Diversification involved a number of important acquisitions. In 1999, the Zegna Group acquired Lanerie Agnona S.p.A. and in 2002 took over Guida, owners of the Longhi brand. In September of the same year, Zegna set up a 50-50 joint venture – ZeFer – with Salvatore Ferragamo Group to develop a global scale footwear and leather goods business.
    In 2003, Zegna extended its operations in China by taking 50% of SharMoon, belonging to the Chen family, which makes high quality clothing for the Chinese market. 2003 also saw the launch of the first Zegna fragrance: Essenza di Zegna, distribuited by YSL Beauté. And in 2005, it added another fragrance ZZegna, it too produced and distributed worldwide by the cosmetics division of Gucci Group. In 2007 has been launched the Zegna Intenso fragrance.
    In December 2004, Zegna entered a global agreement with De Rigo Vision Group to develop, produce and distribute a line of men's eyewear, optical and sun, to sell under the Ermenegildo Zegna label.
    In February 2006, Zegna announced a long-term agreement with stylist Tom Ford. The Tom Ford collection debuted in Spring 2007 and includes a wide range of luxury clothing and accessories.
    And lastly, still in 2006, Ermenegildo Zegna Group and Perofil, the renowned makers of men's underwear, entered a long-term agreement under which Perofil is licensed to design, produce and distribute a line of underwear, including socks and pyjamas, under the Ermenegildo Zegna brand.

14.4 The role of licensing in brand extension

Under a licensing agreement, a trademark owner (*licensor*) gives an industrial or retail partner (*licensee*) permission to use its name (brand/label) and design for production and/or distribution of one/more product category, within a specific territory and distribution channels, for a certain time. For this the brand owner is paid a royalty, the so-called design fee (normally a percentage of wholesale revenues) and a contribution to communication (again, a percentage of wholesale revenues). The licensor brings to the table its reputation, image and creativity; the licensee contributes with its reliability, facilities and distribution know-how.

There are different kinds of licensing agreements, from purely manufacturing, to manufacturing and distribution all the way to until manufacturing and distribution and retail, allowing the licensee to set up its own retail network.

The licensing agreement offers the licensor the advantage of minimizing investments related to brand development during initial stages, when entering new markets, or when seeking growth in sectors that are distant from the core business. Specifically, licensing is the less risky option when a company enters a business with completely different business logic in terms of product development and seasonality, marketing investments, or distribution network. Such is the case with eyewear and fragrances, for example, where licensing is the most common option for operating the business. In cases of extensions into unrelated product categories, a company would have to acquire new plants, resources, and know-how which would call for major investments in time and resources. By opting for licensing, this company only incurs the costs of design and institutional communication, and the expense of a licensing manager or an organization that handles the licensing contract. In addition, royalties allow the licensor to finance development while maintaining (more or less direct) control of the outlet market.

The licensee offers technical know-how, financial and human resources, and additional competencies in distribution. This makes it possible to reach doors that are significantly different (and higher in number) than those of the core business. The licensee, in turn, learns from the licensor how to develop a creative project, and comes to understand the fashion business logic, increases the fashionability of own brands, saturates production capacity, reaches economies of scale, has access to new distribution channels, and improves the brand equity.

Key features of a licensing agreement
Main features of a licensing agreement refer to:

- *Exclusivity*. The licensor grants the licensee the exclusive (worldwide, option) license to manufacture, distribute and sell the products belonging to a specific collection identified by a trademark.
- *Duration*. Licenses are valid for a specific length of time. Duration should allow the licensee to have an adequate return on investment (from five to ten years)[2]. Most contracts set a deadline for the two parties to meet to discuss possible renewal. The agreement should also define cases of breach of contract that may lead to the possibility of an anticipated termination (i.e bankruptcy, takeover by a third party, etc.).
- *Royalties, advertising fee and minimum guaranteed*. Royalties are paid by licensee to licensor as a fee for ongoing use of trademark and designer's creativity. This amount is usually determined as a percentage of wholesale revenues which fluctuates depending on the awareness of the brand and the product category. Regardless the sales' trend, licensor is secured with a minimum guaranteed fee (agreed on seasonal or yearly basis). On the top of royalties, an advertising fee (always calculated as a percentage of wholesale revenues) is paid by licensee to licensor for promotion activities (such as media buying, event management, new

---

2. In case of a change of partner, managing of different licensees has to be carefully taken into account as deliveries and sales of the ongoing collection may overlap with the sale campaign of the next one (managed by the new partner).

product launches, etc.). Other financial obligations may include an initial lump sum, the sample for the fashion show, discounts for licensor's directly operated stores, plus the possibility to substitute a percentage of stock, POS material and visual tools, and other expenses[3].

- *Product and manufacturing approval.* The licensing agreement has to identify the name of the label, graphics, logo, design, materials, and shapes[4]. The licensing contract must stipulate that products will be manufactured by the licensee at that company's production facilities. If the licensee wishes to make use of outsourcers, the approval of the licensor must be given. In the contract, the licensee must agree not to have dealings with countries that allow child labor. Also, for certain lines production must be done in Italy; consequently future productive delocalization in foreign countries must be authorized by the licensor. Lastly, the contract should prohibit the licensee from granting sub-licenses.

- *Distribution plan.* A license may stipulate what territory the rights pertain to. The distribution plan indicates countries

---

3. The percentage of royalties (including the part to be invested in advertising, normally a third) may vary a great deal, depending on the industry's volumes and level of communication investment needed, the importance of the line and the amount of business expected. A trade-off exists between the minimum and royalties: high royalties along with a low minimum give the licensee company a better chance of developing business, which should also enable the fashion house to have a proportional increase in revenue. On the other hand, with no minimum, the risk for the licensor is that the licensee sits back idly and doesn't take any initiative. The real problem arises when both factors are high. When this occurs, in fact, the fashion house exploits the power of its brand, but at the same time risks precluding any chance for development. This is because the licensee company will have a much more difficult time developing the brand, where development means investments in terms of human resources and technology, choice of the best business partners, attention to quality, selection of distribution channel.

4. Licensing agreements define collections' market range. The definition of pricing is a topic of heated discussion while running the business, not when stipulating the contract. Generally, setting a price is innate to defining a line: at a contractual level products are identified, but in a very generic way, which is then interpreted in reference to the target, the market, etc. Markups are not defined at a contractual level either. Since the licensee must bear the expense of production costs, this company must also gain some advantage from its own efficiency.

and distribution channels where the sale of products will be permitted (wholesale or retail), increases or decreases expected in each area in terms of sales, and any other information thought to be relevant. Distribution takes place, depending on specific requirements, through agents or distributors that must have the prior approval of the fashion house. It is also wise to make provisions for the possibility of expanding the sales territory upon presentation of a detailed development plan by the licensee. Potential conflict areas about territory are: duty-free sales; Internet sales; risk of competition between licensees with similar product categories and different price ranges. Worth noting is the tendency for fashion houses to maintain control over certain territories (most frequently Japan and the US), leaving the rest of the world to licensees. In the same way, the licensor normally controls duty-free shops. At times, there is a provision for the possibility of creating pre-collections on some lines and for certain territories. This allows more expedient delivery of merchandise and encourages sales to final clients. Special attention should be given to selling off leftover stock.

- *Reporting from licensee* (information requirements). Normally, the flow of information necessary for regular control activity should include: SKUs, lists of clients and orders by geographic area, sell-in by model, invoices and credits notes, and unsold stock. Deadlines for providing this information vary for each topic.
- *Trade mark registration.* The trademark is and always remains the exclusive property of the licensor, who is responsible for registering it. The fashion house must inform all countries where the request for registration has been made or where the registration process is underway. The licensee must agree not to register the trademark under its own company name, and not to manufacture products with its own name utilizing models created by the licensor. In addition, the contract should clearly state who is charged with the expense of registering and maintaining the validity of the trademark in

the territory. Finally, the licensee agrees to furnish proof of utilization of the trademark, in order to avoid expiration for non-use.

- *Managerial roles.* The key to the success of the licensing relationship is a strong licensing management team both in the organizational structure of the licensor as well as the licensee, more focused on understanding the business than on defining the terms of legal agreements. Licensing management should not be understood in a limited sense as the office that handles legal or administrative questions, but should be a management team that acts as a point of convergence for a wide array of information, and also for solutions to critical problems that can come up in any phase of the relationship, from production to the distribution plan. At an organizational level, the Licensing Office should be situated just below the Managing Director, considering its highly strategic role. Beyond conferring on the decision whether or not to enter into a licensing agreement, the Licensing Office is responsible for certain critical elements such as: with whom to stipulate such an agreement, how to set it up at a contractual level, and which business objectives to pursue.

The licensor and the licensee are two different organizations and each one has its own objectives and strategies: fashion houses have to give strategic orientation to the brand; the licensee has to succeed in exploiting the awareness of the brand. As these are two different jobs, continuous tension is part of the game. The major issue is the balance between the search for an exclusive image and the push towards commercial diffusion. A high minimum, for example, could conflict with the need for a selective distribution. The choice of expensive materials could make it difficult to price the product in the right market range. Generally speaking, the licensor focuses especially on visibility, exposure, the possibility to create a total living; while the industrial partner wants to increase selling, conquer new market segments and create added value to its business.

Given the importance of a precise contract stipulation, combining the different perspectives of a licensor and a licensee requires a great deal of effort on a daily basis. The structure of the relationship is hardly standardizable. What's more, the specific nature and structure of each licensed brand and each licensor has to be understood, and the two partners have to be willing to learn from each other. At the end of the day, licensing is all about building a long-term relationship based on mutual trust.

The eyewear industry has been characterized by a dramatic evolution in recent years, with the increasing importance of fashion contents and continuous worldwide growth of premium and luxury segments. Eyewear has moved from pure function to fashion accessory as a result of the massive entry of designer fashion brands and the overall explosion of total number of brands in the category. Brand extension in eyewear plays a more and more important role for designer brands both as an image builder and a profitability driver.

Luxottica is the global market leader in luxury and premium eyewear. The Group started as a manufacturing company, then evolved into a licensing company, and now is a fully vertical integrated company – from R&D to retailing.

Luxottica leverages on a well-balanced portfolio that comprises leading and best selling premium house and licensed brands[5]. The key to success in partnerships with brands lies in the long-term orientation allowing for optimum planning and investment, and in the business model based on integrated control of the entire value chain: design, production, logistics, marketing distribution, and in many countries, retail. In addition to a global sales network that covers 130 countries, in its primary markets Luxottica manages a number of leading retail chains such as LensCrafters and Pearle Vision in North America, OPSM and Laubman & Pank in Asia-Pacific, and Sunglass Hut throughout the world. As a result, licensed brands are guaranteed not only access to the channel, but also the most appropriate positioning in the sales point for visibility and consistency with respect to overall positioning.

---

5. House brands include Ray-Ban, the world's best selling sun & prescription brand, Vogue, Persol, Arnette and Revo, while licensed brands are high-caliber names such as Bulgari, Burberry, Chanel, Dolce&Gabbana, Polo Ralph Lauren, Prada, Tiffany and Versace.

From opportunistic to strategic licensing

The trend of licensing a brand to a manufacturing firm, of which Pierre Cardin was forerunner, got underway in earnest from the late 1970s (when Armani and Valentino produced on license from the Gruppo Finanziario Tessile – GFT) to the early 1980s. In the 1990s, however, this movement abated because many of the top designers (beginning with Giorgio Armani) decided to take back production and distribution for branded apparel and accessories and handle these activities in-house by buying the relative production units. The aim was to control the entire production cycle and the profits generated from the brand. This was done up until the new diversification cycle began with entry into sectors such as watches, eyewear and perfumes involving production specificities and different distribution channels than clothing.

In the meantime companies have moved away from an approach to brand equity based on exploitation (the 500 licensing agreements of Pierre Cardin at the beginning of the 1980s, or the 60 licensing contracts YSL had in 2001, cut to fewer than 15 the year next by De Sole and Tom Ford). The last frontier is joint ventures (with shareholding of the licensor in the industrial partner or viceversa). To enhance brand equity, duration has increased (5-10 years with renewal); distribution control is more and more strict with exclusivity in each territory; there is a high degree of know-how exchange between licensee and licensor and investments are shared (i.e. royalties are reinvested by the licensor in brand communication). In order to establish a long-term relation, selecting the best partner is fundamental too.

A licensee has to share the brand's core values and development strategies. Other key requirements are: manufacturing quality and reliability (i.e. innovative design, quality of production, manufacturing capacity), capacity in distribution (worldwide distribution coverage, entry to prestigious locations, sales network, efficiency in deliveries), dimension of licensee and experience in managing other licenses (company reputation, image of own brands, healthy financial situation, dedicated people, a fast decision making process). Furthermore, for well established designer-brands, the size and global coverage of the licensee is an increasingly important factor because, for example in fragrances, it can assure the launch of more products, a better penetration into the market, with stronger and broader distribution and more investments in advertising.

After the failure of GFT, which wasn't able to create an alternative for its designer dependency, licensees learned their lesson and built well-balanced brand portfolios. On one hand, they are less dependent on a single brand, and on the other they've bought own brands (such as Gianfranco Ferré by IT Holding or Ray-Ban by Luxottica).

Licensing lifecycle

Figure 14.1 shows the typical evolution of licensing, from line extension to brand extension. Licensing has moved from being a tool for emerging designers to develop their core business into a way for big brands to promote a lifestyle. As a consequence, the dimensions of licensees and licensors have increased to the detriment of small players and licensing is now one of the major sources of income for global brands for brand extended products. Indeed, for small and emerging brands in clothing with a strong reputation but a limited business, manufacturing licensing is still the best, if not the only, option for growth. Given the investments required to affirm a new brand nowadays, finding (more than selecting) a partner has become the major issue for emerging designers. While some brands that used to be famous in the past are now surviving only as licenses without the core business[6], a niche designer can still succeed in working with mass oriented/industrial companies provided his or her signature brings to the industrial company glamorous exposure (such as the Puma's partnerships for co-branding with Jil Sander and Neil Barrett).

---

6. Examples are Oliver, Valentino's former young line from the 1980s, which today is only an eyewear brand by Safilo; or Genny, a brand name for eyewear by Luxottica. Thierry Mugler instead has returned to *prêt-à-porter* after stopping for a few years, following the decision by the Clarins Group to close down the griffe.

FIGURE 14.1   **LICENSING LIFECYCLE**

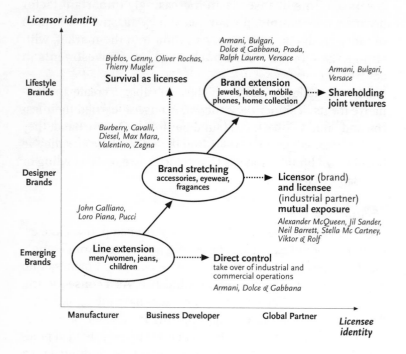

It's worthwhile to observe that in recent times young designers have jumped directly into brand extensions, launching a fragrance or a co-branding for sneakers in order to achieve the awareness that it would have taken years to gain otherwise. This is the case of the Viktor & Rolf/L'Oréal partnership. The fragrance promoted V&R to the general public, a name that was unknown outside of the fashion community. Meanwhile this move gave L'Oréal a different positioning: from the industrial giant working with top designers, very well-established but not cutting edge, to a talent scout in tune with the young generations. L'Oréal took a risk investing in the V&R name, but it paid off as L'Oréal eventually signed with Diesel.

Summing up, licensing has seen various development stages, as we've described in this chapter. It started as a growth engine for brands, with a strong push toward line extensions and diversification. In many cases this led to an excessive dilution of brand equity. Licensing then went through a time of crisis when several designers took back control of their core business. Today licensing is experiencing a "second childhood" thanks to growing revenues from fragrances, eyewear and accessories for fashion and luxury companies. In this evolution, the type of agreement and content of the partnership has radically changed: from opportunistic exploitation of the power of the brand similar to merchandising, to a long-term partnership centered on focusing the utmost attention on the brand and on internal and external consistency by both parties. The starting point for all this is brand vision in the core business that is focused, exclusive, and very clear.

Conclusions

The future forward: What will the future hold for fashion and luxury companies with ever-more elitist luxury and an ever-more aggressive mass market?

Fashion and luxury, as we define them today, have changed vastly with respect to the past. Business logics which at one time applied to a limited number of product categories and a happy few Western markets now extend to an ever-expanding world of products and services, transversal targets, and emerging markets.

- On the product front, we see the coexistence of very exclusive products, to keep the dream alive and maintain legitimization, along with accessible products to pay back investments, keep shops open, and sell (more and more).
- On the consumer front, we see the coexistence of expert consumers and *nouveau riche*. Most importantly, we find consumers who, to varying degrees, can be all things at once: refined and ostentatious, ethical and consumerist, fashionista and radical. The same brand has very different customers in terms of the price range and product cate-

gory it offers; brands have to sell a dream to everyone, but with different strategies.

- On the geographical market front, we see the coexistence of mature markets (Europe, the US, and Japan) and new markets (India, China, and South America). All call for in-depth understanding, bringing together global recognition in advertising and iconic products with adaptations of local strategies in areas such as merchandising, choosing distribution formats, media planning, and Public Relations.

Expanding the field of action in terms of products, customers, and markets corresponds to a deep-seated evolution in business models of companies: from fashion house to vertically integrated conglomerates, from apparel makers to retailers, from specialized brands to total living brands, from independent companies to financial groups. At the same time, new players have established themselves or experienced growth: vertical retailers have won over the cheap & chic market; private labels in hypermarkets have taken over "value for money" markets; diverse industries such as consumer electronics have made their entrance in fashion and luxury through partnerships (such as Prada/LG or Armani/Samsung) or by launching new brand/product concepts (such as Vertu, Nokia's super-luxury brand of cellular phone); luxury and fashion have made incursions into service-driven rather than product-driven sectors (such as Bulgari's in hospitality).

Till today, intensified complexity has translated into opportunities for fashion and luxury companies:

- The increase on average well-being has allowed brands to expand their offering to new consumer segments, enabling luxury brands to avoid growing old along with their core customers.
- Development of new markets has allowed companies to continue to expand even in economically stagnant times (in some cases finding cheaper production sources as well). The luxury market today is a global one, which makes it possible to strike a balance between growing markets and shrinking ones, mature customers and aspirational ones.

- Enhanced fashion content of luxury products has accelerated obsolescence, boosting consumption.

However, there are certain signs that should call for concern:

- Fashion and luxury are expanding to encompass new goods and services but, at the same time, in mature markets consumption has become trivialized for the one product – apparel – which has traditionally represented the core business for numerous high-end brands. Apparel is still what feeds the dream (*couture*, fashion shows, the season's theme) to sell other things. Nevertheless, the passion that inspired the creators of times past seems to have abated. It may be true that *couture* no longer meets the needs of today's customers, but trivializing the product doesn't help premium and luxury brands to distinguish themselves from Zara.
- Brands are decelerating innovation in their core business, and defocusing resources and energy on far away markets where they sell a value system more and more, and competence and know how less and less. In striving for the spotlight, those technical/industrial skills that are the foundation of the true innovative ability of creative companies have been neglected. Now, stores are overflowing with nearly identical merchandise; advertising has raised the noise level even higher, and what counts most of all, consumers are increasingly fed up.
- Tying in to the preceding point is a further consideration: brands are progressively disengaging from the figure of founder/designer/demiurge/entrepreneur, but often a role that serves to inspire and guide in the same way can't be found in-house. The level of managerialization is rising, and this is good, but in some cases it also seems to attenuate the sense of vision, the willingness to risk and experiment. What's more, if the stock market is involved, growing and generating profits becomes an imperative on which the fortunes of managers turn in the short term, but not always the sustainability of brand positioning in the medium-long term. Cost control is a necessary mindset in order for

a firm to be able to dialogue with investors, analysts, and partners, and is clearly a virtue in efficiently managing a progressively complex company. But if the culture of cost control becomes dominant, to the detriment of the culture of research and experimentation (with relative time and risks), the very essence of these businesses is jeopardized.

- Growth by continually adding to the number of sales points might not produce hoped-for results. The number of shops in Europe is not sustainable unless current tourist flows remain steady or rise. On the other hand, in emerging markets new shops are opened with an eye to converging local consumption. The differentials in terms of taxes, customs, and duties still make prices very different from market to market. As a result, international shopping tends to prefer certain bargain destinations over others, where brands open boutiques in a (costly) showroom logic. When these price differentials shrink (which is already happening in several new markets), we may see a shift in consumption between destinations, rather than a proliferation of consumption, which instead seems to be the forecast scenario in the optimistic anticipation behind all these new openings. The number of super-rich, like the wealthy, is said to be constantly on the rise, making it possible to promote local consumption further by differentiating the offering. Nonetheless, the hypothesis of a propagation of the offering (more collections, more lines, more products) to fill up an increasing number of sales points targeting a rising number of customers leads to brands gradually de-specializing and moving away from their "reason why".

- Lastly, the question arises as to how sustainable a model can be in which multipliers of the cost of finished products and the sales price are constantly rising, in which suppliers are choked off and quality suffers to compensate for immense investments in communication and retailing. This is a particularly acute problem in the high-end of the market. Luxury is not ethical if it makes customers pay more for store rent rather than product quality and creativity. While brands don't necessarily define luxury, many

luxury consumers look to the brand and the brand's reputation as a signal of quality. The impending risk is that sophisticated consumers will begin showing less appreciation for a luxury which is seen as synonymous with ostentation and frivolousness. True luxury, instead, is the ex-
act opposite of waste because it's associated with a valuable, enduring product.

Fashion has to become creative and luxury timeless once again.
Both industries need to focus on a product which is beautiful, well
done and different. At this point a market segment opens not so
to much high prices but real quality, true functionality associated
with intangible values linked to a place, a name, a person.

Specialization represents an answer to globalization, standardization, and productive homologation, and most importantly
to price competition from developing countries. After years of
brand stretching, specialization is also a way to rebuild brand
credibility and legitimacy. There is no room for covering all opportunities and being "special" at doing everything.

Pipeline certification represents an answer to the growing need
for ethicalness. Inevitably, brand identity will be tied more closely
to brand and corporate reputation, to what the company represents for the environment, its stakeholders, and for future generations.

Fashion and luxury once again have to become exponents of
beauty that makes us feel good. Beauty that comes from quality:
the product makes the difference; when it's precious and innovative it becomes the only defence against with communication
that is more aspirational and rich in imagery, even in the mass
market. Beauty that comes from proposing an original style.
Brands have personality that often can set a trend in motion, but
can never ever follow one. Lastly, fashion and luxury must offer
beauty because the foundations that underpin them are ethical
and transparent: workers in factories, salespeople in shops, managers in offices, designers in the style office. Nothing is superfluous, but much is necessary in this dream.

Bibliography

AA. VV., *Grande dizionario della lingua italiana*, Garzanti, 1993.

Aaker D., *Building Strong Brands*, The Free Press, 1996.

Aaker D.A., Joachimsthaler E., *Brand Leadership*, The Free Press, 2000.

Aaker D.A., Keller K.L., "Consumer Evaluations of Brand Extensions", *Journal of Marketing*, 54, 1990, pp. 27-41.

Aaker D.A., *Managing Brand Equity*, The Free Press, 1991.

Abell D., *Defining the Business: The Starting Point of Strategic Planning*, Prentice Hall, 1980.

Ambler T., Styles C., "Brand Development versus New Product Development: Toward a Process Model of Extension Decisions", *Journal of Product and Brand Management*, 6 (4), 1997, pp. 222-234.

Anderson Black J., Garland M., *Storia della moda*, Istituto Geografico De Agostini, 1994.

Aspinall K., *Long Term Scenarios for the EU Textile and Clothing Industry*, OETH, 1997.

Barnard M., *Fashion as Communication*, Routledge, 2001.

Barrett J., Lye A. and Venkateswarlu P., "Consumer Perceptions of Brand Extensions: Generalising Aaker and Keller's model",

Journal of Empirical Generalisations in Marketing Science, 4, 1999, pp. 1-21.

Barthes R., *The Fashion System*, University of California Press, 1990.

Baudrillard J., *The Consumer Society: Myths and Structures, (Theory, Culture and Society)*, Sage Publications, 1998.

Baudrillard J., *Simulacra and Simulation (The Body, in Theory)*, University of Michigan Press, 1994.

Bauman Z., *Liquid Life*, Polity Press, 2005.

Blumer H., "Fashion: From Class Differentiation to Collective Selection", *Sociological Quarterly*, 10, 1969.

Bocconi University, ESSEC Business School and Baker & McKenzie, "Business relations in the EU clothing chain: from industry to retail and distribution", European Commission DG Enterprise, 2007.

Breward C., *Fashion*, Oxford University Press, 2003.

Castarède J., *Le luxe. Que sais-je?*, 3rd edition, PUF, 2003.

Chadha R., Husband P., *The Cult of the Luxury Brand: Inside Asia's Love Affair with Luxury*, Nicholas Brealey Publishing, 2007.

Chandran R., Kirpalani J., "Luxury Brands Take Baby Steps in India", June 16, 2006, moneycontrol.com.

Chevalier M., Mazzalovo G., *Luxury Brand Management: A World of Privilege*, John Wiley & Sons, 2008.

CII-KPMG, "Indian Entertainment Industry Focus 2010: Dreams to Reality", Report, 2005.

Corbellini E., Saviolo S., *La scommessa del Made in Italy*, Etas, 2004.

Corbellini E., Saviolo S., *L'esperienza del lusso*, Etas, 2007.

Czellar S., "Consumer Attitude Toward Brand Extensions: An Integrative Model and Research Propositions", *International Journal of Research in Marketing*, 20 (1), 2003, pp. 97-115.

Dall'Olmo F., Lomax W., Blunden A., "Dove vs. Dior: Extending the Brand Extension Decision-Making Process from Mass to Luxury", *Australasian Marketing Journal*, 12 (3), 2004.

Danziger P., *Let Them Eat Cake: Marketing Luxury to the Masses – As well as the Classes*, Dearborn Trade Publishing, 2005.

Davis F., *Fashion, Culture, and Identity*, The University of Chicago Press, 1992.

Deshpande T.A., "Textile Sector Shops for Italian Brands", *Business Standard*, February 1, 2007.

Desiderio E., "Versace 'vestirà' i jet privati e gli alberghi di lusso", *Italian National Daily*, April 7, 2006.

Devoto G., *Il dizionario della lingua italiana*, Le Monnier, 1995.

Dubois B., Laurent G. and Czellar S., "Consumer Rapport to Luxury: Analysing Complex and Ambivalent Attitudes", *Cahier de Recherche du Groupe HEC*, n. 736, HEC School of Management, 2001.

Dubois B., Paternault C., "Observations: Understanding the World of International Luxury Brands", *Journal of Advertising Research*, 35 (4), 1995, pp. 69-76.

Fareed Z., "India Rising", *Newsweek*, March 6, 2006.

Ferré G., "Altagamma sbarca a Mumbai", *Corriere Economia*, June 5, 2006.

Ferré G., "Non chiamatele più seconde linee", *Corriere Economia*, January 1, 2006.

Giannelli B., Saviolo S., *Il licensing nel sistema moda. Evoluzione e prospettive*, Etas, 2001.

Giriharadas A., "Indian Designers Look to Export Their Heritage", *International Herald Tribune*, February 22, 2007.

Giriharadas A., "Global Goals for Indian Designers", *International Herald Tribune*, May 5, 2005.

Government of India – Press Information Bureau, "Satellite Channel FTV Banned", March 29, 2007.

Groeppel A., Bloch B., "An Investigation of Experience-Oriented Consumer in Retailing", *The International Review of Retail, Distribution and Consumer Research*, 1, October, 1990.

Herbig P., Koehler W. and Day K., "Marketing to the Baby Bust Generation", *Journal of Consumer Marketing*, 10 (1), 1993.

Hongwei H., Mukherjee A., "I Am, Ergo I Shop: Does Store Image Congruity Explain Shopping Behaviour of Chinese Consumers?", *Journal of Marketing Management*, 23 (5/6), June, 2007.

Kapferer, J.-N., *Strategic Brand Management*, Kogan Page, 1998.

Kapferer, J.-N., "Managing Luxury Brands", *Journal of Brand Management*, 4, 1997, pp. 251-260.

Keller K.L., Aaker D.A., "The Effects of Sequential Introductions on Brand Extensions", *Journal of Marketing Management*, 29, 1992, pp. 35-50.

Keller K.L., "Conceptualising, Measuring and Managing Customer-Based Brand Equity", *Journal of Marketing*, 57 (1), 1993.

Keller K.L., "Building Customer-Based Brand Equity", *Marketing Management*, 10 (2), 2001.

Keller K.L., *Strategic Brand Management: Building, Measuring and Managing Brand Equity*, 2nd edition, Prentice Hall, 2003.

Khanna S.R., "Structural Changes in Asian Textile and Clothing Industries: The Second Migration of Production", Textile Outlook International, Economist Intelligence Unit, September, 1993.

Klein N., *No Logo*, Flamingo, 2001.

Krishnan H.S., "Characteristics of Memory Associations: A Consumer-based Brand Equity Perspective", *International Journal of Research in Marketing*, 13, 1996.

Leibenstein H., "Bandwagon, Snob and Veblen Effects in the Theory of Consumer's Demand", *Quarterly Journal of Economics*, 64 (2), May, 1950.

Levi Pisetzky R., *Il costume e la moda nella società italiana*, Einaudi, 1978.

Lipovetsky G., Roux E., *Le luxe éternel. De l'âge du sacré au temps des marques*, Gallimard, 2003.

Lopiano-Misdom J., De Luca J., *Street Trends*, Harper Business, 1998.

Lowson B., King R. and Hunter A., *Quick Response: Managing the Supply Chain to Meet Consumer Demand*, John Wiley & Sons, 1999.

Mariotti S., Cainarca G., "The Evolution of Transaction Governance in the Textile-Clothing Industry", *Journal of Economic Behavior and Organization*, 7 (4), 1986.

McDowell C., *Fashion Today*, Phaidon Press Limited, 2000.

Menkes S., "Who's Next in Fashion? No One. A Designer Century Comes to a Close, with New Talents Caught Between Corporate Pressure and Fast Fashion", *International Herald Tribune*, October 2, 2006.

Michault J., "New Year's Coming and No Outfit? Rent It", *International Herald Tribune*, January 10, 2006.

Murphy C., "India the Superpower? Think Again", February 9, 2007, money.cnn.com.

Okonkwo U., *Luxury Fashion Branding: Trends, Tactics, Techniques*, Palgrave Macmillan, 2007.

Pesendorfer W., "Design Innovation and Fashion Cycles", *The American Economic Review*, 5, September, 1995.

Peterson, R.A., Kern R.M., "Changing Highbrow Taste: From Snob to Omnivore", *American Sociological Review*, 61 (5), 1996, pp. 900-907.

Phau I., Prendergast G., "Consuming Luxury Brands: The Relevance of the 'Rarity Principle'", *The Journal of Brand Management*, 8, 2000, pp. 122-138.

Pine J. II, Gilmore J.H., *The Experience Economy*, Harvard Business School Press, 1999.

Polhemus T., *Streetstyle: From Sidewalk to Catwalk*, Thames & Hudson, 1994.

Polhemus T., Procter L., *Fashion and Anti-Fashion: An Anthropology of Clothing and Adornment*, Thames and Hudson, 1978.

Porter M., *The Competitive Advantage of Nations*, Macmillan Press, 1990.

Porter M., *Competitive Advantage. Creating and Sustaining Superior Performance*, The Free Press, 1985.

Ravindranathan C.P., "English – Advantage India", *The Hindu Business Line*, May 12, 2007.

Saviolo S., "China Strategy for International Luxury brands", *Harvard Business Review China*, June, 2007.

Saviolo S.,Testa S., *Strategic Management in the Fashion Companies*, Etas, 2002.

Saviolo S.,Testa S., *La gestion de las empresas de moda*, Gili Editor, 2007.

Seeling C., *Fashion the Century of the Designer 1900-1999*, Konemann, 1999.

Sicard M., *Luxe, mensonges et marketing*, Village Mondial, 2003.

Sharma R.T., "Luxury Malls to Hit India Soon", *Business Standard*, March 31, 2007.

Silverstein M., Fiske N., *Trading Up: The New American Luxury*, The Penguin Group, 2003.

Simmel G., "Fashion", *The American Journal of Sociology*, 1957, p. 544.

Steele V., *Paris Fashion: A Cultural History*, Oxford University Press, 1988.

Strauss W., Howe N., *Generations: The History of America's Future, 1584 to 2069*, William Morrow & Co, 1992.

Sudworth J., "Indians Head Home in 'Brain Gain'", BBC Delhi, August 27, 2006.

Sun Tzu, *The Art of War*, Delacorte Press, 1989.

Tandon T., Sengupta H., "Brands Ready to Rock India", May 4, 2007, moneycontrol.com.

Thomas D., *Deluxe. How Luxury lost its Luster*, Penguin, 2007.

Treacy K., "Made in India: Western Brands Attracted, but Ironing Out Wrinkles", *International Herald Tribune*, October 6, 2005.

Truong Y., Simmons G., McColl R. and Kitchen P.J., "Status and Conspicuousness – Are They Related? Strategic Marketing Implications for Luxury Brands", *Journal of Strategic Marketing*, 16 (3), July, 2008.

Tungate M., *Fashion Brands: Branding Style from Armani to Zara*, Kogan Page, 2005.

UNCTAD, "TNCs and the Removal of Textiles and Clothing Quotas", UNCTAD/ITE/IIA/2005/1.

Veblen T., *The Theory of the Leisure Class: An Economic Study of Institutions*, Macmillan, 1899.

Vigneron F., Johnson L.W., "A Review and a Conceptual Framework of Prestige-Seeking Consumer Behavior", *Academy of Marketing Science Review*, 1, 1999.

Wetlaufer S., "The Perfect Paradox of Star Brands: An Interview with Bernard Arnault of LVMH", *Harvard Business Review*, 79 (9), 2001, pp. 117-23.

Wilson D., Pusushothaman R., "Dreaming with BRICs: The Path to 2050", Global Economics Papers, n. 99, October 1, 2003.

Wong N., Ahuvia A., "Personal Taste and Family Face: Luxury Consumption in Confucian and Western Societies", *Psychology and Marketing*, 15 (5), 1998, pp. 423-41.

Xiao Lu P., *Elite China, Luxury Consumer Behaviour in China*, John Wiley & Sons, 2008.

Finito di stampare nel mese di febbraio 2009
dalla Cartoedit s.r.l. - Città di Castello (Perugia)
per conto della RCS Libri s.p.a.
Via Mecenate, 91 – 20138 Milano